CW00520179

Contemporary society and the growth of leisure

Contemporary society and the growth of leisure

Kenneth Roberts

Longman
London and New York

Longman Group Limited London

Associated companies, branches and representatives
throughout the world

Published in the United States of America
by Longman Inc., New York

© Longman Group Limited 1978

All rights reserved. No part of this publication may be
reproduced, stored in a retrieval system, or transmitted
in any form or by any means, electronic, mechanical,
photocopying, recording, or otherwise, without the
prior permission of the Copyright owner.

First published 1978

British Library Cataloguing in Publication Data

Roberts, Kenneth, b.1940
  Contemporary society and the growth of leisure.
  1. Leisure
  I. Title
  301.5'7   GV173   78–40158

  ISBN 0-582-48990-3

Printed in Great Britain by Richard Clay (The Chaucer Press) Ltd, Bungay, Suffolk.

Contents

Acknowledgements

We are grateful to the Centre for Urban and Regional Studies for permission to reproduce material from *School Children and Leisure* by Ed Derrick, Martin Davey, Jon Edwards and Erica Watson

Chapter 1

The character of modern leisure

Sociology has always sought to identify the sources and consequences of major currents of change. In the nineteenth century the discipline originated as a series of debates about the nature of industrialism, urbanism, secularisation and the new type of class society that was being created. Subsequently these 'classical' problems have remained central to sociological enquiry. For example, attempts to chart changes in the system of stratification and patterns of class conflict have continued as major areas of interest. The study of leisure cannot be claimed as part of this sociological tradition but it stands in the line of descent, for the growth of leisure is one of the main currents of change underway in the advanced industrial societies. Leisure is no longer peripheral and therefore deserves sociological attention. Sociologists who remain disinterested are mistaken. They prove only that it is possible to remain so blinded by their discipline's traditional concerns as to fail to perceive its contemporary subject-matter.

What is leisure?

Even among those who recognise its importance, there is little agreement about leisure's role in society. It has been 'praised as the best means of enhancing self-expression and blamed as the artificial epiphenomenon of a sick society'.[1]* Of course, much depends on what we mean by leisure. Definitions are important. Answers to questions such as whether leisure is growing together with its sources and consequences can depend upon how the phenomenon is defined. Hence the need at the outset of this study to define the nature of the leisure to be examined.

Among contemporary leisure scholars there is general agreement that a satisfactory definition of leisure must incorporate at least two dimensions. According to Parker, 'Leisure is time free from work and other obligations and it also encompasses activities which are characterised by a feeling of (comparative) freedom.'[2] Dumazedier agrees that leisure must be distinguished, in the first place, from working time,

*References are listed at the end of the book, p. 169.

and second that its uses are characterised by being relatively freely chosen as opposed to obligatory.[3] Other writers have offered more complex definitions that attempt to capture the rich variety of leisure experience. Kaplan defines leisure, initially, as 'relatively self-determined activity-experience that falls into one's economically free-time roles', but then proceeds to add that it is '. . . seen as leisure by the participants, is psychologically pleasant in anticipation and recollection . . . potentially covers the whole range of commitment and intensity . . . contains characteristic norms and constraints, and . . . provides opportunities for recreation, personal growth and service to others'.[4]

This writer prefers simplicity. Kaplan's definition may convey certain qualities of leisure experience, but it is unnecessarily elaborate and therefore confusing. No researcher has ever found it practical to work from so elaborate a definition. Furthermore, whether 'relatively self-determined activity-experience that falls into one's economically free-time roles' is psychologically pleasant, and whether it really results in personal growth and service to others, are better regarded as hypotheses requiring investigation than issues to be resolved by definition.

Even more basically, it is desirable to distinguish instead of compounding stipulative and lexicographic definitions. Lexicographic or dictionary-type definitions describe how words are conventionally used. Sociological definitions, in contrast, are normally stipulative, simply stating how a given author intends to use a term. There is no sense in which stipulative definitions can be proved right or wrong; they just turn out to be more or less useful. In formulating stipulative definitions of terms such as social class, role and leisure, it is often unwise to remain *wholly* faithful to everyday meanings. If it restricted itself in this way, sociology would never advance far beyond common sense. One of the aims of the subject is to perceive social phenomena in original ways thereby eventually offering better understandings of the familiar. Kaplan's insistence that before he will regard it as such, leisure activity must be seen as leisure by the participants, is therefore unnecessarily restrictive.

If they wish to be understood by the wider public, sociologists must use terms in ways that broadly correspond with their everyday meanings. Although it would not be scientifically improper, it would be poor public relations for a book titled 'leisure' to be addressed to issues that are normally termed 'educational'. Furthermore, sociologists normally seek to take people's everyday knowledge into account whatever areas of social life they are endeavouring to explore. But this need not inhibit sociologists from 'sharpening' or otherwise attempting to improve upon common-sense definitions. Actually very little is known about what the term 'leisure' means to members of the public. It is quite possible that the expression means very little. People can smoke, drink, watch television and drive their motor cars to the seaside without being mindful that the sum total of such activities amounts to something called leisure. Investigators who have probed what leisure means to the public have found general agreement with scholars' definitions.[5] People see leisure as different from work. The fact that an activity is remunerated is sufficient to place it outside leisure. Furthermore, people have positive expectations of leisure; they expect to enjoy the experiences that it provides. Situations defined as leisure are characterised by the participants' ability to determine their own behaviour and environments, and by the 'friendly' quality of the social relationships that are encountered. Despite its apparent simplicity, regarding leisure as relatively freely undertaken non-work activity is broadly consistent with the everday use of the term, and can also be a penetrating sociological formula.

Leisure as non-work

It is common in social science to protest about the complexity and variety in social life. As a result, definitions are always hit and miss affairs, and there are many instances where defining leisure as non-work is inconvenient. What about leisure in work; the lunch-hour card game, music-while-you-work, and sociability on the job? Then what about work as leisure? Some individuals including sportsmen make careers out of others' leisure activities. And what about work in leisure time? Individuals' jobs can overlap their non-working lives. Some people spend some of their leisure talking shop and reading professional literature, and do so at least partly out of interest. There are many people for whom the boundaries between work and non-work are too imprecise to be usefully included in a definition of leisure. Nevertheless, to understand leisure in modern societies it must be seen, in part at least, as the obverse of work. Things were different before industrialism. When the term was used, 'leisure' conveyed a different sense from that being suggested here. There was an ideal of leisure that can be traced back to the ancient Greek philosophers which applauded the 'whole man' who developed all aspects of his nature. The original Olympic Games embodied this ideal. They were not purely sporting contests but also artistic and religious festivals, and the champion who was able to excel in only one sport was considered a perversion of the true Olympic spirit. Leisure was a quality of a life that enabled man to develop and express all sides of his intellectual, physical and spiritual natures. Educational thought was oriented towards this ideal, and in so far as one could talk about a leisure class, the referent would not be people who did not work, but those whose overall lives possessed a wholesome, leisurely character.

To understand this traditional concept of leisure the point to grasp is that in pre-industrial times work, play, worship and education were all blended as part and parcel of community life. Malcolmson describes how, in eighteenth-century Britain, popular recreations arose out of the community at markets, work, weddings and funerals, and how 'the popular playgrounds were usually constructed from the materials of everyday life – the market place, the public thoroughfare, the churchyard, an uncultivated close, the open fields'.[6] Life possessed a wholeness that was lost with the industrial revolution.

One of the basic features of industrialism is that it transforms work into a segment of life. Under industrialism work is undertaken in particular places – in factories and offices, at specific times, and amid work-specific relationships. The boss has authority at work but his writ stops at the factory gates; a quite different relationship from that between lord and serf in feudal times. Once work is segmented, a type of leisure that was previously impossible results; time free from work which you can use as you please, to do what you choose, with whoever you will. In industrial societies we can only understand leisure by distinguishing it from work, but this definition must be recognised as historically specific.

In its modern sense, leisure could not have existed for most people in pre-industrial society, but to conclude that these people had no leisure whatsoever would be ridiculous. In pre-industrial Britain there was plenty of time for play. At the beginning of the nineteenth century the Bank of England closed for 34 Bank Holidays and most London businesses followed this practice. In rural areas life followed the agrarian and ecclesiastical calendars which offered a generous sprinkling of saints' and feast days. For villagers in medieval Europe, in general the demands of work were no more onerous than for the modern factory employee. People had plenty of time for play, fun, sport and other amusements. These experiences were simply not packaged in the type of leisure that occurs in industrial societies. Myerscough recognises that although the modern concept of leisure is a product of nineteenth-century industrialism, 'this does not mean to say that recreation and play had not existed earlier; leisure and pleasure must not be confused. Rather, the new ways of allocating time and the changed perceptions of work, which industrialism brought, gave free choice non-pecuniary activities, undertaken in time off work, a fresh meaning.'[7]

If it is unrealistic to judge life in pre-industrial times by modern standards, it is equally inappropriate to use the Greek ideal of leisure to evaluate modern life-styles. The result cannot be other than critical. Sebastian de Grazia[8] deplores the free time that has been substituted for the genuine leisure of previous eras. In de Grazia's view, modern man's free time is not leisure; it occurs in useless fragments when people are not working and is spent uncritically receiving entertainments to which no active response is possible. It is certainly legitimate to debate the quality of contemporary mass culture, but pointless to evaluate it with concepts forged in antiquity that have little relevance in modern times. Subjecting modern leisure to this type of critical treatment is as false a practice as concluding that pre-industrial life was totally devoid of leisure. In industrial societies leisure is different from earlier times and must be appropriately conceptualised, and this means, first, seeing leisure as non-work.

As already acknowledged, there are individuals for whom the distinction between work and leisure is far from clear. For some people, particularly academics and priests whose occupations have yet to feel the full impact of the industrial revolution, the distinction is hardly appropriate. But most people today have little difficulty in deciding when they are at work and when not. Leisure, as being currently defined, is less difficult to apply to hard cases than most social science concepts. The majority of individuals can report exactly how many hours a week they work, and how many weeks holiday they take each year. For the mass of the public, industrialism has made work a demarcated area of life, and leisure occurs in the remainder.

Leisure as relatively self-determined activity

Leisure is not the whole of non-work but, within this area, includes only those activities (and inactivities) that are relatively self-determined. If it is difficult to draw an absolutely rigid line between work and leisure, this problem is magnified with the phrase 'relatively self-determined'. The one thing that this phrase makes clear is that the boundaries at the margin of leisure are far from precise. To say that activities are relatively self-determined does not mean that they are products of pure free will, nor that they are completely free from influences external to the actor. The criterion is that individuals can nevertheless feel that they have scope for choice.

The options open to actors are always limited by the availability of facilities, individuals' limited knowledge of the opportunities that are available, and constraints such as time and money. Few of us can choose to risk large fortunes at gaming tables. Relatively self-determined simply means that actors are left with some scope for choice. If we cannot afford Monte Carlo, most of us are nevertheless able to visit a local betting shop, but none of us has to do either; there are many alternative ways in which we can elect to spend our time and money.

The choices that actors make can never be entirely free from external influence. Individuals are invariably influenced by the opinions of spouses, parents, neighbours and friends as to what constitute desirable uses of leisure time. However, our associates' expectations vary in precision and intensity. At work employers usually have quite precise expectations concerning the jobs that employees will perform, and these expectations are backed with monetary and other sanctions. In contrast, my neighbours might well object if I keep lions, but there are wide limits to the uses of my garden that they will tolerate. They

reward me with approving comments if they enjoy my roses, but I can
live quite happily without this approval. Leisure occurs when others'
opinions are not decisive but are simply taken into account when we
decide how to act.

In making choices individuals are guided by their own values which
are usually the internalised expectations of others. As with others' life
expectations, however, our values can be set with tolerance limits
which mean that we do not feel duty-bound and conscience-stricken if
we fail to play golf or visit the coast. Amid all the above limitations on
pure free will, individuals can feel that they possess scope for choice,
and this is one of the definitive features of leisure.

Some areas of non-work are therefore excluded. To begin with, we
can exclude activities that are physically necessary such as eating and
sleeping. Then there are activities inspired by social or moral 'obliga-
tion'. Individuals may feel that they have to visit ageing relatives, tend
their gardens, decorate their lounges, and take their children for family
holidays. Whether or not these activities count as leisure will vary from
case to case depending upon the precision and intensity of the pressures by which the actors are surrounded. Gardening can be a hobby or
a duty, as can love-making and participating in community associations. Activities that are considered irksome by one person may be
freely chosen by another. Applying the relatively self-determined
criterion in real life is less easy than on paper. People may have to eat
and sleep but where, when and with whom leave scope for choice. The
difficulties encountered in deciding whether a particular activity is
relatively self-determined, however, are not signs of an unsatisfactory
definition. The definition is simply true to reality. Leisure shades
imperceptibly into other spheres of life making it impossible to measure *exactly* how much of it individuals have, and how much money
families devote to leisure expenditure. When we picture leisure dia-
gramatically, as in Fig. 1., it is advisable to leave the lines broken in
order to indicate the fluid boundaries between leisure and other parts

Fig. 1.1 Leisure and life-space.

		Time	
	Work	1	Non-work
	Unfree	1	
Activity	---------	1	---------
	Relatively self-determined	1	Pure leisure

of life. An easy-to-measure concept of leisure would sacrifice authenticity, and to understand modern leisure the 'relatively self-determined' formula is of fundamental importance.

A feature of industrial societies is that many of the social and moral constraints that formerly structured individuals' lives are relaxed. Individuals' duties to relatives and neighbours, for example, are no longer clearly defined by law, custom or religion. Nor are the sports and games in which individuals participate so stipulated. Since the industrial revolution people have constantly been able to talk about a 'decline in morality' and the advent of what is now termed a 'permissive society'. All sections of the population have gained greater freedom. Adolescents are now able to cultivate preferred life-styles in their own youth cultures, while ageing members of the community are often left 'old and alone', free from being the responsibility of younger generations.

There are a number of reasons why industrialisation relaxes traditional constraints and generates relative individual freedom. Money-wages bestow financial independence, as does a market economy, while the urban mass enables the individual to escape from pressures that can operate in a village community. Hence the scope for choice that is characteristic of modern leisure. How individuals use their leisure certainly remains influenced by their education, family circumstances, work and peers. Nevertheless, the point holds that leisure is an area of contemporary life in which individuals can feel relatively free to choose.

Recreation and leisure

Despite its simultaneous simplicity and imprecision, the definition of leisure offered above is valid in respect of industrial societies, and its utility can be demonstrated immediately by clearing up some common misconceptions. To begin with, it enables us to see the difference between leisure and recreation. Leisure is sometimes studied by presenting individuals with checklists of activities such as bingo, ballet and television, and measuring rates of participation. These forms of recreation certainly fall within our definition of leisure, but they do not exhaust it. A person's leisure can also include serving on a trade union branch committee, or just talking to relatives and friends.

Recreation is a narrower concept than leisure and is best approached through the notion of play. In his classic treatise, *Homo Ludens,* Huizinga defined play as '. . . a voluntary action or occupation executed within fixed limits of time and place according to rules freely accepted, but absolutely binding, having its aim in itself and accompanied by a feeling of tension, joy and the consciousness that it is "different" from "ordinary life".'[9]

One of the central features in Huizinga's conception of play is its separation from 'real life'. Play is cut off from ordinary affairs by time, place and distinctive rules, and, according to Huizinga, it is a basic human function, vital rather than peripheral in all civilisations. Consequently Huizinga expressed misgivings about the regimentation and systematisation in twentieth-century sport that he saw as militating against pure playfulness.

Subsequent writers have both broken down Huizinga's conception of play and disputed this latter judgement. Callois[10] has classified the games people play according to whether the predominant feature is competition, chance, pretence or vertigo, and also argues that organisation can be a way of introducing gratuitous difficulty rather than incompatible with fun, suggesting a continuum from *paidia* (unorganised play) to *ludus* (organised sport). Keating has made a further distinction between sport and athletics, sport being a diversion which contains its own reward, while athletics is essentially a competition for a prize.[11] All these distinctions, however, remain within the realm that Huizinga recognised as different from ordinary life, and this entire realm is recreation. Play is the psychological concept which draws attention to the individual's orientation and experiences. Recreation is the social parallel, denoting activities that are socially recognised as playful – fundamentally divorced from the serious business of living, and in modern societies recreation is served by its own commercial, voluntary and public organisations, staffed by people many of whom regard themselves as recreation professionals.

The study of leisure encompasses this territory, but it is important to insist that leisure is a broader phenomenon. Leisure is the whole of non-work where individuals are free to choose, and can occur in settings that have not been constructed purely for recreational purposes. Education, family and church-life can be leisurely. If leisure is growing its implications will not be confined to recreation, and furthermore, as will be argued in later chapters, to understand recreation and its many uses, it needs to be set in the context of leisure as a whole.

Life minus work equals leisure?

A further way in which the value of our definition can be demonstrated quickly is by exploding simplistic notions that equate leisure with the absence of work. Occasionally it is suggested that individuals outside the labour force including the retired and the unemployed enjoy lives of leisure. More frequently it is argued that the problems of the retired and unemployed are essentially problems of developing satisfying uses of leisure time. If leisure were a unidimensional phenomenon, simply non-work, these inferences would follow. With a more realistic definition, however, we can see that treating the out-of-work as a leisure class makes a travesty of leisure and distorts the predicaments of the individuals concerned.

If all other things remained equal, release from work would certainly bring about an increase in leisure. Unfortunately, perhaps, other things rarely remain equal. Lack of work tends to reduce individuals' capacities for self-determined behaviour. Income is forgone, and the status along with the social relationships that accompany a work-role are lost. Far from being a leisure class, it is arguable that many of the economically inactive are deprived of leisure.

The definition that has been proposed enables us to identify the real conditions that must be satisfied in order for leisure to grow. A growth of leisure requires that the demands of work are contained, and also an expansion of the scope for individuals to be self-determining. Whether these conditions are currently spreading will be considered in the next chapter. The conception of leisure offered above provides the necessary foundation, enabling us to discount oversimplifications, and identify the types of evidence that are genuinely relevant to the issue.

Social and sociological problems of leisure

The study of leisure can do more than titillate academic interests. Scholarly research for its own sake need not be deplored; it has a contribution to make, but the study of leisure can also enjoy a broader social purpose. Leisure bestows scope for choice upon both individuals and whole societies. Neighbours can put their leisure to contrasting uses, and so can larger communities. An aim of this volume, therefore, is to clarify the options. We all have our own preferences, but we have no necessary interest in persuading others to share all our idiosyncrasies, let alone in foreclosing their options. In leisure we do not need to speak with a single collective voice.

An implication of any growth of leisure is that we must begin thinking about social issues in maybe unfamiliar ways. All manner of leisure problems have been alleged. Since the birth of modern leisure fears have been repeatedly expressed that the public, particularly its younger members, will devote free time to mischief. Critics have deplored the quality of popular culture, while others have voiced alarm at an impending wilderness of spare time. These and similar misgivings will be examined critically in the following chapters, and few will survive the scrutiny, but there is at least one broader sense in which we can all recognise a leisure problem. In so far as leisure means scope for choice the public must decide which options it prefers. The conventional welfare approach with which social problems including crime and poverty have been tackled, where experts devise solutions, obtain public consent, then take appropriate action through bureaucratic apparatuses, is out of harmony with the opportunities that leisure bestows. Leisure research and theory can clarify the options, but respect for the integrity of the subject-matter, leisure, forbids pre-empting the public's right to choose. This is why it is so important that the character of modern leisure should be properly and widely understood. While they will have heard of the term, most citizens will probably not be conscious of leisure exactly in the stipulative sense outlined above. Many people will be unaware of any sense in which leisure is a problem. Ordinary citizens are quite capable of having, enjoying and being depressed by some of their leisure without being aware of all its properties. Ignorance may sometimes be blissful, but leisure analysis need not be pursued solely for its own sake: it is also justified by the belief that the common good will be served if more people can be made more aware of the leisure opportunities that most of us now possess.

This book is titled as a study of contemporary society, though strictly speaking the analysis focuses upon leisure in modern Britain. The details of how leisure is used inevitably vary between societies, as indeed is the case between regions, even neighbourhoods, within any one country. Largely as a result of their island's geography, people in Great Britain are more likely to spend vacations at coastal resorts than, for example, is the case in North America. This type of contrast could be multiplied a hundredfold, but the following pages do not attempt to compile an encyclopedic store of detailed comparisons. Detailed illustrations are drawn mainly from modern Britain, but the argument concerns trends and consequences of leisure that are common throughout the Western industrial world. Hence the title's reference to contemporary rather than British society. The analysis is not meant to be valid in relation to the non-industrial world. Nor are its descriptive conclusions meant to apply in communist societies. Indeed, one of the book's arguments is that leisure is different in societies that retain market economies, private property and democratic multi-party political systems. The presentation is hostile towards claims that an inescapable logic of industrialism produces convergence. Indeed, any growth of leisure will favour divergence. Leisure allows individuals to decide whether to watch soccer or rugby, and there are larger options, where the choices must necessarily be made collectively, which concern the type of future society in which we will live. Leisure opens alternative futures that we will build for ourselves either purposefully or by default. Do we want governments to marshal the resources that leisure unleashes, to promote and educate the public to appreciate approved pastimes, and maybe to produce Olympic champions? In the socialist world governments purport to know how people should spend their leisure and pursue policies accordingly. Appeals for similar guidance from above are not unheard in Western countries. This is one possible future that beckons. Do we wish to appoint armies of recreation professionals to organise our sport, arts, tourism and other uses of leisure? Most local authorities in Britain now have departments providing leisure services. Does any growth of leisure call for a comparable increase in their budgets? Or do we want to leave consumers with money in their pockets to play the market and organise their own voluntary associations?

This volume does not aim to make up its readers' minds, but it is intended to illuminate the issues at stake. We shall not only be concerned to understand the character of modern leisure and its pace of growth. These are merely preliminary issues preparing the way for an analysis of leisure's contemporary role. How are leisure and its uses structured by political, economic, educational and other social forces? What role does leisure play in the lives of different sections of the public? How do the public leisure services contribute to the quality of life? To what extent is leisure constrained by the institutions of capitalism – the market and private property? We need to pose these questions if we are to make informed decisions about our futures.

Some sociologists have drawn upon theories initially constructed for other purposes in order to make sense of leisure. Theories of mass society portray the public as helpless before large-scale organisations including the mass media, which broadcast a mass culture in which creativity is stifled and tastes reduced to a common denominator. Other theories treat citizens as victims not of impersonal mass forces, but ultimately of dominant class interests that control both commercial and state-sponsored leisure industries. In contrast, theories that conceive modern societies as socially plural, containing multiple centres of power, that regard democracy as a reality rather than an ideology, and insist that there are real senses in which the market bestows consumer sovereignty, lead to quite different interpretations of leisure. These theories that attempt to relate leisure to the macro-social order, along with the substantial body of theory and research that recreation itself has attracted, are examined in Chapters 3 to 6. In Chapters 7 and 8 the analysis moves inside the larger social system to consider variations in uses of leisure, and how these are related to individuals' other social roles in the family, at work and elsewhere. Here we shall be concerned not only with whether and to what extent, but how individuals' uses of leisure are shaped by their experiences in other spheres of life. Chapters 9 and 10 switch from considering how leisure is shaped by to how leisure affects other social institutions. Is leisure changing family life, education and work? Is it the case, as some commentators assert, that we are moving towards a society in which leisure will be the dominant social process? The final chapter relates the preceding arguments to social policy issues, and as should already be evident, these do not concern only the number of sports and arts centres to be provided. Leisure raises broader issues about the type of society in which we want to live.

As will become apparent, in this writer's view there most certainly has been a growth of leisure since that formative, classical period in sociology's history when the subject's main theories were constructed and its problems defined. It will be argued that the subsequent growth of leisure has changed society, and in the process has left some of sociology's grander theories in need of replacement, or at least drastic revision. Sociologists who remain more loyal to their discipline's traditions than the societies they purport to study, and who attempt to embrace leisure wholesale within their favoured classical theories, not only distort their subject-matter, but obscure instead of clarifying the problems and opportunities that leisure creates.

Chapter 2

Is leisure growing ?

The anti-leisure thesis

The belief that leisure is growing is part of our society's conventional wisdom. During the 1950s, amid the excitement of the emergent affluent society, we became accustomed to futurologists envisaging automated factories and 20-hour 3-day working weeks within the lifetimes of their audiences. Since then every upswing in the unemployment statistics has stoked prophecies of the human worker being replaced by increasingly efficient machines, as happened to the horse. Commentators have advised us that we are going to be immersed in more and more leisure whether we welcome it or not. However, one body of opinion has vigorously disputed this growth of leisure. A series of claims have been made disputing that work is in decline, and asserting that time off work is becoming less rather than more leisurely. Taken together, these arguments insist that what is growing is a condition of anti-leisure.

Wilenski [1] was among the first writers to challenge the conventional wisdom and express doubts about the supposed decline of working time, arguing that the actual take-off into industrialism, when long hours of work did become common, should be considered an exceptional period. During the twentieth century, Wilenski argues that the decline in hours worked has been modest and unevenly spread. Managers and professional workers have not benefited from any such trend. Time freed from work has been concentrated among the retired, the unemployed and the intermittently employed, whose overall circumstances cannot be legitimately described as leisure.

Burck [2] has extended these arguments, drawing attention to the swing in the labour force away from manufacturing and into service occupations such as teaching, medicine and social work, where productivity is hardly improving, if at all. Given these facts of the situation, Burck argues, not only are real incomes destined to rise more slowly than we have come to expect, but the demand for services will militate against any decline of work. In Britain the evidence from Young and Willmott's research has lent some support to these suspicions. [3] In their survey investigation they found that many respondents in higher status managerial and professional occupations felt that the demands of work were increasing, and the majority claimed that work was interfering with their leisure.

Linder has injected a new dimension into this debate with his notion of a harried leisure class.[4] Treating leisure from the perspective of classical economic theory, Linder points out that time is a scarce resource whose supply in all but the very long term, is absolutely fixed. Consequently, as incomes rise, time becomes relatively scarce and therefore increasingly valuable thereby creating a harried leisure class. Rather than finding uses for more and more leisure time, Linder argues that lack of time will increasingly become mankind's major problem.

Bell[5] has further disputed the growth of leisure with some additional observations on the quality of non-working life. He rejects the fear of the late 1960s that the post-industrial society will be a doomsday of depleted resources, but is equally firm in dismissing talk of a work-free utopia. Bell agrees with Linder that time is becoming a scarce resource, and identifies additional problems besides. According to Bell, we are marching towards new kinds of scarcity. The inhabitants of post-industrial society will have more than enough to persist, but producing and consuming these goods and services creates a surfeit of information which individuals have difficulty in absorbing. Furthermore, there are new problems of coordination and management. More people taking more holidays involves more planning and, paradoxically, less individual freedom.

Godbey[6] has synthesised these arguments to conclude that in North America what is increasing is anti-leisure. Like Burck, Godbey comments upon the shift in labour towards services in which hours of work are not generally declining and, Godbey guesses, with visions of ambitious managers and professional men working into their weekends, may actually be increasing. What is more, in Godbey's view, outside work, self-determined activity, is in decline. Non-working time is increasingly filled with anti-leisure: 'Activity which is undertaken compulsively, as a means to an end, from a perception of necessity, with a high degree of externally imposed conditions, with considerable anxiety, with a high degree of time consciousness, with a minimum of personal autonomy and which avoids self-actualisation, authentification or finitude.' Godbey endorses Linder's forecast of a time famine, and argues that a work ethic is spilling into spare time. Hence not only the popularity of quick meals but also the decline of mistresses who have become too time-consuming. Like Bell, Godbey sees increasing societal complexity and change leading to information overload, while limitless materialism leads to the acquisition of new wants immediately old wants are satisfied. Amid this situation of complexity and flux, individuals are provoked into constant activity in a search for self-definition. In Godbey's opinion, spare time is becoming decreasingly leisurely.

The containment of work

In this writer's view, advocates of the anti-leisure thesis exaggerate the significance of their evidence. Despite their protests, leisure *is* growing because the demands of work *are* being contained. For over a century in Britain, the trend has been towards trimming the working day, week and year, while at each end of the working life time has been freed for education and retirement respectively. These trends are unmistakable and are repeated throughout the industrial world,[7] though two qualifications must be added.

The first is to admit that the containment of work is a slow and long-term rather than a cataclysmic impending change. The anti-leisure school is correct to refute forecasts of work becoming a spare-time activity. Looking back over a century we may be impressed by the extent to which the demands of work have been lifted, but this has not been the ordinary citizen's experience of life. As a result of its slow and gradual nature, it is doubtful whether the historical trend has ever made many people conscious of needing to develop new ways of using extra leisure time. Since the 1940s the actual working week of the typical factory employee in Britain has declined by only three hours, more slowly than the standard work-week. The age when work will become an incidental pastime remains firmly in the realm of social science fiction. Riva Poor has documented and recommended the spread of the four-day work-week in North America.[8] She is correct to point out that the three-day weekend is arriving, but on present trends it will take a long time before it is the norm.

The containment of working time is not an accelerating trend. In Britain the most rapid decline in hours worked occurred between 1850 and 1918. Between these dates the typical work-week in industry declined from over 70 to 54 hours. Economists have calculated that since then the working population has exercised a 4:1 preference for taking benefits from increased productivity in higher incomes rather than free time.[9] In 1960 the average factory work-week was still 48 hours long, and by the mid-1970s it had dropped to only 44 hours.

But however gradual it might be, the direction of the historical trend is unmistakable. With the trimming of the work-day, evenings have been freed for leisure. At the end of the nineteenth century these leisure occasions were spent mainly in public houses and music halls whereas today they are typically spent in front of television screens. Towards the end of the nineteenth century the one-and-a-half-day weekend became the norm allowing the spread of Saturday spectator sports, principally football, and subsequently the five-day work-week has become standard. In the nineteenth century paid holidays for manual workers were rare but by the 1930s, when they became a statutory requirement, they had become the norm. During the last 30 years 'annual' holidays have been the main form in which extra time freed from work has been taken. As recently as 1960, 97 per cent of manual workers were entitled to only two weeks' basic holiday each year, but by 1974 61 per cent were taking over three weeks. One recent estimate suggests that by the end of the century working time per person per year will have declined by just 13 per cent, and the extra leisure will be taken mainly in the form of additional holiday entitle-ment – an extra three weeks.[10]

At the moment there is little widespread clamour for shorter hours of work. Ask simply whether they would prefer to work fewer hours and most trade unionists will naturally vote in favour, but in practice the issue is never this simple. There is always a trade-off to be made between time and money. Actual hours of work in industry have been falling more slowly than the standard work-week, suggesting that overt demands for shorter hours often conceal a covert demand for overtime instead of basic rates of pay. Surveys show that more pay is a stronger demand than the desire for more leisure time, even among under 25-year-olds.[11] Katona's research in several European countries and America actually found greater demand for more rather than fewer hours of work.[12] Similarly in my own survey investigation on Merseyside, most respondents expressed satisfaction with their exist-ing working hours, while among the dissatisfied complaints about inconvenient hours and demands for more overtime outweighed pre-ferences for shorter hours.[13]

Public opinion seems unlikely to bring about a rapid collapse of working time, and one hoary myth that must be nailed is the prophecy of human beings being inexorably driven out of work by machines. This simply cannot happen. A market economy does not work in the way that such forecasts imply. Even if there ever came a time when machines could perform all jobs more efficiently than humans (an unlikely prospect), the optimum arrangement would not be a fully automated economy. The optimum practice would be to use machines where their comparative advantage over humans was greatest, and to use humans on those tasks where their comparative disadvantage was least. Students of economics will recognise that the same principles explain why trade is still beneficial to both countries even when one can produce everything more efficiently than the other. Technological change can make particular skills redundant and result in particular groups of workers losing their jobs. However, these need be no more than short-term dislocations. If governments want to maintain full employment, in the long term technological progress will not stand in the way.

In absolute terms there has been no decline of work. Kreps[14] has calculated that, in the USA, on average, workers today put in 1,200 fewer hours each year yet work 6,800 more hours during their lifetimes than in 1890. The decline in mortality rates has extended lifetime, and leisure has expanded not so much at the expense of, as more rapidly than and alongside work. Work has been contained rather than declined.

In terms of international comparisons, hours of work in British industry are roughly midway up the range found among the advanced industrial societies. Experience elsewhere, therefore, does not indicate that a sharp decline in time worked is imminent. Talk about the collapse of work is an exaggeration. Nevertheless, the continuing trend is towards a containment of working time.

The second cautionary note that must be attached in discussing this containment is that, as the anti-leisure school correctly observes, not all occupational groups have seen their hours of work contracting. The containment of working time is an uneven trend rather than a consistent development affecting the entire population. In some occupations annual and weekly hours of work have increased. The transformation of professional status from a leisurely way of life to a type of work has been completed during the twentieth century, and as a result, Kreps estimates that leisure has actually declined among America's upper middle classes.[15] Likewise Kaplan quotes the case of senior levels of government employment in France where annual hours of work increased from 2,500 to 3,000 between 1800 and 1950.[16] However, rather than using these exceptions to contest the growth of leisure, it is more realistic to see them as part of a movement towards the democratisation of leisure time.

Top managers alongside self-employed businessmen and professional people now feature among the groups for whom relatively long hours of work are common, though it must be pointed out that they are usually well rewarded for their efforts with money. Democratisation does not mean that leisure time is now distributed equally throughout the whole population. This is clearly not the case. But inequalities in time free from work have ceased to correlate with other indices of socio-economic status. In teaching and senior levels of government employment in Britain, annual holidays have traditionally been generous, but there has been no increase in holiday entitlement for these groups during the last 40 years. Meanwhile other employees, including manual workers, have been closing the gap. In many spheres of social life, including the availability of health and education services, middle class occupational status has ceased to be regarded as a legitimate claim to privilege, and likewise with leisure time. That white-collar workers should automatically be required to work fewer hours than men on the shop floor is no longer considered acceptable.

Married women comprise a major section of the population where the general trend has been against the overall historical tide. Since the beginning of the century, in Britain the proportion of married women in employment has risen from approximately 10 per cent to over 50 per cent. Household gadgets, canned and frozen foods, and, even more important, the advent of the small planned family, have released the wife/mother from total domesticity, but for paid employment rather than a life of leisure, again testifying to the public's preference for higher incomes and standards of consumption rather than more free time.

When account is taken of the uneven and gradual character of the lightening demands of work, there are no grounds for supposing that man stands on the verge of an age in which abundance will solve the age-old economic problem of scarcity and in which work can become a minor activity. It is purely mischievous to suggest that we are reaching a stage where the problem of unemployment can be solved by calling it leisure. Rather than an eclipse of work, the actual trend amounts to no more than a gradual shift in the overall balance. The direction of this shift is nonetheless unmistakably towards more leisure.

Some of yesterday's wilder aspirations have become not only today's reasonable expectations but are being redefined as civic rights. For example, a report sponsored by the English Tourist Authority and the Trades Union Congress in 1976 defined holidays as a 'social need', lamented the fact that 8 million people in Britain had enjoyed no holiday away from home for at least five years and, among other proposals, called for increased support from public funds to enable individuals to exercise their 'right to a holdiay'.[17] Many ordinary features of contemporary life-styles would have been regarded as extraordinary by our grandparents. This is one of the consequences of the slow but progressive containment of working time.

Scope for choice

As argued in the previous chapter, leisure is not merely non-work. It is also relatively self-determined activity. Hence the need to query whether the trends have enabled the public to gain more scope for choice during non-working time. Two historical currents – demographic change and the spread of affluence – have wrought exactly this effect.

The significance of demographic change is underestimated in many standard texts on leisure. Since the nineteenth century fertility and mortality rates have declined. People are now living longer so that today it is unusual for children not to survive working life and into old age. Fertility has also declined. The small, planned family has become the norm, and the net effect of these trends is a population containing a larger proportion of old people and fewer children than a century ago. It is this pattern of demographic change that has made it possible for people to work more hours during their lifetimes, yet fewer hours each year during their occupational careers. The lifetime of the average citizen has increased, enabling non-working time to expand considerably without hours of work falling sharply. This new demographic pattern has also enabled the ends of the life-cycle to be released for education and retirement, which amounts to a major change since the nineteenth century when people began their working lives in childhood and, for the bulk of the population, there could be no such thing as retirement.

As far as creating greater scope for choice is concerned the decline in the birth-rate has been the critical development. The lives of women in particular have been transformed by this trend. In both Britain and

America, today the typical mother has her youngest child in school when she is in her early thirties, and with survival into old age having become the norm, she can anticipate another 30 years or more of active life. Adult women have been released from the routines of darning, mending, cooking, cleaning, child-bearing and child-rearing that once made home-keeping an all consuming occupation, often interrupted only by death. We must certainly bear in mind the move-ment of married women back into the labour force, and the fact that expected standards of home and child care have been rising. But the plain fact is that mothers, and fathers as well, now have time to spare after playing their necessary parts in rearing the successive generation. Hence the greater scope, both inside and outside the family, for relatively self-determined activity.

Money has been the second great liberator and has gradually been enlarging the public's scope for choice. However many well-paid intel-lectuals bemoan materialism, for ordinary people the growth of pros-perity has meant release from grinding subsistence and freedom to choose. Most of the gains from increased productivity in industry may not have been taken in the form of extra leisure time, but they have been used to increase spending power thereby extending consumers' scope for choice and making non-working time more leisurely. Until the 1930s, among the British working class, subsistence level poverty was a normal condition. By redefining it in relative terms, researchers have been able to rediscover poverty in contemporary 'affluent' societies, and it cannot be denied that the poorer sections of the community still have little money to spare beyond what the necessaries of life require. But standards of living among the working population, particularly those outside the child-rearing phase of the life-cycle and in households containing more than one earner, have advanced con-siderably over the last generation. There was a time when the mass of the people had little choice but to spend their non-working time on the street or (when drink was cheap) in public houses. Today the condition of the people is vastly different. Families have money to spend on their homes, clothing, meals out, entertainment, sport and transport.

Little of this was envisaged even 30 years ago. As recently as the 1950s in Britain, local authorities were building council estates with-out garages assuming that working class families requiring public housing would be unable to afford motor cars. The number of roads today that are half-used as car parks proves how wrong this assumption was. The spread of car ownership in Britain since the 1950s has greatly enlarged leisure opportunities. The countryside has beome a mass playground with consequent pressure upon resources. There may be no absolute shortage of land for leisure in Britain, but popular destina-tions close to the major conurbations become heavily congested at weekends and during the summer season. People can now be observed queueing for leisure not only outside cinemas and football grounds, but also at the foot of some of the better-known climbs in Snowdonia, and above the more popular pot-holes in the Yorkshire dales.

These trends have led to some controversy over whether access to the countryside should be rationed. In Britain there is opposition to the spread of camping sites on the ground that they blight the environment, and instead of building new motorways it has been suggested that road networks into the Scottish Highlands be allowed to deteriorate in order that genuine mountain lovers can remain in peaceful isolation. Likewise some users of the national parks are proposing that the hordes of casual visitors be discouraged in order to leave the spaces open for those who *really* know how to enjoy them. For example, 'We have got to restrict access in some of the really over-used places. I don't think you can afford to allow cars to be driven freely to certain places, or approach them, and permit people to stroll in and meander around. It may be that you should prove you are a serious rock climber, or know your way around the mountains. I think it must come to that.'[18]

Many leisure industries have been obliged to adjust to the population's new mobility. Hotel architecture has changed to reflect the reduced demand for lounge accommodation and the increased demand for car parks. The spread of the motor car has lowered demand and therefore standards in public transport, with the result that the non-motorised public has become less rather than more mobile. Between establishing independence from parental supervision and acquiring the incomes necessary for personal transport, young people are probably more confined than a generation ago with the motor car having reduced the availability of public transport and transformed the bicycle from a means of transport into a toy. Affluence and its accompanying freedom are not evenly spread. Nevertheless, among the population as a whole, mobility has increased and discretionary spending has grown; symptoms of the self-determined activity that is a basic element in leisure.

It is always important not to confuse temporary quirks with longer-term historical trends. The growth of leisure has not been steady from year-to-year. At the moment, in the late 1970s, economic growth has halted, in Britain standards of living have fallen, and it has become unfashionable to talk the language of perpetual progress. But such pauses, and there have been many, have not undone the longer-term containment of work and the rise of prosperity. Holman[19] has calculated that in the USA, during the first half of the twentieth century, the proportion of lifetime unaccounted for by work and other necessary activities rose from 27 to 34 per cent, the gains mainly taking the form of longer weekends. Since 1950 vacations, education and retirement have pushed up time free from work still further, and living standards have risen simultaneously. This longer-term trend may or may not resume, but it is unlikely that the developments of the past century will be undone.

The recreation explosion

Without postulating a growth of leisure it is difficult to make sense of the known trends in recreation. Between 1971 and 1973 the number of golf balls sold in Britain rose from 13 million to 20 million, whilst UK manufacturers' home sales and imports of fishing rods, reels and other tackle grew by 66 per cent. A 41.9 per cent increase in the number of pleasure craft using rivers, canals and reservoirs occurred beween 1967 and 1971, membership of the Ramblers' Association rose from 11,000 in 1963 to 25,000 in 1975, while the Caravan Club grew from 41,000 members in 1965 to 143,000 in 1974. These figures are admittedly hand-picked, but they indicate a general trend which has been variously termed a boom and explosion. Across virtually all fields of recreation, participation has been growing, and sharply rather than marginally. Hence the spate of magazine and newspaper articles with titles such as 'The busy world of leisure'.[20]

This trend is evident not only in sport and other active forms of outdoor recreation, but has equally affected indoor and 'cultural' pursuits. Attendances at the four main London art galleries rose from 2.6 million in 1965 to 3.2 million in 1973, and at the ten major national museums from 7 million to 12 million. The number of gramophone records sold increased from 85 million to 161 million between 1966 and 1973, and during this same period there was a trend away from singles towards long-playing records. It is difficult to see how this boom in recreation can be explained apart from a growth of leisure.

There has been an all-round growth in participant recreation. Favoured activities have not been expanding at the expense of others. Rather than locked in competition, all forms of participant recreation seem to have benefited from a 'multiplier effect'. As a result of the social contacts and information that it supplies, involvement in any one type of recreation tends to stimulate interest in others. Hence whether we examine participation in sport, the arts, countryside recreation or the use of libraries, the same sections of the population, the middle classes, repeatedly turn out to be the most participant. Not every single form of recreation has benefited from this multiplier effect, but the exceptions have been governed by special circumstances. There are fewer cyclists than a generation ago, but to explain this one does not need to look beyond the congested roads. There are also fewer amateur boxers. The Boxing Association attributes this to school teachers' unwarranted prejudice, but the schools are probably only reflecting a diminishing tolerance of interpersonal violence in society-at-large. Certain sections of the population have been left behind by the recreation boom. Among the socially and economically deprived, the multiplier effect operates in reverse gear. When the ageing, poor and disabled are confined to their homes and television, they are denied the possibility of latent interests being stirred through social interaction. Hence the identification of new forms of deprivation. In a society in which participant recreation has become a normal use of time, concern has been expressed for those who are deprived of recreational opportunities.

Developments in central and local government parallel the growth of recreational activity among the public. At central government level there is now an Arts Council, a Sports Council and a Countryside Commission – all post-war creations. In addition, bodies originally created principally for other than recreational purposes including the Forestry Commission and the water authorities have increasingly found themselves in the leisure business. Catering for leisure is now accepted as a legitimate function of government which no longer needs to be justified in terms of improving the health, work efficiency or moral fibre of the population.

In local government there have been equally dramatic developments. Particularly since the reorganisation of local authorities in 1974, departments under recreation, leisure and similar titles have been blossoming throughout the country, headed by well-paid directors sitting at the head of expanding bureaucracies. Under their supervision, sports, leisure, recreation, neighbourhood and arts centres have been appearing throughout the land. At more modest levels in the occupational hierarchy, the staff formerly known as baths' attendants have reappeared as managers of leisure centres, while the traditional park-keepers are now administrators of recreation complexes. Public recreation services are being consolidated and professionalised. Courses, conferences, textbooks and diplomas are increasingly thick on the ground, and in Britain it is now possible to take a degree in recreation studies. In America the recreation services have travelled even further along this road. Recreation has become a standard college subject, and the parks, sports complexes and wilderness areas are now well staffed with professionally qualified personnel. What can all this mean, other than a growth of leisure?

How free is spare time?

Perhaps the most challenging part of the anti-leisure thesis is the claim that non-working time is becoming less self-determined and leisurely, but some of the trends towards which these arguments draw attention, such as the increase in compulsive activity, undertaken from a perception of necessity and with considerable anxiety, are impressions rather than conclusions derived from firm evidence. In so far as the argument contains a valid core, it is doubtful whether it deserves so provocative a title as anti-leisure.

Linder's prophecies about a harried leisure class are difficult to challenge. Although leisure is growing, it is unlikely that 'finding things to do' will become a major problem. There is little prospect of mankind being stranded in a wilderness of boredom. The development of leisure is not heralding an age of either gracious or boring idleness. Because lifetime is scarce, rather than finding things to do, the challenge of leisure is more a matter of finding the time to spend with our families, to visit our relatives and to associate with our friends, to watch our favourite television programmes, to visit the theatre, to travel, to use our boats and caravans, and to play our games of badminton and golf. The sharpest increases in recreation demand, therefore, are likely to involve not the more time-consuming activities but quickies – squash rather than cricket. And for this same reason among others, the private motor car is unlikely to lose its popularity.

Pressures of time mount and, as Bell rightly points out, there is a growing problem of handling all the information about how we might use our leisure. Furthermore, having decided what to do, we are increasingly likely to find ourselves among armies of fellow 'trippers' or sportsmen whose behaviour needs to be managed. Packaged holidays are one indication of these trends. Yet none of this needs to be seen as the antithesis of leisure. Defining leisure in unrealistic terms can lead to all manner of peculiar conclusions. Adopt a Greek definition, and as de Grazia skilfully shows, modern leisure appears grotesquely deformed. We can accept that the ways in which people choose to spend their leisure are becoming increasingly packaged and condensed to avoid 'wasting' time. This may well be the character of modern leisure, and the quality of experience that it offers is a legitimate subject for debate, but refusing to call it leisure makes as much sense as relabelling rotten wood as steel.

Chapter 3

Recreation theory and research

Is leisure fun, or a problem?

Despite its historic growth, in some quarters the study of leisure is still dismissed as the coffee table subject par excellence; incidental chat serving as light relief from the serious business of confronting society's principal institutions. The very concept of leisure conjures impressions of joy, amusement and euphoria. In common sense leisure is fun, by definition it is relatively self-determined activity, so what can be the point of studying it save as a diversionary pastime? Other writers have questioned whether leisure is necessarily a good time. Scholarly volumes have dwelt on the 'problem of leisure'. Rater than fun, some writers have interpreted leisure as a threat and a challenge. Fears surrounding the devil's ability to employ idle hands enjoy a distinguished history, and the quality of popular culture has been a topic of habitual concern among those who ascribe to themselves more cultivated tastes. And there is more to this concern than a paternal disdain for popular pastimes. Many members of the public will openly confess that their leisure is sometimes desultory, while some of the most common leisure activities, including television, are rarely named as particularly enjoyable.[1] Studies of young people offer ample evidence that leisure is far from all fun and excitement. Every recent investigation has confirmed how drab, monotonous, dull and boring spare time can be.[2] 'What to do?' seems to be a perennial topic of peer group conversation. Today's youth have time and all the other qualities that generate leisure in abundance. Their predicament is not simply a lack of resources to do things they enjoy. Another problem is not knowing what they would really like to do. Young people are aware of many things that they could do. There is immense variety in young people's leisure.[3] Adolescents are constantly trying out activities and seeking new experiences in sport and entertainment, with alcohol and other drugs, at pop festivals and elsewhere. Yet the experience of this age-group offers clear evidence that leisure is not always fun.

It may seem a paradox if self-determined behaviour proves anything but satisfying. How can this be so? Surely individuals will choose to do things that they enjoy? While mistakes may be made, must not leisure in general necessarily be a source of experiences that individuals value? Sociologists have plundered their armoury of theory to resolve this paradox. For example, the theory of mass society has been imported to leisure analysis. In this theory contemporary man is seen as the victim of impersonal forces such as bureaucracy, technology and the media. These institutions, it is alleged, threaten to reduce the public to a helpless mass, swamped by a mass culture which stifles individuality and creativity, and lowers tastes to a common denominator. Solutions to the malaise are sought either through paternal control of leisure by cultivated élites who can protect the public from cruder temptations, or through 'participation' – somehow giving the public genuine control over the institutions that currently dominate leisure. Another body of theory that has been recommended for grappling with leisure talks the language of social class conflict, and interprets leisure and its maladies in terms of class domination. The public's uses of leisure are seen as constrained by class divisions rooted in the broader economic and political order. Threats to the quality of life are identified as stemming not from impersonal forces but dominant class interests. Like man at work, man at leisure is conceived as alienated, and the solutions to his problems are seen as contingent upon a revolution in prevailing class relationships.

Sociology enjoys no monopoly in the study of leisure, and the majority of leisure researchers have seen little need to resort to these theories. Compared with mainstream leisure analysis, sociological theory appears only to complicate the issues. The growth of leisure has inspired its own body of recreation theory and research, whose explanations for any shortcomings in the quality of leisure probably correspond more closely with everyday common sense. According to this school of thought, leisure problems result principally from an imbalance between the demand for and the supply of leisure goods and services. It is argued that recreation provision has not kept pace with a growing demand. Facilities for sport and the arts, for example, are criticised for being too few in number, often of the wrong type, and sometimes in the wrong places. Other imbalances occur because members of the public lack information about, or lack the necessary education to use the facilities that are available. In addition, particular sections of the public can be constrained by lack of time, money or transport. This approach calls for more research to probe the character of 'latent' in addition to already manifest recreation demand. It calls for improved provision, education for leisure, and more effective 'delivery systems' to make recreation opportunities available where the need is greatest. Are sociologists merely demonstrating a customary perversity in clouding leisure with their theories of massification and class conflict?

Sociologists have returned this scepticism. In general sociologists treat the recreation movement, composed of researchers and practitioners, with suspicion. They express two major reservations. First, the recreation approach is criticised as too narrow. It is argued that recreation is only a part of leisure. Suggesting that the quality of life depends upon sports complexes and fun centres smacks of 'bread and circuses'. The second objection is that the recreation approach is asociological, meaning that it takes too little account of how both the supply and demand for recreation facilities are likely to be influenced by the wider social system. Instead of encapsulating themselves within recreation research, sociologists have preferred to draw upon their broader bodies of theory to illuminate leisure.

As a sociologist, my own sympathies are inevitably biased towards the sociological accounts that explicitly relate leisure to the wider social order, though as will become increasingly apparent, some of the theories that sociologists offer are less than wholly convincing. Before looking at sociology's theories in detail, however, we must systematically consider the claims of recreation theory and research. This is the approach to beat if sociology is to prove its relevance in the study of leisure. Does the analysis of leisure need sociology? Sociologists may consider this self-evident, but the wider public is entitled to demand evidence. Why is specifically recreation research and theory inadequate? The main reason is that recreation is only a part, not the whole of leisure, but in addition to this, mainstream recreation research's concentration upon activities and facilities fails to do justice even to recreation itself.

Surveying recreational activities

Precisely separating leisure from the rest of life, from work and other activities where individuals have little choice, becomes difficult when we move from abstract concepts to real cases. Hence the impossibility of giving *exact* answers to the questions of how much leisure people have, and by how much it has grown. These difficulties, however, pale to insignificance when we try to look inside leisure and distinguish among its many uses. Recreation alone is a truly complex field. Researchers find themselves grappling with a subject that dissolves in their hands the moment it is touched.

The orthodox approach in analysing recreation behaviour is to construct inventories of activities before surveying the public to determine who does what. In Britain, since the mid-1960s, there have been several large-scale investigations of this type,[4] and from this research we learn which leisure activities have a mass appeal and which are relatively select, the latter group being by far the more numerous. Many interests that are thought of as enjoying mass appeals actually involve only small minorities. For example, on a typical match-day professional football in Britain attracts less than half a million spectators out of a population of over 50 million. When we calculate the numbers playing sports such as golf and tennis, or visiting the theatre each month, the percentages fall well down into single figures. Leisure interests are far from uniform, and it is unnecessary to seek out every odd pastime to compile an inventory of activities running to several hundred items.

From activity surveys it is possible to discern relationships between 'independent variables' such as age and income, and uses of leisure, and once established these relationships can be used to identify 'latent demand', and to predict trends in recreation behaviour. We can discover which sections of the population are generally inactive, then probe the reasons, identify any exceptional constraints, and tailor future provision accordingly. As far as predicting future trends is concerned, if it can be shown, for example, that affluence is currently related to high levels of participation in particular types of pursuits, this is a basis for predicting trends as incomes generally rise. This standard methodology can be given a variety of embellishments. A cross-cultural perspective can be added, as in the surveys of sports participation sponsored by the Council of Europe.[5] Certain relationships such as between age, social class and participation are found in all countries, but their strength varies, and this suggests, for example, that a sharp decline in sports participation with advancing age need not be accepted as inevitable, and enables the types of recreation provision and other circumstances that minimise the constraints normally associated with advancing age to be identified. This Council of Europe study was unusually sophisticated in its measures of participation. The investigators compared the *penetration* of different sports, meaning the percentages who had ever played, and also developed a measure of *fidelity,* the percentages of some-time participants still active. The object of this analysis was to enable resources and publicity to be directed towards sports to which initiates tend to remain loyal, and on this basis sailing and golf emerge as more attractive propositions than team games and gymnastics. Measuring rates of participation in recreational activities is certainly not a useless exercise.

Yet the yield from this type of research is not entirely satisfying. One problem is that levels of participation in most activities are so low that, even with large samples, it is difficult to draw any reliable conclusions. To compound the resultant problems, the relationships that can be established beween uses of leisure and independent variables tend to be disappointingly loose. More men play sports than women, but there are thousands of sportswomen while the majority of adult males are not active sportsmen. Knowledge of such loose relationships may be useful in predicting trends, but from the point of view of explaining leisure behaviour it is difficult to know what to make of them. Recreation research yields a plethora of data whose meaning baffles even its collectors. The classic example is the 12-nation time-budget study.[6] Investigators in 12 different countries conducted enquiries which involved itemising their samples' uses of time. Each project was allowed scope to tailor its research methods to its own national conditions and problems, but some overall coordination was attempted. The end-result has been an enormous multi-authored volume amounting to 868 pages packed with masses of data. What does it all tell us? What conclusions emerge? Not even the volume's editor attempts to summarise or offer an overall interpretation of the findings.

Sociologists are entitled to protest at this rampant and expensive fact-gathering. Recreation research has been less influenced by sociological thinking than the routine attention paid to 'sociological' variables might suggest. Socio-demographic variables are related to levels of participation in most kinds of activity. Age, sex, marital status and a series of factors linked with social class including occupation, income, education and car ownership have emerged as useful predictors which enable plausible assessments to be made of future trends. Sociology is certainly responsible for promoting the use of these variables in survey investigations, and recreation research has borrowed this sociological equipment. The objectives and conclusions of recreation research, however, have remained specifically recreational rather than sociological. The emphasis has been upon activities that make demands upon land and other facilities, and it is easy to understand why. Recreation policy-makers and administrators in both the commercial and public sectors need to assess the types of provision that will match demand, and welcome guidance on how to market their existing facilities. Orthodox recreation research has its uses. No one urges its abandonment. But properly to understand recreation itself, let alone the rest of leisure, supplementary research is needed switching the focus away from activities and facilities, and towards genuinely sociological processes.

Television, drink, tobacco, sex and gambling

It is informative to list the leisure activities that prove the most common. Judged in these terms, leisure is not so much a matter of sport, the countryside and the arts, as television, alcohol, tobacco, sex and gambling. These big five are far and away the most popular forms of recreation in Britain today.

British adults average approximately 19 hours of televiewing each week, roughly equivalent to a quarter of all leisure time. Since the 1950s, television has reigned as the supreme time-filler, and during recent years time spent with television has been edging up, partly due to the spread of colour sets which seem more effective in holding their audience than monochrome models, and to the extension of broadcasting into afternoons and late evenings. There are variations, but television is a common pastime among all age groups, sexes and social classes. Children are very regular viewers. The television often acts as the staple form of recreation between school and bedtime.[7] In America station operators have become well aware of this child audience. Although adults may be viewing as well, when children are in the room they tend to control the channel selector. Hence the cartoons and other programmes aimed at tempting the young channel selectors to stations which can then attract the advertising that is usually intended to reach the adult audience.[8]

Alcoholic drink is another leisure pastime with a truly mass appeal. A government social survey in Britain has found that nine out of ten adults drink alcohol at least occasionally, while 67 per cent of all males, and 76 per cent of 18- to 24-year-olds, visit a public house at least once a month.[9] Teetotallers are left adrift from a substantial area of normal social intercourse. Spending on alcohol is judged sufficiently important to be measured separately in the Family Expenditure Survey, and tobacco is an equally significant object of recreational expenditure. In 1977 cigarettes were smoken by 40 per cent of all adults. Government campaigns publicising the dangers of smoking to health largely account for an 8 per cent decline between 1973 and 1977. However, this decline is most evident among upper middle class males, and partly represents a movement to pipe and cigar smoking rather than the total abandonment of tobacco. The working class has proved more resistant to government propaganda, while a feature of female emancipation over the last generation has been a growing use of cigarettes. There is now little difference between the proportions of men and women who are cigarette smokers. During recent years new drugs such as cannabis have made some impact, especially among young people. As they are illegal, these inroads cannot be precisely quantified, but at the moment the positions of alcohol and tobacco at the head of the leisure drug market do not appear to be under serious challenge.

Sex is another important form of leisure behaviour, but as in the case of illegal drugs, its prevalence eludes precise quantification. Casual observation suggests that a great deal of leisure activity among young people evolves around making and cultivating relationships with the opposite sex. After marriage its importance depends upon how broadly the term sex is defined. The conjugal relationship supplies a framework within which considerable leisure time is spent. On the narrowest definition, however, sex is one of the few leisure activities where participation among the entire adult population averages more than twice a week.[10]

Gambling completes the big five. In Britain betting is a national pastime and another important object of recreational expenditure. The typical adult stakes well over £1 per week, though losses are considerably less. Newman has calculated that in 1967 outlay on betting totalled £27.20 per head of population, but as the greater part of stake money is returned as winnings, net losses amounted to only £4.85.[11] Hence Newman's conclusion that, for most punters, gambling is better regarded as a common pastime than an addiction. Over half the total staked is concentrated upon horse and greyhound racing. High street betting shops alongside the 'runners' who still operate in most places of large-scale employment offer opportunities for a quick flutter to both the shopping and working publics. In 1976 a single horse race, the Derby, attracted stakes of £25 million. In 1968 Downes and his colleagues conducted interview investigations in Woodford and Wanstead, Sheffield and Swansea. They found that 44 per cent of the men and 9 per cent of the women used betting shops at least once a year, staking an average of £85, but for a net loss of only £3.[12] Football pools were patronised by 53 per cent of the men and 26 per cent of the women, while the fruit machines that have taken gaming into most public places were used by 29 and 17 per cent respectively. Bingo was an important venue for evenings out, particularly among older women, and also a frequent pastime in working men's clubs. On average the males interviewed were involved in 123 gaming sessions each year, while the women participated in 35. Gambling was somewhat less common among the middle than the working classes, though within the latter the relatively poor were the least frequent gamblers. Young people gambled more frequently than older age groups, and a host of additional variables including low job involvement, little interest in hobbies, a belief in luck and willingness to take risks all proved related to participation. But the main point at issue here is that gambling is a normal rather than an exceptional pastime. Gamblers are not a deviant minority. As in the case of alcohol, it is total abstainers who are exceptional. Gambling is interwoven into ordinary life. Becoming involved requires no great initiative; remaining aloof is the greater problem.

Reflecting upon these common uses of leisure can be instructive. Most people necessarily recognise the list as valid in relation to their own lives. Yet simultaneously many feel that stressing these activities does not convey the true character of their leisure. When presented with the above items, many people find the resultant portrait of leisure unattractive. Frequency of participation does not always correlate with enjoyment. For instance, as previously observed, although it is the most common single use of leisure time, television is rarely named as a favourite activity.[13] If leisure equals television, drugs, sex and gambling, how do we feel about its continued growth? How many people fancy more hours spent in front of the television, more alcohol in their blood-streams, and more money lost on pools and horses? Is this really all that we have to look forward to? In fact it is not *all* that we can anticipate; the emphasis upon activities is misleading.

Doing and experiencing

Silly questions deserve silly answers. Researchers find that when asked to name their favourite leisure activities, individuals will usually mention something that can be recorded. Yet it remains possible that many people only acquire favourite leisure activities under the pressures of an interview situation. Similarly researchers often ask their subjects what they did during the previous evenings and weekends. Recordable answers almost invariably follow, eventually, but the difficulties that individuals sometimes face in constructing answers indicate how inappropriate the question can be. The vacant stare or the snap answer, 'Nothing in particular', frequently come closer to the truth. Quite a lot of leisure is spent doing nothing, and this does not necessarily indicate a reprehensible waste of time. Bertrand Russell's praise of idleness was by no means idiosyncratic.[14] Relaxing and idling time can be agreeable experiences. People who work outside and inside their homes become physically and mentally tired, and in these circumstances simply recuperating is a perfectly sensible use of time. Apart from this, a great deal of leisure comes in inconvenient batches, such as a few hours in the evening, when there is not really time to do anything in particular. This is an aspect of leisure that tends to be missed in research that concentrates upon activities and the use of facilities.

Members of the public like to give researchers the types of answers they seem to require, and when pressed most people can manage to name an activity that occupied a particular occasion. If the television was on in the room where a person was doing nothing, he will probably allow himself to be recorded as watching television. One wonders for how many of the 19 hours a week that we average, the television set is little more than background noise. Likewise in other environments where leisure activity takes place, the activity itself is often secondary. The public house and the bingo hall can also be places where individuals simply relax.

Many popular uses of leisure time sound banal when only the activity is named. Gambling can sound particularly moronic. But when we approach closer to taste the real flavour of gambling, this initial appearance cracks. We realise, to begin with, that gambling is not a unitary phenomenon. Different people engage in different types of gambling for all manner of reasons. In some cases economic motivation is important, and not necessarily misplaced. There is always the chance of a coup, the big strike, and for the working class this can be as rational a strategy towards acquiring wealth as effort and application in employment. Newman's interviews with London East Enders and his observations in betting shops revealed a variety of additional satisfactions.[15] Horse-betting enables punters to exercise skill, decision-making and judgement. Furthermore, individuals can publicly display these talents and earn reputations among fellow punters who share a sense of community. Bingo offers tension, excitement, laughs and, once again, the community spirit that seems so elusive in contemporary society. Listing the frequency with which individuals gamble, their expenditures and losses, fails to convey the quality of experience that punters are seeking and obtaining. Whether the behaviour is alcoholic, sexual or televisual, there is invariably a deeper, psychological, experiencing dimension to leisure.

People

'Who were you with?' rather than 'What were you doing?' would often be the more appropriate question for researchers to address. Leisure is sometimes more a matter of doing people than things. When individuals talk informally about their uses of leisure time, it can quickly become apparent how secondary their activities are.

Among young people leisure tends to evolve around friends, sometimes one particular friend, and the activities with which they occupy themselves are often incidental. Peer groups hang about on street corners, frequent pubs and visit coffee bars. Ask any individual why he was participating and the most honest answer he can give is that his friends were there. A great deal of leisure behaviour remains barely comprehensible until the people are brought into focus. The British public's fondness of drink is a prime example. To explain the attraction of public houses it is necessary to shift attention away from the alcohol and towards the people the activity involves. Of those recorded as visiting pubs frequently in the government social survey, the 61 per cent who said they went mainly for the company considerably outnumbered those who reported drink as the main attraction.[16]

Countryside recreation also becomes easier to understand when this social dimension is added. In its absence, the behaviour of many visitors to the countryside remains puzzling. For example, of the trippers interviewed on summer Sundays at six West Midlands sites, 28 per cent did nothing but sit in or near their motor cars.[17] Similarly a survey in the Dartmoor National Park found that 70 per cent of the visitors to a 'moor walk' journeyed less than a mile from their vehicles, and 40 per cent did not venture more than 100 yards away.[18] In the Goyt Valley a scheme is operated in which cars are banned at weekends from several miles of road, while bicycles are on hire to enable visitors to move around. It has been found, however, that many visitors hire the bikes so that their children can ride around the car park.[19] One wonders why individuals spend the time, use the petrol and endure the congestion that these trips involve. What can the gratifications be? One answer lies in the trip's social functions. Car-borne trippers are rarely solitary individuals. People visit the countryside in groups, usually family groups, and both the trips and the countryside destinations can only be understood in terms of how they provide environments in which members of the family can interact. Elson's study of 700 car owners found that 75 per cent made Sunday motoring trips at least once every three weeks, and in explaining the popularity of this use of leisure Elson stresses the importance of shared recreation in fostering family unity.[20]

Burch has made comparable observations in relation to visitors to wilderness areas in America.

'Though solitary contact with untouched nature is a central motive offered by wilderness visitors only 2 per cent enter the wilderness alone, certainly a far lower proportion of solitariness than is found in urban life. Of course, nature as a goal is important. But it is important primarily as a setting for reaffirming and strengthening already estab-

lished social bonds. Solitude is a euphemism for keeping the group together, while the greatest proportion of time is devoted to interaction and adjustment within the group, rather than with pristine nature.'[21]

Neil Cheek and his associates have demonstrated how much can be learnt from detailed observation of what people actually do in 'recreation places'.[22] It is surprising how rarely recreation researchers have delved closely to describe how people really behave in sports centres, the countryside and other leisure milieux. Cheek's research was conducted mainly in rural locations, and one of the initial observations concerned how rarely visitors were unaccompanied. Countryside recreation is usually group behaviour. It was found that the type of activities with which visitors occupied themselves depended largely on the nature of their companions. Casually observing nature and beachcombing were characteristically family activities, while hunting normally took place among friends. This research pointed strongly to the conclusion that satisfactions from leisure derive largely from group interaction. Activities are typically means to ends, rather than ends in themselves. Cheek's enquiries also suggested that childhood socialisation influences later uses of leisure mainly as a result of the 'personal communication', that is the types of social relationships that are developed, a point to which we shall return in a later chapter. Furthermore, whether leisure interests are continued beyond childhood depends considerably upon whether the social relationships in which they are developed are sustained. Peer group pastimes tend to be dropped as the groups in question disintegrate. Interests acquired in the family, a life-long milieu, are more likely to be preserved.

Sport is also illuminated when a social dimension is introduced to its analysis. As mentioned in the previous chapter, participation in sport is growing, and it is informative to identify the types of sports where the upward trend is most marked. Although they are not declining, the traditional team games of soccer, rugby and cricket are not recording the most dramatic gains. The growing popularity of participant sport is most evident in what have previously been regarded as minority, rather select games including sailing, horse-riding, badminton and squash. The number of registered badminton clubs almost quadrupled within the space of two years between 1966 and 1968. This rate of expansion is exceptional, and can only be achieved from a very low take-off point, but comparably impressive if not quite as dramatic figures could be presented for each of the sports listed above. It is interesting to note certain characteristics that these boom sports share. They do not require any high level of physical fitness. Aspiring squash champions must be fit, but this is not necessary simply to play. Neither is any high degree of skill required. Again, it is different if you want to win tournaments, but to enjoy golf, squash or badminton all that is necessary is an opponent of comparable ability. Furthermore, none of the boom sports requires 22 or 30 people to gather at prearranged times. Squash, golf and sailing are 'social' sports. Groups of friends, neighbours, workmates and members of families can play at times to suit their own convenience, and as the demands upon skill and fitness are not great, few individuals are barred and the sports can be played throughout the greater part of the life-cycle. There is no need to argue that people play golf *only* for the subsequent drinks or to transact business in order to suggest that these social dimensions are often relevant. Catering for sport is no doubt partly a matter of enabling individual enthusiasts to pursue their interests. To some extent, however, it is also a matter of providing milieux for sociability that, in all probability, would otherwise find alternative supportive environments.

Tourism is another growth area where we can only begin to make sense of the participants' behaviour when we probe behind their more easily observable activities. Year by year more people are taking more holidays both in Britain and abroad. Time freed from work during the last 30 years has been taken mainly in the form of holiday entitlement, and the tourist industry has been a beneficiary. Despite the affluent society, the trend is not towards expensive hotels but towards camping with tents and caravans.[23] Taking to the tent is no longer the resort only of Boy Scouts and other impecunious holiday-makers. Camping holidays are now actually most common among the higher socio-economic strata, probably on account of their ability to afford the initial outlay for equipment. Again, the gratifications are far from self-evident. During the summer season congestion on camp sites in the main tourist areas greatly exceeds anything that would be considered tolerable in urban residential developments, and however many miles touring might be accomplished, any one camp site looks and feels like very many others. Tourism is another instance where we need to probe behind the visible activities in order to understand recreation. As in other spheres, the experiences that tourists are seeking often derive as much from the social interaction as the activities involved. Hence the need to insist, when analysing leisure, that the relatively easy-to-measure activities are firmly located amid the surrounding experiences and interaction.

The social construction of recreation

A further limitation of orthodox recreation research concerns its tendency to offer a static account of leisure activities. Investigators diligently record numbers of participants and forecast likely trends, but the activities themselves as opposed to their popularity are not treated as requiring explanation. The activities are simply on offer, awaiting customers. In actual fact, however, forms of recreation are not simply 'given'. They have not been on offer since time immemorial. All recreation is socially constructed and persistently susceptible to change. Artistic forms change over time, as is the case with sport. The modern game of soccer has not been played throughout history. Its ancestry can be traced to the Middle Ages and even beyond, but the older riotous game was reshaped during the nineteenth century.[24] Its rules were recast to adapt the sport to the limited space available in urban areas, and to allow the completion of matches within periods of time consistent with the rhythm of industrial life. Soccer was promoted along with other team sports, particularly in education, under the belief that such pastimes would nurture moral and civic virtue. Some now famous football league clubs in Britain were originally founded by religious bodies that were impressed by the moral potential of the medium. There is no good reason why soccer should continue indefinitely in its present form. Indeed, as a participant sport the better-known game is currently being partly replaced by five-a-side, a trend that awaits systematic investigation, but which no doubt reflects changes in the surrounding social and educational practices.

Countryside recreation may be conventionally regarded as simply 'doing what comes naturally', but it is as socially constructed as motor racing. To begin with, most of the countryside in Britain is man-made, albeit often centuries ago. There are few parts of the British Isles where the landscape has remained unchanged since the dawn of human history. The rural heritage that concerns conservationists is more frequently a social phenomenon than the unaided work of nature. The belief that sailing ships and tents somehow bring men closer to nature than motorways and hotels is more an ideology, itself requiring explanation, than a statement of scientific fact. Furthermore, the definition of the countryside as a suitable place for leisure is historically relative, largely a reaction to industrial and urban life. Among the leisured classes in eighteenth century Britain, 'High mountains were mostly considered monstrous and frightful, inconvenient obstacles in the way of civilised man'.[25] The European grand tour of that age was framed around cultural and architectural sights rather than the countryside, while the seaside and spa resorts were regarded more as health and pleasure centres than venues for enjoying nature. During the nineteenth century the countryside was redefined as offering not only healthy opportunities for relaxation and recuperation, but also character formation. The new wisdom maintained that, '. . . mountain air regenerates and cleanses the city dweller, the sight of a mountain summit provokes moral ideas, and to climb it, with the assistance of local guides, is an aspect of civic virtue.'[26] Hence the subsequent definition of climbing, hiking, cycling, camping and such-like as especially meritorious forms of recreation.

If the very definition of the countryside as a leisure resource is a social construct, this applies equally to what counts as recreation. Natural resources are cultural appraisals.[27] Conceptions of natural beauty vary according to time and place, while the uses of the countryside that can be regarded as recreation are highly elastic. Hence the crucial role of entrepreneurs and 'gatekeepers' who act as social filters in the leisure field.[28] Public authorities, private land-owners and a variety of voluntary associations all play a role in packaging and presenting images of the countryside in ways that encourage certain activities while implicitly discouraging others, and attract certain groups whilst repelling other sections of the public.

The social construction of recreation takes as its building materials not only physical resources, but also attitudes and values that are invariably rooted in the surrounding society. Hence the proposal that the analysis of leisure be grounded in a broader study of culture.[29] Eugene Bammel has drawn attention to what he terms the mythologies and mystiques, the popular beliefs that usually prove less than rational in a strictly scientific sense, by which leisure behaviour is surrounded.[30] Whether golfing or smoking 'pot', we entertain conceptions of the types of people who are likely to practice the forms of recreation in question, and these cultural conceptions are rarely irrelevant to the explanation of our behaviour.

Rather than fixed and determinate, all types of recreation are delicately poised upon particular constellations of social, economic and cultural circumstance, which is why historical change not only affects levels of participation in given activities, but is also likely to change the activities themselves. In our own time, new recreational uses of the countryside are being actively pioneered. Contemporary urban man venturing to the countryside for recreation, is less likely to be a dedicated hiker or mountaineer inspired by moral purpose than a casual visitor, rarely without a motor car, and often equipped with tent or caravan. Organisations offering more regimented countryside experiences such as the Youth Hostels' Association and the adventure training centres which flourished until recently, have found their popularity waning, and are being obliged to change their own characters in order to arrest their decline.[31] Similarly the traditional holiday camps are transforming themselves into venues where families can spend more loosely-structured, self-catering holidays. Its traditional devotees resent the invasion of their countryside by untutored hordes. Hence the opposition to the spread of caravan and camping sites which are accused of blighting the environment. These sentiments are less conservationist than simply conservative. Like all other forms of recreation, uses of the countryside will continue to adapt to social change. Recreation is historically dynamic. Despite the version of social reality encountered in orthodox recreation research, uses of leisure are not selections from fixed lists of possible activities. Recreation is fluid, subject to constant modification. When recreation research asks only where, when and how much, it overlooks one of the most important qualities of its subject-matter.

Life-styles

In their study of *Leisure and the Family Life-Cycle* Robert and Rhona

Rapoport have expressed impatience with orthodox recreation research, and have argued a need to search beyond 'palpable demand' in order really to make sense of the public's leisure behaviour and problems.[32] This is the essence of the argument in the present chapter. Recreation can only be fully understood when we probe behind the immediately visible activities to explore not one but several underlying realities. Behind the apparent solidity of current leisure habits we can discover an historical fluidity in which new forms of recreation are constantly invented and more traditional pastimes reshaped using the physical and cultural capital furnished by a changing society. Behind activities we also discover social relationships along with the psychological, experiencing dimension of leisure. All these underlying realities need to be brought into focus, and 'life-style' is a helpful concept to understand how they fuse to produce the leisure that we know.

This becomes clear in the Rapoports' study. They distinguish a trio of life-strands in work, the family and leisure which interact in the sense that an individual's circumstances along any one of these career lines have implications in the other spheres, and their book attempts to chart the effects of developing work and particularly family life-cycles for uses of leisure. Their study focuses on major junctions or status transitions such as marriage and retirement. These are critical points during which ways of life can unfreeze and patterns reform, laying the processes influencing uses of leisure unusually bare. The Rapoports argue that successive stages in the life-cycle are characterised by their own preoccupations, which lead to relatively conscious interests, which in turn lead to particular uses of leisure. For example, it is suggested that during adolescence a major preoccupation concerns the individual's identity. A young person wants to know 'Who am I?' which leads to interests in obtaining new experiences, and hence considerable variety and novelty in leisure behaviour. The Rapoports do little more than illustrate such arguments with a handful of case studies, and it could be said that the evidence does not enable them to prove their points conclusively. Nevertheless, their book is important because of its insistence that we probe behind leisure's surface appearances, and once we do this we recognise the need for the totalising perspective that the life-style concept can supply. Particular leisure activities must be located in the context of individuals' overall life-styles for, as the Rapoports illustrate, the significance of the same leisure activity can change as the life-cycle unfolds, and preoccupations and interests develop accordingly.

Real life possesses an holistic quality. Individuals do not so much engage in *ad hoc* miscellanies of activities as develop broader systems of leisure behaviour consisting of a number of interdependent elements, and specific leisure interests are often only explicable in the contexts of the wider life-styles to which they contribute. The golfers and swimmers that surveys identify mostly participate in these activities for only a fraction of their leisure time, though their propensity to participate may influence and be influenced by their behaviour on other occasions. It can be misleading to judge the importance of activities solely in terms of the time they account for. The occasional game of golf can be important in maintaining a lifelong friendship, while the football match that fills only one and a half hours per week may furnish constant topics of conversation throughout the following days. The study of leisure loses something of importance if overall life-styles become lost from view as uses of time are broken down into discrete categories of activities.

Much nonsense has been written as a result of considering trends in specific leisure activities in isolation. Soccer's missing millions are a prime example. Football league clubs sold 41 million tickets in 1948–49, but only 25 million during the 1973–74 season. During this decline in the national game commentators have repeatedly speculated about whether spectators are being driven away by dull and defensive tactics, or by violence on and off the field. In fact there is little that could be done within the sport to restore football's former appeal. Its decline has been modest compared with other longstanding spectator sports. Attendances at greyhound tracks fell from 36 million in 1945–46 to 7 million in 1972, while the 1,500 professional boxers in 1952 had slimmed to 350 by 1973. Spectator sports in general have suffered since the advent of television and the spread of the family motor car which has widened the public's leisure opportunities.

Surface changes in leisure behaviour are easily misinterpreted. Every innovation in recreation since time immemorial appears to have been accompanied by forecasts of moral decay. During the inter-war years 'mixed' youth clubs were a controversial innovation. Many felt that a girl's proper place was in the home. Similarly when 'modern' dancing developed earlier in the century with its close physical contact between couples, many eyebrows were raised. Fears of promiscuity and the dissolution of the family that surround 'pot' and pop festivals today have been awakened among earlier generations. Insisting on looking at the totality of leisure reduces the likelihood of exaggerated reactions to specific changes. Viewing the recent upsurge in participant recreation in isolation can be misleading. Although participation in sport is growing, the proportion of leisure time that it accounts for remains miniscule compared with television. Beneath all the surface flux, historical shifts in the balance between the various elements in the public's life-styles have been subtle rather than dramatic.

Orthodox recreation research says little about life-styles. As a result, it offers a far from complete understanding of recreation itself. Worse still, it tells us little about the interrelationships between recreation, the rest of leisure, and the rest of life either at the individual level or in terms of their roles in the larger social system.

Recreation and the quality of life

This is an appropriate point to confess that as yet social science has made little progress towards measuring the quality of life. Interest in life's quality is as old as human society itself, but present-day attempts at measurement date from the inter-war years when American scholars first began adding 'social indicators' to the economic statistics already employed to assess well-being.[33] Economists have agreed ways of measuring our 'standards of living', but should a rise in the gross national product be equated with a growth in the quality of life? It is plausible to argue that assessments of housing conditions, educational opportunities, crime, racial harmony and suchlike be added to the standard economic indicators. During the 1960s a further methodological innovation occurred. Scepticism was expressed as to whether more education, bathrooms and other material assets determine well-being any more faithfully than GNP. Do people become more happy or satisfied when they are 'better' housed and educated? The response was to develop 'subjective indicators', and it has now become a standard practice for investigators to query whether their samples are happy and satisfied with their jobs, homes, marriages, health and life in general.

When research data are presented in research reports they readily acquire a spurious facticity. With all the indicators now in use, it is easy to convey the impression that the quality of life is being adequately measured. But as Mark Abrams has argued,[34] this remains far from the case. It may be desirable to add social to economic indicators of well-being, but exactly which social phenomena should we measure and how should we weight them? How important are schools relative to hospitals? When laymen are asked what *they* consider important, happy marriages and home lives are frequently mentioned, but are laymen necessarily well informed about the conditions that determine their well-being? The weights that researchers assign to both objective and subjective indicators remain arbitrary. As for subjective indicators themselves, it is doubtful whether responses to a question such as, 'Are you happy with . . .?' can really be equated with the quality of life. What do people mean when they express satisfaction with their jobs, marriages and so on? There is evidence that many respondents interpret this kind of question in comparison with other people they know, in which cases expressed satisfaction will be socially relative rather than an absolute indicator of well-being. High levels of expressed satisfaction may mean only that individuals are resigned to their predicaments, and it can be argued that a critical abrasiveness indicating an awareness of imperfections in existing circumstances is a preferable quality to such passive complacency.

Having mentioned the imperfections in our current measurements we are entitled to observe that, for what they are worth, other indicators of the quality of life do not correlate strongly with recreation opportunities. After relating various indices of social pathology and well-being to recreation facilities in American cities, Diana Dunn concluded that, 'There is no evidence that the quality of life in US cities would be diminished appreciably nor improved substantially if dramatic changes occurred in the amount or kind of recreation opportunities afforded urban residents or if all minimum recreation standards were met or exceeded.'[35] It could be the measures of well-being that are faulty. The quality of the available evidence hardly justifies wholesale closure of sports complexes and urban parks. But at best the case for recreation remains unproven. Citizens are not marching upon or petitioning town and county halls in their thousands calling for better recreation facilities. Recreation has yet to emerge as a politically sensitive issue, except in so far as rate- and tax-payers query levels of expenditure. Hall and Perry's interviews in two urban areas where recreation provision was being deliberately improved in a quality of life experiment found less than 17 per cent of the respondents naming recreational activities and facilities among the three most important contributors to their satisfaction with life.[36] Health, jobs and homes proved the main satisfiers, while lack of genuine democracy, income and the quality of education were the main sources of grievance.

To narrate these findings is not to argue against public support for the arts, sport and other forms of recreation. The evidence is simply a reminder that recreation is not the whole of leisure. Scope for choice in non-working time need not be put to purely playful purposes. Once institutionalised and professionalised, every activity gains an in-built momentum for growth, and this is very evident in the case of recreation. Its past development has produced a vocal recreation lobby in which researchers and practitioners unite to proclaim the value of their interest. It is deceptively easy to equate the growth of leisure with pleas for resources to satisfy a seemingly inexorable growth in recreation demand. In fact, however, to the extent to which we are moving towards a society with greater leisure, the options are wider than voices lobbying on behalf of already institutionalised forms of recreation tend to indicate. To understand leisure together with the opportunities and problems that it raises, the first requirement is that we extend our gaze beyond the relatively easy-to-measure recreational facilities and activities.

Chapter 4

Mass society theory

Mass media and mass culture

The word 'mass' has become a common article of twentieth century speech. Mass media which allow a single communicator to address the entire nation instantaneously have become a part of everyday life. In addition to his daily entertainment, modern man obtains most of his information about the wider world through the media.[1] We no longer depend upon face-to-face gossip. The world's latest fashions, sports events and political dramas can be delivered into virtually every citizen's home. Since the advent of television, it has been possible to live as a recluse yet actually witness events in every corner of the globe. The arrival of the mass media has been accompanied by the growth of a mass or popular culture. Tastes and ideas no longer need remain confined within a variety of regional, occupational and religious communities. The whole nation hears the same news and is enthralled by the same television soap operas. In the jargon of the advertising industry, the nation now comprises a single admass that will respond to the same images and accents.

It has been estimated that, when their audiences are aggregated, the mass media account for as much as a half of the contemporary public's leisure time, and among the media television enjoys unrivalled prominence. In Britain the typical adult views for three hours every day, and the average family's set is switched on for five hours – equivalent to the greater part of every evening. It is difficult to exaggerate the importance of the media when examining modern leisure. Whether people are seeking entertainment, information or merely diversion, the television is the most popular resort. The broadcast audiences for religious worship and sports fixtures vastly exceed live audiences. Boxing, tennis and cricket, if Kerry Packer proves successful, are now exploiting the mass marketing possibilities of the media to yield huge returns for promoters and star performers. Commercial organisations are prepared to invest considerable sums in sponsoring media-covered sports events to reap the publicity and prestige that accompany association with a popular sport. In addition to direct sponsorship, sport and advertising are now linked in a host of intricate ways which range from bill-boards alongside playing areas, through adverts on racing cars to the provision of clothing for leading golfers and kits for soccer teams. None of this would occur if it were not for the mass media in general and television in particular. Older amateur ideals have been placed under enormous stress by these developments. Lords and Wimbledon have succumbed to professionalism. It remains to be seen how long the Olympic movement can continue as the world's major athletics festival and remain amateur in the traditional sense.

The technological progress characteristic of industrial society has made mass communication a reality. Developments in printing technology and, equally important, the creation of a railway system allowed the mass circulation of daily newspapers before the end of the nineteenth century. Electricity, the telegram and the telephone increased the speed of information gathering and dissemination. The camera and cinematography, the gramophone, radio and, more recently, television technology have created new media of mass communication. It is unlikely that we have yet seen the end of this sequence.

Through the mass media the few address the many, and over time the few have become fewer and the many have become more as the media have 'invaded' country after country. Golding has distinguished two phases in the growth of the mass communication industries.[2] He terms the initial phase industrialisation, meaning specialisation, with distinctions appearing, for example, between newspaper publishers, printers and distributors, and their numbers multiplying. The British press went through this stage during the second half of the nineteenth century – the classic period of liberal journalism when scores of publications served a variety of publics.[3] By the turn of the century, however, Golding's second phase had begun; a period of concentration with the strong dominating the market and crushing or taking over competitors. Today this process of concentration is well advanced. Newspapers have merged, publishing has been integrated with printing and distribution, and the press is now linked with other media industries such as commercial television. Concentration has acquired an international dimension. As Tunstall has provocatively observed, the media are American.[4] Not wholly American, but throughout the world American feature films appear on television screens and international news consists of information judged important through Western, mainly American, eyes. This development has been sinisterly but appropriately described as 'cultural imperialism'.

The media's importance in the public's leisure commends their analysis as an approach to understanding leisure itself. Contemporary leisure is mass leisure, based upon a mass culture propagated by the mass media, and sociology has a ready-made body of theory, the theory of mass society, to aid the interpretation.

Mass society theory

The mass society theory is not new. It pre-dates all the contemporary mass media. In his excellent discussion, Giner has shown that its

principal ideas can be traced to the ancient Greeks.⁵ Massification is
seen as the consequence of two processes. The first is the breakdown of
a society's internal social organisation, meaning a weakening of the
social institutions such as family, church and neighbourhood that
otherwise mediate between individuals and the wider social order. The
mass society theory is not only about leisure. Massification has been
seen as a consequence of the growth of cities and the eclipse of
tighter-knit rural communities, the decline of the traditional extended
family, and the spread of affluence together with the related commodity consciousness and status striving that can divide neighbours. It is
alleged that these developments atomise the public into a disorganised
mass of individuals, and this condition allows the second massifying
process to operate. Individuals stand helpless before forces ranging
from bureaucracy to political demagogues who can manipulate the
public for their own purposes. Bereft of primary group loyalties and
religious values, the theory argues that people are predisposed to seek
security in mass movements created by manipulative leaders who are
able to whip up fanatical support with extremist ideologies. In a mass
society, democracy, equal rights and universal suffrage have been
regarded as dangerous developments. Mass society theorists regard
the public as victims and simultaneously as a threat to order. The
masses are susceptible to manipulation and in this sense are helpless
victims. But the masses tend to be restive and, once mobilised, can
become rebellious and threaten values and institutions that have previously resisted massification. This is the theory behind the fear that
enfranchised workers will be persuaded to use their votes against their
own better interests, and behind the suspicion that affluent workers
will be tempted to part with their money for candy floss instead of
upgrading their basic living standards. Mass society theory is tainted
with an age-old aristocratic pessimism towards the lower orders.

Paternalism has become unfashionable, but this does not mean that
the theory must be dismissed. It offers an explanation for such twentieth century political phenomena as the rise of authoritarian, 'extremist' movements both left and right of the ideological spectrum. And
many pundits consider the theory particularly relevant for understanding the implications of the mass media. Golding argues that, 'The
kernel model of mass communication [is] the few addressing the many
with omnipotence.'⁶ The mass media allow only one-way communication. It is impossible for the receiver to make any immediate response
to the television presenter or journalist. The audience is sentenced to
passivity. Furthermore, the members of an audience cannot communi-
cate with one another. They comprise a mass of individuals rather than
an organised public. Their only link is through the communicator.
With the mass media, the twin processes of massification operate
jointly and on an unprecedented massive scale. The audience is fragmented and simultaneously rendered available for persuasion.

When political propaganda was channelled principally through
doorstep canvassing and public meetings, politicians were forced into

face-to-face interaction with their constituents. The audience at a meeting could hear each other's arguments as well as the speaker's, who would therefore stand exposed to the force of public opinion. Today's party leaders speak to the nation through the media. Individuals listen in their homes rather than public places. Participation in public debate is therefore inhibited. To obtain 'feedback' the parties commission market research, the results of which do not so much constrain the leaders as enable them to package their policies and present their images more persuasively. The constrast between the folk cultures in which participants fashioned their own amusements and elevated their own folk artists, and the entertainment that is dispensed on television and cinema screens is directly analogous. According to the mass society theory, the rise of the mass media has contributed to a psychological rape of the once great public. The citizenry is transformed into a mass of passive consumers of prepackaged information and entertainment.

It is alleged that ease of consumption and persuasive delivery blunt the critical power of the masses. Because it is atomised the public is unable to nurture its own standards against which to judge media products. And because of this atomised helplessness, the public is susceptible to whatever amusement, values and facts the media broadcast. Critics deplore the way in which media output is styled to make the widest possible appeal. To maximise audiences it is necessary to strike a 'common denominator' that inevitably fails to tap the authentic tastes and interests of any section of the community. Unhappily the mass is helpless to resist. Its critical potential is neutralised by the ease with which mass culture can be assimilated. The media are seen as seducing passive innocents. The plights of children and the working class can be portrayed in especially pitiful terms. Since it is aimed at the mass, the quality of pop culture is necessarily mediocre, but it nevertheless erodes high culture in a manner comparable to that in which political demagogues who arouse the fanatical support of the masses can sweep opposition aside. Herein, according to the theory under discussion, lies the problem of modern leisure. Mediocrity is broadcast with an irresistible power which suppresses individuals' latent capacities for self-expression. The net result, according to Rosenberg, is a public that is 'anaesthetised' and left unaware of its own potential.[7] Likewise Stuart Hood deplores the 'narcoticising' effects of television, claiming that news, sport and beauty contests are all presented as equally worthwhile, leaving the impression that nothing is important.[8] Wilenski argues that ' . . . the good, the mediocre and the trashy are becoming fused in one massive middle mush.'[9] Ernest van den Haag echoes these sentiments. 'The total effect of mass culture is to distract people from lives which are so boring that they generate obsession with escape. Yet because mass culture creates addiction to prefabricated experience, most people are deprived of the remaining possibility for autonomous growth and personal enrichment, and their lives become ever more boring and unfulfilled.'[10]

The medium and the message

Part of the critique of the mass media and the culture they broadcast maintains that the media are not neutral purveyors of communications; that they cannot be so innocent – their very nature forbids it. It is claimed that the output, whether entertainment or news, is inevitably fashioned by the medium itself. The best-known version of this argument is summarised in McCluhan's dictum that the 'medium is the message' (and often a soothing massage as well), and his observations on how electronic technology has reshaped so many aspects of personal life while transforming the world into a 'global village'.[11] News reporting through both press and television has understandably been a major object of research, and claims that the media merely report events as they actually happen have been ruthlessly exposed.

One of the earliest and still among the most systematic investigations in this area was conducted by Galtung and Ruge into the coverage of the Cuban, Congo and Cyprus crises in four Norwegian newspapers.[12] They discovered that the likelihood of events becoming news depended upon a number of factors, all confirmed in subsequent enquiries, that had less to do with the intrinsic importance of the events than the nature of the medium. First there was a *periodicity* factor. Newspapers that appear once a day are best able to report events that develop in this sequence. Developments that unfold gradually over weeks or months are more difficult to handle. Similarly events that produce a sequel in less than 24 hours are not treated as fully as when the pace of development is more consistent with the rhythm of the medium. In any case, however the flow of events is paced in the real world, the mechanics of daily news reporting impose a day-to-day rhythm on the output.

Second, Galtung and Ruge found that events were most likely to be reported if they were *unexpected yet meaningful*. As the cliché informs us, 'Dog bites man' is not news. Ordinary day-to-day life – the typical, the average, the expected is drained from the images of the world dispensed through newspapers and television screens. The public has an unquenchable appetite for sensations but does not need the media to supply details of ordinary, humdrum, often boring everyday life. To become news an event must be unusual, and its chances of being 'taken up' are increased if it is nevertheless instantly comprehensible. Presenting news is not like writing a book. Reports must be immediately intelligible to the audience. Contrary to the saying, 'Man bites dog' is not an ideal news story – the motivation is far from self-evident. Experienced reporters claim to possess noses that immediately scent news value. They learn from experience to recognise events that will earn space and headlines. Bensman and Lilienfield write about 'the journalistic attitude' that includes an ability to identify the appropriate 'angle'.[13] Freelance reporters operating from magistrates' courts throughout the country can produce a constant flow of copy for the nationals and income for themselves if they can spot news value. An ideal angle will surprise readers but remain within their comprehension, and the operation of this news value is illustrated in Halloran's research into the media's coverage of the London anti-Vietnam war demonstration in October 1968.[14] The run-up to this event was reported almost entirely in terms of the likelihood of violent clashes between demonstrators and police. The organisers insisted throughout that their intentions were non-violent and that their motivations were political. They hoped to publicise their arguments against US policy in Vietnam. But the anti-war arguments were well worn, not news. In contrast, the mere possibility of violence contained enough sensation to capture the public's imagination, and the plot could be made readily comprehensible – demonstrators versus police. There was little trouble on the demonstration itself. Needless to say, the minor incidents that did occur were given extensive media coverage, and the absence of any major violence made another news story.

Galtung and Ruge's third news-making factor is *human interest.* To merit news coverage, it is helpful if events involve specific persons. People are more interesting than cold events. Collective behaviour and decisions are difficult to report. News must be personalised to give it human interest, warmth and audience appeal. The news value of political events increases when conflicts can be presented as gladiatorial contests between personalities. Bensman and Lilienfield list an eye for human interest, the angle allowing the public to identify with people in the news, as a major element in the journalistic attitude. Who remembers what the Congo crisis was about? Probably fewer people than can recall the name of Lumumba. Most people will have heard of Fidel Castro, but how many could describe the Cuban brand of communism? Holding their audiences' interest is a preoccupation among television producers. John Whale, a broadcaster who has worked on both British and American television, describes his medium as the 'half-shut eye'.[15] Stories must be picture-centered and ideas kept simple. Even in documentaries and news programmes, 'talking heads' must be kept to a minimum. Ideas must be contextualised with eye-catching pictures. In his study of the television production of seven half-hour documentary programmes on the nature of prejudice, Elliott was impressed by the extent to which 'professional standards' took precedence over both the subject-matter and the anticipated effects of the series.[16] The producer wanted interesting programmes, so interesting film sequences had to be used irrespective of their relevance to an argument, and the entire presentation had to be geared to material that could be filmed.

The fourth factor that Galtung and Ruge list as increasing the likelihood of events being selected as news is that they should involve *élite individuals or nations.* In Britain everything that the Prime Minister says is news.[17] With other citizens and even Cabinet Ministers more discriminating criteria are applied. Few people might quarrel with this bias. Nevertheless, the fact remains that the picture of world affairs presented through the media is systematically distorted.

In some instances the news is not only selectively filtered but actually manufactured by the media. In 1977 Tate and Lyle obtained a court injunction postponing an ATV documentary film which allegedly portrayed the company's black employees in South Africa. The company was able to produce sworn affidavits supporting the claim that interviewees had been paid to 'act' the parts that the film-makers were seeking. During the firemen's strike, also in 1977, it subsequently emerged that live television reports apparently showing firemen responding to exceptional emergencies had been artificially staged. However, claims that the media manufacture news are not drawing attention only to such cases of outright deception. A more typical example of news 'manufacture' concerns the operation of the 'lobby' in British politics. Over a hundred lobby correspondents are recognised by the Serjeant-at-arms on behalf of the Speaker and granted access to the House of Commons lobby along with other privileges including early sight of documents and informal briefings by politicians. Tunstall interviewed 39 of these correspondents and his findings offer unique insights, for one of their own rules forbids lobby journalists mentioning the lobby itself in their reports, meaning that correspondents never disclose where their information was obtained.[18] Lobby reporters guarantee the anonymity of informants, unless otherwise instructed. The material processed by these journalists is not 'hard news' – real events that happen independently of journalism. The lobby deals essentially with 'soft news', rumours and insights that often owe their existence to the fact that there is a lobby, though reports are normally presented as if they were the results of investigative journalism. It has been suggested that street demonstrations and civil disobedience are encouraged by a quest for media publicity, and the media have frequently earned rebuke on this account. No doubt there is some truth in this complaint, but it is not only fringe groups that play to the media. Leading politicians are as skilled as anyone at the art.

No one is more aware that the medium is often the message than mass communicators themselves. It is not journalists and broadcasters but sociologists along with other members of the public who need convincing with evidence from research. Features of the media that excite mass society theorists because of their implications for society-at-large also concern the communicators, though usually for different reasons. While the mass society theory portrays the atomised public as helpless before the bombardment of media output, unable to respond and thereby influence the communicators, media personnel develop their own sense of helplessness. Journalists and broadcasters receive no representative feedback from readers and listeners. Yet they are subject to remote control by this mysterious mass that can switch off its television sets and cease buying particular newspapers. In private, media personnel often display cynicism towards the public. The communicators do not regard themselves as servants of the community, but construct and take refuge in their own private worlds.[19] They decline to judge their work in terms of audience appeal, preferring to insulate themselves behind professional standards. Tunstall has described how, among journalists, the most prestigious types of work are diplomatic, foreign and political news-gathering, though these are known to do little to increase newspaper revenue. Motoring correspondents on the one hand, whose value to their papers largely derives from attracting advertising revenue, and crime and sports reporters on the other hand whose contributions attract readers, are in less prestigious branches of journalism.[20] From the public's point of view, the ways in which the media select and manufacture information are problems, if at all, on account of the tendency for news to be systematically distorted. For media personnel the problem is seen in terms of organisational constraints upon creativity. Several reactions are possible.[21] A common response is for communicators to 'distance' themselves from their eventual products, disclaiming responsibility for the final outcome of their work as it appears in newspapers and on television. Among themselves, and with any members of the public with whom they have direct contact, little secret may be made of their low opinions of the quality of the work they are obliged to produce. In so far as they defend their efforts, the commitment of media men is normally segmented. They identify only with their particular contributions to the production process. Within journalism there is at best an uneasy truce between news gatherers and processors. Reporters complain vociferously about the sub-editors who mangle their copy. For their part, the processors may accept no brief for the contents, but will commend the lay-out achieved on a given newspaper page.

As in most occupations, the media offer scope for the development and display of esoteric skills that can only be fully appreciated by colleagues. The performances and products seen by the public often overlay private games of which the wider audience remains unaware. In their report on a provincial repertory company, Taylor and Williams comment on the practice of 'corpsing' – on-stage attempts by actors to make their colleagues lose composure.[22] Part of the skill involves concealing these manoeuvres from the audience, the point being to display to fellow actors technical skills that the untutored public is considered unable to appreciate. Broadcasting, where a greater part of the production process is off-stage, offers plentiful scope for personnel to acquire reputations within their profession by developing skills whose relevance may never become known in the outside world. In recent years, mass communicators themselves have been the subject of considerable research. Their private worlds invariably prove fascinating, but apart from this, the output becomes increasingly comprehensible the more we move away from treating the media as neutral channels conveying news and entertainment, and towards taking account of intra-media processes.

Is this relevant to the quality of leisure? It must be if only because there is more to leisure than entertainment. Large sections of the public devote some of their leisure to keeping themselves informed about the world around. But the above arguments about news reporting can be applied with equal force to the media's entertainment function. Here the argument is that the media are not offering wares that the public would independently demand. By their nature, the mass media are incapable of such a response. At the time of the media's birth, optimists hoped that means were arriving to present mankind's artistic treasures to the millions. We now know that the media do not function in the manner that this optimism assumed. The bulk of televised drama is written specifically for the medium, and one of the forces to which this production is subject is the need to appeal to a mass (often world-wide) audience. In light entertainment the mass media have created the 'star system'. Popular performers can be offered to the millions which reduces demand for other artists and strips away the middle rungs that once slowly led to the top of entertainers' career ladders. In our modern world of entertainment, stars are born overnight, apparently created by popular appeal. But stars fade with equal pace. It is not the elementary public response that produces these phenomena, but the manner in which the mass media are interposed between performers and their publics. Mass entertainment is as prefabricated as news reporting.

Solutions to the malaise

In so far as the unsatisfactory quality of contemporary leisure is the result of its mass character, what is the solution? Two answers are suggested. The older and better-known advocates paternalism, while the more trendy response favours participation. Paternalist solutions recommend that media be run or at least subject to control by responsible and cultivated élites who can protect the public from vulgar temptations, and who should in turn be protected from the competition of those whose aims are more sordid – profit or demagoguery. In its early days the BBC's aims were explicitly paternal. Under the leadership of Lord Reith, the Corporation's mission was to educate the public and raise levels of popular taste. It is only since the 1950s that commercial competition has been permitted in British broadcasting, and that the BBC has felt a need to compete for audience ratings. State sponsorship of approved forms of recreation including the classical arts, is also justified on paternal grounds. Britain has plenty of experience with this attempted answer to the problem of popular culture, and the difficulties are now only too evident. The crux of the problem concerns how to decide who are the cultivated élites. In practice the arbiter is power. Paternal control of culture requires a parallel political economy. Fascism, communism and feudalism furnish preconditions for paternalism. Would we really recommend the types of cultural control that operate in the Soviet Union where Smith comments on '. . . the refusal of music monitors of the Komsomol and Ministry of Culture to permit groups to play their own compositions on the grounds that these tunes were not written by official, regime-approved composers'?[23] Despite these controls, in the USSR 'pop culture has seeped right through the ideological walls that conservative elders have tried to create'[24] in a manner comparable to the spread of 'pot' on American campuses. Is the quality of culture so serious a problem to justify abandoning democracy and the market economy? It is because we have preserved these institutions that cultural paternalism in twentieth-century Britain and America has made even less impact on the public's leisure than in the socialist world.

Distaste for paternalism's political implications has led recent critics of mass culture to seek different solutions, with one school of thought proposing to extend rather than suppress democracy by promoting participation. During the 1970s 'participation' has become one of the 'good things' that everyone favours. In town planning, industry, education and numerous other spheres, 'power to the people' has been hailed as the solve-all. Managers, trade unionists and politicians of all major parties claim to favour workers' participation in industry. Needless to say, closer inspection proves that participation tends to mean rather different things to these different interest groups, and it is important to identify the ways in which it is envisaged that participation might cure mass culture's ailments.

In Britain one of the most sustained and coherent arguments for participation has been made by Brian Groombridge in relation to television broadcasting.[25] Groombridge's main complaint is that television has become the public's main source of information about current events, and is lamentably failing to deliver information effectively. On political and social issues, the knowledge of the typical man in the street tends to be pathetic. As an educational medium, television has been less than wholly successful, and Groombridge's answer is to bring the medium into closer contact with the public that it serves. He advocates a 'journalism of explanation' instead of concentration upon interesting pictures, but places a greater stress on a need for reporters to operate like community workers. He does not argue for 'direct access', as in the BBC Open Door series where interest groups are allowed to produce and broadcast their own programmes. Open access is just one way in which participation could be extended, and Groombridge is aware of the disadvantages of this particular method – it could fragment programming and result in a low-quality output. He insists that programmes be professionally produced and presented, but seeks a greater responsiveness to the public's interests, the aim being to actually involve the public in the analysis of current affairs. Instead of broadcasts being framed by alien professional standards for passive viewers, Groombridge seeks programmes that are sensitive to ordinary people's interests.

The spread of film clubs and community newspapers has been advocated on similar grounds, and there have been parallel proposals to democratise the arts. The case for *animation* envisages cultural workers leaving their artistic enclaves to work among the public thereby unlocking the potential creativity of the masses. Participation offers an end to passivity and manipulation. It seeks to place both media technology and the traditional arts at the disposal of the masses – to transform the public from consumers to creative producers of their own culture. All manner of splendid results are envisaged, and the likely effectiveness and desirability of schemes to extend participation will be examined more comprehensively in Chapter 11. Here we are concerned specifically with the mass society critique which is just one of the positions from which participation can be urged, and before proceeding to assess the cure, it is necessary to ask whether the diagnosis is valid. Is mass culture the dreadful beast that its critics allege? Do the mass media as currently organised really detract from the quality of life and leisure in the ways that the theory specifies? As we shall see, although the case sounds persuasive when well presented, it is doubtful whether the mass society theory is realistic in relation to modern leisure.

How powerful are the media?

In their early days the mass media were held in considerable awe. A sentence had only to be broadcast and, some pessimists apparently believed, it would be imprinted forever on the public's consciousness. Politicians everywhere have treated the media with suspicion. Throughout the world television and radio have been subjected to some type of government control. For their part, in addition to charting audience size and character, mass media researchers have traditionally been preoccupied with the (short-term) effects of mass communication. Just how powerful are the media in shaping tastes and opinions?

One conclusion now firmly established is that the media's powers of persuasion are less magical than was once variously hoped and feared. Contrary to some impressions created by debates that the media themselves host, viewers of sexploitation films do not rush from cinemas in their thousands intent on acts of rape. Nor does television screen violence provoke nationwide carbon-copy murders. A handful of individuals with violent predispositions may find encouraging models to mimic, and repeated exposure may foster a blasé attitude when real acts of violence occur, though the concern that media violence continues to arouse argues otherwise. Advertising executives have learnt to their cost that the promotion of a brand on television does not automatically lead to soaring sales. Likewise politicians find the public less easy to manipulate than mass society theories would lead them to expect. The influence of television on general election campaigns has been carefully monitored, and all the evidence has shown its impact to be marginal. This is partly because the parties' efforts cancel each other out, as is the case when advertisers promote competing brands. But in addition the public displays a capacity for discrimination. A well organised advertising campaign can pay off, but it is helpful to have a product that is in demand. As far as politics are concerned, people are most likely to expose themselves to opinions with which they already agree, and often dismiss the other side's arguments on grounds of their source. Plugging a record on the radio will not necessarily make it a hit. Nor will a BBC ban always prevent a record climbing the charts, as the Sex Pistols have proved. If public taste could be so easily shaped, by now the British public would be addicted to classical music which has always received enormous backing from the BBC, originally founded on the paternal belief that the public could and should be educated to a higher level of musical appreciation. Clayre has observed that,

'One of the most cherished beliefs of those responsible for music broadcasts is that the BBC (with its magnificent music broadcasts since its very early days in the 1920s) has created a great new audience for classical music listening to the radio. . . . But when audience statistics began to be gathered in the 1930s there was no significant increase from year to year in the population listening to classical music, and the audience today is very much as it was in the 1930s.'[26]

No one claims that the media have no effects whatsoever upon their audiences. Whether trading in musical tastes or political opinions, the media can consolidate existing dispositions. The processes whereby new trends become fads and fashions, only subsequently to be overtaken, are accelerated by the media. Students have latterly been declaring that to assess the media's total impact we must concern ourselves not only with short-term and easily anticipated effects, but also with longer-term maybe less obvious influence. It has been suggested, for example, that radio and television's political neutrality towards the major parties may have spread the belief that there are two sides to every argument thereby diluting partisanship. While rarely changing already formed opinions, it has been argued that over a period the media may define the issues on which both politicians and the public are expected to hold points of view.[27] It has also been argued that in the longer term the media may modify the primary social relationships among which citizens spend their everyday lives. Clayre has speculated about the differences between families that listen to the radio which leaves the senses free for eye-to-eye contact, and the television-watching household.[28] Television has been blamed for reducing interaction between parents and children. Indeed, Bronfenbrenner accuses American parents of abdicating to the media their responsibilities for socialisation.[29] Throughout the world the media in general and the transistor radio in particular have been seen as contributing to the breakdown of traditional cultures by spreading modern aspirations and life-styles. In advanced countries including Britain the media have helped to dilute regional contrasts in the face of a national culture. Raymond Williams[30] and Richard Hoggart,[31] in their well-known works on the subject, have drawn attention to the role of the media in the evolution of working class culture since the nineteenth century. The media play an important role in contemporary life. No one denies this. But the evidence now available suggests that their influence hardly matches the allegations of the mass society theory which portrays the public as passively seduced and manipulated, grasping at whatever tastes and wares the media choose to propagate.

Are primary groups destroyed?

A major error in some versions of the mass society argument lies in its conception of the public as a disorganised rabble with no sources of support other than those delivered through the media. In practice this is not the condition in which people normally receive mass communications. The public at the receiving end of television is more organised than mass society theorists have supposed. Audiences are not reduced to helpless aggregates of solitary persons. Readers, viewers and listeners are mostly members of families and other social groups from which they acquire tastes and opinions which influence their uses of the media and filter the messages that are received. In their review of the evidence on how the public responds to television, Baggaley and his colleagues have concluded that viewing must be regarded as a dynamic rather than a purely passive exercise.[32] Rather than simply assimilating pictures, viewers are noticing different things, and interpreting cues differently depending on their prior frames of reference. Mass media researchers are now abandoning former models in which the receiver was treated as a passive receptacle to be investigated only to discover media effects, in favour of more complex models that examine the various uses that people make, and the diverse gratifications that are derived from the media.[33] Families do not passively absorb whatever the moguls care to broadcast. They decide, for example, which channels to select. Their decisions depend upon what they are seeking – information or entertainment. And these decisions are often reached collectively; hence the influence of children's tastes upon adult viewing.

How seriously should we treat the lyrics of popular songs? Spiro Agnew appeared to take them seriously and accused the pop industry of corrupting the minds of young Americans with unpatriotic and psychedelic lyrics. Some social scientists have devoted equally serious attention to the hit parade in so far as they have amused themselves by analysing the content of popular songs, and during the last century two main currents of change have been discerned. In the nineteenth century lyrics dealt with a wide variety of themes including work, poverty, war, the nation, death and love. Subsequently, in the period up to the 1940s, songs became increasingly stereotyped with heterosexual love as the predominant theme. Since the 1950s a number of subtle developments can be distinguished within one major pattern of change; the percentage of hits with non-love themes has increased. Songs with protest, psychedelic and other non-love themes have remained a minority, but a growing one.[34] This is what concerned Spiro Agnew, the underlying assumption being that changes in the content of popular songs reflect or cause changes in their listeners' values and behaviour. However, other investigators have studied not the songs but the public and found that most 'listeners' do not know the lyrics of even the main hits.[35]

Changes in the content of songs are most easily explicable not in terms of listener characteristics, but in terms of the character of the industry producing them.[36] In the nineteenth century songs were composed and presented by a large number of independent musicians who travelled the country entertaining wherever they could find audiences. Around the turn of the century pop music became a real industry the control of which, particularly in America, became concentrated in a handful of organisations that were collectively titled 'Tin Pan Alley'. The mass marketing of music became possible with the introduction, first of sheet music, and later the gramophone record, combined with radio as a medium for publicising songs. In this new market situation the leading publishers sought a winning formula and stuck close to it, and the best winner of all was love. Since the 1950s the music industry has become relatively fragmented, with the result that a larger number of formulae are now used, and a wider range of tastes catered for. This history of popular music is an interesting topic in itself, which endorses the proposition that the medium shapes the message. But it also implies that both social scientists and politicians are unwise to attach more importance to the content of songs than the majority of listeners. Like television, popular music is often little more than background noise. It can be a background for talk, relaxation or dancing, its importance often residing in creating an agreeable environment for social intercourse. The public does not just listen to popular music. The public uses the music for its own purposes as is the case with television, and these purposes are often group purposes.

Faced with the evidence that audiences are not helplessly atomised, researchers have further revised their models for examining the influence of the media. In addition to taking account of how members of the public elect to use the media, it is also considered necessary to explain how any effects are filtered through the informal networks of friends and families by which individuals are surrounded. Information and tastes are seen as spreading through a two-step flow of communication, in which media effects are dependent upon whether messages are taken up by opinion leaders and thereby reinforced through informal communication. We live in an age of mass media and mass culture, but mass society is a less obviously useful concept. The evidence now available strongly contests the value of likening the public to a disorganised mass. As Gans argues, closer inspection reveals a plethora of smaller taste publics that continue to nurture their own special interests and devise their own uses for the media.[37] We noted in the previous chapter that leisure interests are far from standardised and uniform throughout the land. Most uses of leisure involve minorities. The mass society theory is mistaken. It is less useful in leisure analysis than has been supposed. The public has not been reduced to an amorphous mass, linked only through the purveyors of a mass culture.

The quality of popular culture

The popular arts have always attracted censure from those with the status and power necessary to propagate a view of their own tastes as superior. Popular music, journalism and television are repeatedly dismissed as inferior, trashy, aimed at the lowest common denominator, and confined to what can be assimilated instantly, without effort. Shils assesses the quality of popular culture as ranging from mediocre to brutal, and doubts whether most people are capable of appreciating anything better due to '. . . natural limitations to the spread of the standards and products of the superior culture throughout society'.[38] Many commentators who quarrel with Shils's verdict on the capabilities of the masses nevertheless indict popular culture for crushing more discerning tastes and sensibilities. Even writers with a basic sympathy for the working class and its culture, including Richard Hoggart[39] and Raymond Williams,[40] have criticised the service it receives from the media. Critics who see some good in the popular arts mostly qualify their praise by insisting that the public be educated to distinguish the tasteful from the trashy.[41] Gans defends popular culture, but even he judges its aesthetic standards inferior to those of high culture.[42]

Personally I doubt whether these assessments of the quality of popular culture reflect anything more than the relative power and prestige of the judges and judged. In the nineteenth century there were successful campaigns against bull-baiting and cock-fighting while the gentry's hunting remained above attack.[43] More recently misbehaviour around soccer grounds has been readily attributed to 'hooligans', a label less hastily applied when comparable damage occurs outside Twickenham. Wright insists that all aesthetic judgements are relative.[44] In his discussion of music he argues that musical meaning is not intrinsic to musical objects, but is determined by an individual's culture. Hence the inevitable differences in musical tastes and judgements of value. For purposes of the present argument, however, it is unnecessary to insist that objective aesthetic judgements are absolutely impossible. Even if such judgements were possible in principle, the fact would remain that we have no objective evidence whatsoever, in the ordinary meaning of the term, proving that high culture is especially effective in promoting well-being. Critics of popular culture offer only opinions. The fact that so many people have said it so often in no way proves that popular culture offers an inferior quality of experience to the classical arts. What is so different about high culture apart from the status of its public? No one has yet offered convincing evidence that the quality of experience at symphony concerts is superior to that obtained at pop festivals. Opinions, however strongly and repeatedly stated, and whatever the academic and social status of their orators, do not count as evidence. If push-penny must be considered as good as poetry until someone proves otherwise, in honesty we must continue to profess agnosticism. Being among the many who prefer Sinatra to symphony and a football league to live theatre, I am reluctant to believe that the traditional arts offer a superior kind of experience. Faced with convincing evidence, I would be prepared to confess cultural impoverishment, but to date it has been unnecessary to rebut a single shred. Philistines should be more assertive. Beneath its aristocratic airs and graces the opposition's case is paper thin.

Are the arts different?

The classical arts can be distinguished from popular pastimes, but not necessarily in terms of the quality of experience that they offer. Art is a type of play in so far as it is set apart from the 'serious business' of life, though a minority of professionals can work in the arts. Unlike many other forms in which play can be institutionalised, art is non-competitive. The display of artistic talent rarely takes the form of a contest. Yet there are agreed standards among both audiences and artists in terms of which performances can be evaluated. Art implies an appropriate 'form' and learning to appreciate an art is a process of learning the relevant norms, which can take considerable time and practice.[45] This is why an uninitiated philistine simply cannot appreciate a work of art in the way that is possible for those with 'cultured' tastes. Pop music differs from classical music in that there is less agreement about standards among the audience. 'Do I like it?' is therefore a perfectly adequate question with which to evaluate any particular work, and any one person's opinion is as good as another's.

Needless to say, this difference is one of degree rather than absolutes. There is some dissensus within the classical arts, the status of abstract painting being a case in point, while discerning taste publics nurture their own standards for the appreciation of rock, traditional jazz, modern jazz and soul music. In sport, also, connoisseurs learn to appreciate individual skills and team tactics, thereby making performances into aesthetic experiences in addition to opportunities to support one side in a contest. There are 'serious' journalists who offer criticism of soccer, soap operas and even beer drinking, using the idiom normally reserved for ballet, symphony concerts and wine-tasting.

In so far as there is such a thing as a special artistic or aesthetic experience, it is not simply intrinsic to particular activities such as looking at paintings, but is created through processes of interaction among performers and audiences during which the necessary tastes are developed and sustained. Aesthetic experience should be understood as a product of such total settings. The craft component in art is not irrelevant. Performances in both opera and soccer require basic skills which are then employed for playful rather than purely instrumental purposes, and it is unlikely that all crafts are equally capable of sustaining artistic standards. Crafts can be compared with respect to the scope for improvisation and interpretation that they allow, and in this sense cricket is probably superior to shot-putting. But it is less certain that classical music is superior to jazz and, in any case, it would be pointless to urge that all people should be educated to appreciate whatever art forms might prove superior. Even if the classical arts were shown to be aesthetically superior, we would still be faced with the evidence suggesting that their enjoyment depends upon a particular type of education and a broader life-style consistent with the tastes in question.[46] The classical arts are probably too distant from the lives of working class individuals to be capable of a mass appeal. In other words, in a differentiated society it is doubtful whether any one art form could prove best for everyone.

As previously stated, there is in fact no evidence that the classical arts really do offer superior experiences, but there is evidence showing that self-rated happiness is positively related to social participation, measured by the frequency of voluntary contacts.[47] Rather that 'what' people do with their leisure, 'how' they do it may be more relevant to the quality of the experience, and the social context is an important part of the 'how'. In so far as high culture offers any exceptional experience, it is more likely to be a product of the social processes of entry and participation than a pristine response to the intrinsic properties of the works appreciated.

Is passivity encouraged?

One of the main charges against mass culture concerns the passivity that it is said to encourage. It is claimed that individuals become so accustomed to consuming prepackaged entertainment and opinions that they develop an incapacity for more demanding types of recreation. Ease of consumption, it is alleged, drives out more demanding, but ultimately more satisfying uses of leisure. This is the ground on which the spread of popular culture is regarded as a threat to more discerning, minority tastes. It has been claimed that the habit of consuming opinions and information is liable to spread into all areas of life including politics.

In fact, however, the evidence is wholly contrary to this admittedly plausible argument. The classical arts appeal only to minorities but, as we saw in an earlier chapter, if anything these minorities are growing rather than shrinking. Visits to art galleries and museums, and sales of classical music records have been increasing. Likewise participant sport is a growth industry. The public has not been lured from the playing fields by an epidemic of spectatoritis. If anything publicising sport through the media tends to stimulate participation, the case of Olga Korbut and gymnastics being but one example.

It is informative to ask what leisure was really like in the good old days before the advent of television and other forms of mass entertainment. Confronting the evidence explodes myths of an age when people devised their own amusements and evolved tasteful participant folk cultures. A hundred years ago, before the mass media era, drinking was the staple form of recreation.[48] Drink remained far and away the most important single object of recreational expenditure in Britain until the First World War. The public house and music hall were well frequented recreation places, by men in particular. The image of the old-fashioned local where regulars sipped half-pints and made intelligent conversation is false to the facts. More typically the public house offered a bawdy, drunken scene. Alcohol remains an important recreational lubricant to this day, but by the heroic standards of the past, beer consumption is paltry and consumption of spirits moderate. The modern British boozer is a model of sobriety compared with his ancestors. In the 1680s alcoholic drink accounted for approximately one-fifth of the nation's total calorie intake. Today the proportion is around one-twentieth.[49] During the late eighteenth century 800 pints of beer per year per man, woman and child were being consumed. By the mid-nineteenth century this had fallen to 200, and by the 1930s to less than 100 pints per year, since when the total amount brewed has increased only marginally. In 1870 10 pints of spirits per head of population were consumed annually. Today we manage only approximately half this amount. The one exception to this overall downward trend has been rocketing wine consumption since the 1950s. The pattern of historical change shows that consumption of alcohol is highly responsive to changes in price. Consumption falls in times of economic depression, and in the mid-ninteenth century relative changes in price led to tea replacing beer as the staple drink of the poor. But a pint can now be 'earned' with fewer hours work than in the nineteenth century.

Broader changes in social habits have also been encouraging the trend towards sobriety. Between the World Wars two major innovations hit the leisure scene – radio broadcasting and the cinema, and studies at the time found them replacing mainly the public house and music hall. Membership of clubs, hobbies and sport were virtually unaffected.[50] Subsequently television has arrived and mainly diminished time spent listening to the radio, visiting the cinema and watching spectator sports. Once again, however, participant sport, hobbies and membership of clubs have suffered no decline.[51] The mass media in general and television in particular have been blamed for virtually all modern ills from the decline of church-going to rising crime statistics. One of their main actual effects, however, has been to increase the sobriety of the population. The media have neither standardised nor pacified popular recreation. Ever since the industrial revolution, and long before, people have spent a great deal of leisure passively, doing nothing in particular. Today television is typically in the background, whereas previously it was the public house and music hall. New forms of recreation tend to have replaced former pastimes that performed similar functions in individuals' overall life-styles.

Uses of leisure are not dictated by the media. In most cases it is media offerings that are assimilated into the independently preferred and varied life-styles of different sections of the public. Popular culture has been short-changed by many social scientists. Television's unglamorous image has been reinforced by researchers who have noted how rarely it is named as a 'most enjoyed' use of leisure despite the amount of time that it accounts for, and who, albeit with exceptionally heavy viewing in mind, have labelled it a residual time-filler[52] and a second-rate form of para-social involvement.[53] These judgements illustrate only that social scientists have frequently misunderstood how people actually use television. Goodhardt and his colleagues have assembled all the available information on *how* television is used and, at first sight, some of the evidence appears to confirm suspicions about the undiscriminating audience.[54] On average there is only 55 per cent audience continuity between weekly serial episodes, a lower rate than between adjacent programmes of completely different characters. Television stations are well aware of the importance of 'capturing' their audiences in the early evenings. There is only a weak tendency for viewers to concentrate upon particular types of programmes. Furthermore, light viewers are no more systematically selective than frequent viewers. This evidence could be read as confirming the stereotype of the passive viewer, exposing himself to whatever the broadcasters choose to display on his television, but first impressions can be deceptive. The sum of Goodhardt's evidence portrays uses of television as products of the broader life-styles to which individuals are independently committed. Whether or not individuals view at particular times depends mainly upon whether they are 'out' or at home. The absence of high levels of audience continuity between weekly episodes is evidence of the inability of most television programmes to determine leisure habits. People rarely stay indoors in order to watch television. It is more typical for television to be viewed because individuals happen to be at home. Why are viewers so undiscriminating in selecting programmes? Which programmes are viewed tends to be determined by what happens to be available when individuals have no other commitments. In addition, individuals' choices are constrained by other members of their households. Television is typically a social rather than a solitary use of leisure.

As we shall see in a later chapter, simply being with the family is a major and valued aspect of leisure among large sections of the public and, in addition to its convenience and low cost, the popularity of television can be fully explained only when its compatibility with family life is taken into account. Television has become part of the normal background for social intercourse in the home, but even mass media researchers tend to have neglected this social function of television. For example, McQuail's sophisticated typology of satisfactions that can be derived from televiewing involves only slight recognition of its social aspects.[55] Careful distinctions are drawn between satisfactions that individuals can derive such as diversion, increasing knowledge and consolidating a personal identity, but beyond acknowledging that programmes might subsequently be discussed among friends and neighbours the social functions of television are virtually ignored.

Exceptionally heavy televiewing, for 30 hours per week and more, is common only among the very poor and other disadvantaged sections of the population such as the elderly and the disabled whose circumstances deprive them of the scope for choice that is a feature of genuine leisure.[56] Deploring the need for time-filling and this substitute for real social intercourse may be appropriate in these cases. But for the bulk of the viewing public, television is not a cultural calamity. It has not set passivity spreading like a disease throughout society.

What remains of the mass society theory?

Like other grand theories in sociology, the mass society arguments contain elements of truth. The twentieth century has seen the spread of a mass culture. The mass media have encouraged the development of tastes and interests whose appeal transcends regions, age, sex and social class boundaries. It is true that the mass media make it easier than formerly for individuals to be passively entertained and to absorb ready-made opinions. But the mass society theory tells only part of the story. Individuals are not rendered helpless but are able to resist the lure and persuasiveness of the media. They can preserve their own minority pastimes both alone and in informal groups. They can retain previously formed values and opinions in the face of propaganda. Sections of the public are even able to 'hit back' in their different ways and use the media for their own private purposes.

Giner admits that the mass society theory makes some valid points, but challenges its utility as a general interpretation of contemporary society,[57] and his reservations are entirely justified. Viewing leisure through the mass society theory goes beyond simplification to misleadingly distort a more complex reality. This view needs to be counterbalanced, partly by the imagery presented in recreation research which portrays individuals selecting from a multitude of leisure activites according to their varying interests and circumstances.

Chapter 5

Class domination theory

A post-capitalist society?

Talk about leisure, particularly its growth, can make life sound good. It seems a far cry from theories of society that bristle with references to alienation and portray contemporary man as the oppressed, programmed and dehumanised product of industrial capitalism. Writers who believe these theories contain a valid point have endeavoured to accommodate leisure within their perspective. To some extent their theories echo the mass society critique, but rather than seeing the public as victims of impersonal forces, class domination theorists argue that the crux of the problem resides in the media and other agencies that structure leisure being responsive to the interests of a dominant class. They insist that while we inhabit a class society, leisure must be correspondingly deformed.

A similarity with the mass society critique is that the class domination interpretation of leisure also draws upon a broader body of sociological theory, which in this case usually claims Marxist inspiration, and reinterprets what are ordinarily considered liberal and democratic institutions, insisting that beneath surface appearances their actual role is one of social control. No one disputes that since the creation of the first industrial society in Victorian England, the political economy has been transformed. Trades unions have won emancipation, the political system has been democratised, and the state has accepted responsibility for intervening in social and economic life to promote the common good and to enhance the welfare of the people, resulting in the apparatuses of economic management, education, health and other services that are now generically known as the Welfare State. The combination of a Welfare State with widening rather than declining civil liberties including the right to own property and the maintenance of a market economy has embellished our vocabulary. Writers speak of the 'mixed economy', 'liberal democracy' and 'welfare capitalism' – phrases that are often wielded in denials that society is still capitalist in the classical sense. It has been claimed that power no longer follows property, that the former establishment has disintegrated, that power has been dispersed resulting in a society containing numerous interest groups including those representing labour and capital that are able to organise industrially and politically to pursue diverse objectives, without any being able to gain an overriding dominance. This 'liberal' interpretation of Western society treats both the state and business corporations as servants rather than masters of the public's many interests. Politics and industrial relations are seen as arenas in which all major interests can be recognised and compromised, resulting in a never-ending series of truces.[1] Leisure itself can be regarded as having contributed to the liberalisation of the social system, with affluence and the growth of leisure time bestowing greater scope for choice, and commercial and public providers responding to popular demands.

Class domination theory contests the significance of the trends to which the 'post-capitalist' case draws attention. It is argued that the historic process of liberalisation, including the growth of trades unions and the extension of the franchise, has managed to retain effective power in the hands of a dominant class, and that apparently democratic institutions in industry and politics are little more than façades concealing the realities of power. The Welfare State is indicted as a capitalist state which strategically intervenes to consolidate rather than check the power and privileges of economically dominant strata. Beneath the appearance of equal opportunity, it is alleged that education is managed so as to keep the working class in its place.[2] And, in a comparable manner, it is claimed that mass leisure is controlled through institutions, including the media, that are responsive principally to the interests of a dominant class.

Are the media biased? The case of news reporting

British broadcasting is proud of its political independence while the press normally distinguishes editorial comment from factual news reporting, but this has not inhibited strident and repeated complaints of media bias, and within sociology a substantial body of opinion has judged this bias to be systematically conservative. This argument assumes a variety of forms, and it is desirable to separate the 'vulgar' from the more plausible in order to do justice to the latter.

The less plausible accounts allege that the media systematically endorse the values and arguments of some sections of the community at the expense of others. It is claimed that the media embrace the values of the authorities – the police, employers, governments and the courts, while undermining the credibility of other interpretations of events. This bias is not attributed to the conservatism of individual reporters but to pressures under which they work that make their own views irrelevant. Some of these alleged pressures operate directly on the individual reporter, while others make their impact indirectly, through the occupational culture that surrounds news gathering and reporting, and which is assimilated, mostly subconsciously, by individual journalists.

What evidence do claimants of conservative bias offer? Chibnall's study of relationships between police and crime reporters illustrates the direct pressures to which journalists can be subject.[3] He interviewed thirteen Fleet Street crime reporters, and concluded that they would be more appropriately titled police reporters. Chibnall points to the reporters' dependence upon the police for information about pending court cases and the progress of criminal investigations. Few journalists have comparably helpful contacts with criminals. Crime reporters could not operate without police cooperation. A wealth of police contacts is the stock-in-trade of the successful crime reporter. Given this dependence, Chibnall asks, is it likely that the press will criticise police procedures and evidence? Is it at all likely that journalists will actively pursue stories offensive to the police, such as following up complaints of police corruption? This dependence of reporters upon the authorities is also the theme in Murphy's examination of the local press. The book's title, *The Silent Watchdog,* summarises the argument.[4] Murphy points to the limitations of local newspapers as investigators of malpractice and sustainers of protest. A major obstacle is their dependence upon town halls and other local centres of power for information. Friendly complicity is the logical working relationship. Couple this with the pressures of deadlines under which journalists work and the threat of libel laws, and it becomes easy to appreciate why only the exceptional reporter will risk offending his local notables. Murphy's own book illustrates his argument in a presumably unintended way, for his otherwise ruthless exposure of local newspapers' timidity protects the anonymity of the two specimen papers on which the enquiry concentrated.

By their nature, less direct forms of control are more difficult to illustrate, but a number of writers with 'inside' experience have reported considerable government pressure on the broadcasting authorities in Britain. John Whale[5] and Stuart Hood[6] claim that both the BBC and the commercial broadcasting network are subject to government influence. This influence is said to be exerted in a number of ways: by financial controls, and by ministers talking persuasively to top executives, aided by a similarity of social and educational background. The result, it is claimed, is that 'establishment' values pervade the broadcasting organisations and are assimilated by employees aspiring to successful careers. It is alleged that these values set limits to views and discussion considered reasonable, and result in the government's view being treated as the clearly reasonable norm, while contrary arguments are subject to more rigorous scrutiny. In a broadly comparable way, it has been argued that the newspapers' dependence upon advertising revenue (and the government is the largest single purchaser of advertising space) has a similar effect upon the 'climates' within which journalists operate.

Media coverage of industrial relations has been systematically monitored by both Morley[7] and a research team at Glasgow University,[8] and each claims a bias in favour of managements and against labour. The two sides might be granted equal air time on television, but they are treated differently. News writers and presenters appear prepared to concur with the view that managements, particularly when their stands are consistent with government policies, are representing the national interest. Furthermore, location interviews with managements tend to be conducted in congenial surroundings, such as boardrooms, and interviewers treat their subjects with respect, even deference, presuming that they possess reasonable cases to argue. Trade union officials and 'unofficial' strike leaders are likely to receive different treatment. Interviewers are more likely to assume inspiration by self-ish, sectional interests. The factory gate is a common interview location where workers are encouraged to 'perform'. Neither the location nor the interviewer's style is likely to make for the presentation of a 'reasonable' case.

Those who allege conservative bias in the media in general and the press in particular, do not find it difficult to discover explanations. The media are dependent upon the 'powers that be' for much of their information. And the media themselves are among these powers. Newspapers are privately owned. Is it surprising that none of the major nationals is committed to socialist politics? The boards that control broadcasting are appointed by the government which, in the case of the BBC, also holds the purse-strings, while the 'independent' channels are operated commercially, in most cases by companies with stakes in other sectors of the economy. Given the media's structural position, impartiality seems unlikely.

The drug LSD has a chequered history of press publicity which has been used to illustrate the media's responsiveness to vested interests.[9] Before 1964 LSD was hailed as a 'miracle drug', achieving all manner of marvellous results in treating mental illness. Then, rather abruptly, LSD became the 'killer drug'. Neither of these extreme views was ever justified by the evidence.[10] Their propagation could be attributed simply to press sensationalism, but so simple a verdict would ignore that until 1964 the press was uncritically accepting the drug manufac-turer's claims. Once LSD was adopted by the 'hippie fringe' media attitudes towards this section of the community coloured appraisals of the drug. Different sources of information are not treated with equal credibility.

Although these allegations of bias can sound impressive when listed consecutively, the argument is not entirely convincing. It is probably no accident that those alleging right-wing bias tend to be of left-wing persuasion. Contrary examples are plentiful. What about Watergate? In Britain we do not need to search back to 'That was the week that was' for examples of the media offending the powers that be. During the mid-1970s, the press helped to expose police corruption in Soho and provoked an outcry over a possible 'slush-fund' at British Leyland. The initiatives of just one newspaper, the *Sunday Times*, included exposing collusion between cabinet ministers and major oil companies in breaching sanctions against Rhodesia, withstanding litigation to campaign against thalidomide's manufacturers and in favour of the affected families, publication of the Crossman Diaries, and publication of some of the more questionable aspects of Jim Slater's financial career. For their part, the television networks incurred the wrath of governments by the credibility accorded to IRA complaints of police brutality in Northern Ireland, and annoyed a number of multinational companies with their programmes on labour conditions in South Africa and Sri Lanka. Organisations situated on the right of the political spectrum do not find the media consistently helpful. The Aims of Industry[11] has accused the media of a left-wing bias, while Anthony Jay has argued that the BBC current affairs department is a haven for left-wing intellectuals whose views are unrepresentative both of the country in general and the political élite in particular.[12]

Maybe the correct conclusion to draw is that all interest groups feel that their own points of view are unfairly treated. This was certainly the case during the strike at Pilkingtons in 1970 when press reports, not surprisingly, focused upon the occasional scenes of violence that erupted. The strike leaders felt that this was part of a campaign intended to smear their motives and tactics, while for its part the company condemned the press for increasing non-militant workers' fears of crossing the picket lines.[13] Media authorities have a habit of regarding the complaints they attract from all sides as evidence of a net impartiality. This is a comforting posture for media men, but maybe it is not wholly unreasonable. Some independent investigators have endorsed the view that, in general, the media do hold the middle ground. This is the interpretation that Warner places upon his observations in three American television newsrooms.[14] He found that the personal politics of their staffs were mainly left-of-centre, but the policy of all the newsrooms stressed the desirability of 'balance', and this policy not only controlled but was assimilated by the reporters. Attempting to be anything other than neutral was considered unprofessional. In Britain Tunstall has rejected the idea that the lobby can be manipulated by the political establishment.[15] Lobby correspondents might 'manufacture' news, but Tunstall claims that politicians are unable to manipulate the process. This is because correspondents have many sources of information. They need not fear being blackballed by any one informant. Individual politicians are discredited as reliable sources if their briefings prove misleading. Journalists are able to play off sources against each other, and in this way can avert the danger of becoming vehicles for establishment propaganda. Following his own experience in the medium, Kumar has revealed some of the strategies that are employed within television broadcasting to ensure that political balance is preserved.[16] He highlights the roles of announcers, news readers and presenters who are carefully selected, promoted and gradually built into prestigious personalities whose reputations carry a guarantee of impartiality. According to Kumar, the role of these personalities goes beyond ensuring that programmes are not pulled off-centre by outside interests. They also carry weight within broadcasting organisations themselves, thereby acting as a control over producers and other members of programme teams.

To do the argument justice, it is necessary not to carry allegations of bias to vulgar extremes. It is simply impractical for the media to accord equal credibility to every possible point of view on every issue. The media inevitably tend to reflect viewpoints that are prevalent in the societies that they serve. In this sense bias is unavoidable. And the various viewpoints represented among the public are not backed with equal power. Absolute neutrality between different interests is hardly likely. Allegations of bias almost certainly contain some substance, though it is equally certain that complainants sometimes exaggerate.

In addition to favouring establishment over other points of view, there is a more subtle and possibly more important way in which, it has been claimed, the media exert an ideologically conservative influence. This rests upon the claim that the 'middle ground' may be apparently neutral, but in fact it is often implicitly conservative. Morley's analysis of the media's treatment of industrial relations develops this argument.[17] He claims that media reports frequently assume, as background imagery, an economy composed of competing interest groups including workers with different types and levels of skill, managements and shareholders. Given this background assumption, it can appear neutral to treat talk and compromise as desirable strategies, and to regard holding out for sectional interests as less worthy. No partiality towards any one side is explicit. Things look different when industrial disputes are regarded as struggles between dominant and subordinate classes rather than evenly balanced interests, but, Morley argues, this interpretation is never considered in media reports. Hence the claim that the media are biased towards managements not only in the sense of according their arguments the greater credibility, but also in setting discussion within implicit background assumptions from which behaviour consistent with managements' interests inevitably appears the more reasonable.

Cohen and Young argue in parallel but broader terms that the media propagate a consensual image of society that rules out the possibility of genuine and irreconcilable conflicts of interest, and therefore enables sustained dissent to be dismissed as 'deviance'.[18] They note how the media select rather than merely discover news, and in addition to the medium being a part of the message, they claim that the selection depends upon how closely information accords with a preferred world-view – a consensual image of society, enabling elements outside the consensus to be labelled as irrational, sick or otherwise deviant. They quote their own research illustrating how drug users,[19] mods and rockers[20] have been subjected to this labelling and argue that the net effect is persistently to reinforce consensual imagery, stressing the opinions and interests that are common throughout the public, with inevitably conservative implications.

Halloran's study of the 1968 Vietnam demonstration supplies an independent illustration of these processes.[21] As indicated in the previous chapter, the possibility of violence featured as the main news angle, although no violence was threatened and little occurred. In their investigation, Halloran and his colleagues endeavoured to go beyond noting the media's tendency to sensationalise and examined the effects of this coverage. They questioned samples of students and police who were not directly involved in the events, and the findings suggested that the views of these sections of the public were significantly affected by the media. The demonstrators were regarded as people out to make trouble, which confirms the role that Cohen and Young attribute to the media. A message implicit in the treatment of the Vietnam demonstration was that taking to the streets was not an act to which reasonable, responsible citizens would ordinarily resort. The demonstrators were cast as an unrepresentative and unreasonable minority rather than as representatives of the public served by the media. They were typed as outcastes, a troublesome minority, whose arguments were not entitled to rational consideration, and who merited only the attention offered to other threats to law and order.

A difficulty in evaluating this allegation of bias arises from the ambiguous connotations of the term 'conservative'. One of the major British political parties is called Conservative, and in a party-political sense a non-conservative view of the world can be attributed to over half the population. However, the examples of bias quoted by critics of the media all involve support for points of view that are anything but confined to the Conservative Party and its supporters. Most people in Britain are against the use of LSD and heroin for kicks, juvenile delinquency, strikes and the global expansion of communism. There is a broad consensus on these matters, and in reflecting this consensus the media are not favouring views exclusive to the Conservative section of the community. Cohen, Young and Morley may not be part of this consensus, but it is hardly reasonable to criticise the media for according less weight to the opinions of certain social scientists than is attached to the views of the public majority. This would be merely another case of crying bias when one's own values were violated. At the same time, in a non-party political sense, it is correct to draw attention to the fact that in reflecting any consensual viewpoints, the media will necessarily reinforce the consensus, and the implications will be conservative in the sense of consolidating existing values. It is hardly reasonable to assume that any consensus on the drugs, strikes and crime issues must have been forcibly implanted by the media. In cases where there are clear divisions of opinion among the public, as over comprehensive schools and nationalisation, the media do not impose a consensus. But in so far as they seek mass audiences, the media must aim to accord with whatever general tastes and opinions are current. Some journals act otherwise, but their appeal is confined to minority groups; they have little hope of building mass circulations.

It is impossible to conceive of any society in which mass media, however organised, would display no tendency to reflect and reinforce majority opinion. As matters could not be otherwise, it is clearly mistaken to portray this conservative role of the media as a problem to be cured. But it is perfectly fair and legitimate, and sociologically significant, to draw attention to the fact that one of the media's functions is to consolidate a consensus, to point out that the content of this consensus will necessarily be compatible with the surrounding political and economic system, and that if the latter were changed, the consensus enshrined in media output would be correspondingly modified. It is equally fair to point out that those who are relatively privileged have the most to gain from preserving the consensus that supports existing social arrangements. The media's influence can be socially conservative, without reporting favouring the politically Conservative section of the population. This is probably the strongest ground on which conservative 'bias' can be claimed.

Socio-cultural control

Receiving news information accounts for only a tiny fraction of all leisure time, but it offers the clearest illustration of a broader theory asserting that the operations of the mass media and other leisure industries are best understood as processes of socio-cultural control. The more 'vulgar' versions of this theory, which come close to suggesting a deliberate conspiracy, are difficult to apply to the greater part of leisure. Whatever happens in the USSR, in Western countries authors and composers are not overtly pressured into applauding politicians and businessmen. Nevertheless, some writers have given the impression that, even if they neither declare nor even view their own intentions in such terms, political and industrial élites act so as to encourage uses of leisure that are compatible with vested interests.

It has been argued, for example, that the modern leisure we enjoy is not a natural human function; that capitalism rather than humanity needs the type of leisure we are granted. Employers purchase labour power rather than workers as individuals who must, therefore, be given time to refresh – to re-create themselves. Equally important, workers must be given the time and money-wages to consume the non-essentials that enterprises have to produce for capitalism to flourish in affluent societies. Simultaneously members of the public must be persuaded to use their leisure time and money to purchase the goods and services that commercial enterprises purvey. Hence the key role of advertising. As at work, people must be induced to devote their leisure to furnishing the propertied classes with profit regardless of whether the resultant life-styles maximise well-being. Attention is drawn to the manner in which the state subsidises uses of leisure that can then be commercially profitable. As in other sectors of the mixed economy, the state plugs gaps in the market. The state sponsors sport, principally through education, but also with sports centres and playing fields, and thereby creates a profitable demand for sports equipment. And by encouraging specialisation and high standards of performance, as in athletics, demand for an increasingly wide range of exotic equipment is manufactured.[22]

While encouraging some, the state discourages and sometimes prohibits uses of leisure that would interfere with individuals' performances in other social roles, particularly at work. The sale of alcohol is regulated while the use of other drugs is outlawed not only for medical reasons, but also, according to Young, because 'pot' and comparable substances are associated with life-styles inconsistent with the ethic that industrial capitalism requires.[23] Gambling is also regulated, maybe partly to protect individuals from themselves, but possibly also because it threatens to become an alternative channel for economic ambition that is otherwise directed into more orthodox work. Similarly charges of obscenity and pornography laws can be used to suppress forms of recreation that, rightly or wrongly, are seen as threatening the values on which society is based. Commercial enterprise has to be regulated lest the profit motive sows the seeds of its own destruction. It is argued that the state promotes leisure industries which are at least innocuous or, better still, encourage life-styles and values whose implications are politically and economically conservative. It is possible to point to a long history of British governments sponsoring uses of leisure that contribute to physical health and fitness, including parks and open spaces in urban areas, and justifying this provision in terms of nurturing more effective workers and soldiers. There is also a distinguished history of state sponsorship for pastimes such as school sports and the youth movements that have been judged of beneficial character-forming potential. Nowadays the vocabulary is rarely so explicitly paternal, but the desirability of public recreation provision is still discussed in terms of keeping young people off the streets thereby acting as an antidote to delinquency. Numerous illustrations have been offered of how state recreation provision is allegedly riddled with middle class values. How else can we explain that across virtually every form of public recreation, the clientele is biased towards the middle classes? Bacon gives examples of how leisure that is organised within secondary associations, which are known to draw mainly middle class support, is more likely to receive encouragement from local authorities than less formal modes of working class recreation.[24] Consequently the working classes lose out, unless they become contaminated by middle class values. Attention is also drawn to how governments use sport, particularly international sport, to consolidate national identities and endow states with prestige. In the Western world it is not uncommon for such charges to be brought against communist states,[25] but are ostensibly democratic governments entirely innocent?[26] Exponents of the social control theory have argued that parallel uses of sport occur within localities, where community leaders, usually from middle class backgrounds, exploit sport's ability to encourage identification with communities and their teams transcending class boundaries.

These arguments make good debating talk, but the class domination theory tends to increase its own credibility when it disclaims conspiratorial implications in preference for identifying the latent, usually unintended social structural consequences that inevitably accompany the leisure that can be developed within a given type of society. Mirroring the argument that irrespective of media men's personal convictions, the news that is produced within a capitalist society must inevitably carry the imprint of that society's consensual and otherwise dominant values, it is alleged that, albeit in less obvious ways, the same applies to other uses of leisure and the surrounding mass culture promoted by government and commercial agencies. Raymond Williams' appraisal of television is an example of this style of argument.[27] Television technology, as against the uses to which the technology is put, is ordinarily regarded as commercially and politically neutral. Williams' case, however, is that television technology did not develop in a vacuum. It was produced under the stimulus of commercial interests intending to sell domestic sets, admittedly aided by a demand for communications from privatised families. Given a capitalist context, it may be difficult to conceive television developing differently, but in his book Williams sketches some alternative forms of television that might be developed under modified political and economic conditions, such as those designed to maximise local, democratic control.

Without implying any conspiracy, Gruneau draws attention to the extent to which the rationality of industrial capitalism pervades contemporary sport; how '. . . the meritocratic emphasis of the sporting ethos today often symbolises the ideological manifestations of the capitalist infrastructure'.[28] An introduction to sport is an initiation into the norms of competition, individual ambition (within a framework of rules), and teamwork (while seeking personal glory). Hence the claim that sport helps to inculcate a bourgeois ideology while defining it as apolitical. A number of researchers have discovered that organised sport, within and outside education, tends to nurture and attract those who already possess conservative values.[29] All this is comprehensible without claiming that sports' administrators are paid agents of a ruling class. How could sport, or any other form of mass leisure, escape influence by the surrounding political and economic structures and their associated values?

It is one thing to demonstrate a correspondence between forms of recreation and the wider social order, but what are the mechanisms that allow us to conclude that class domination is entailed? Perhaps the most explicit account is offered by Pierre Bourdieu, a French sociologist who has written widely on the sociology of culture, but remains best known to the English reading public for his work on education, in relation to which he has developed a theory of socio-cultural control and reproduction, the main elements of which are directly applicable to leisure in general.[30] Bourdieu begins by insisting that, 'All pedagogic action is, objectively, symbolic violence in so far as it is the imposition of a cultural arbitrary by an arbitrary power',[31] meaning that school curricula represent not merely an objective stock of human knowledge but a selection therefrom which is inevitably guided by certain values. Hence the labelling of such curricula's imposition upon students as symbolic violence. Bourdieu proceeds to argue that, 'Every power to exert symbolic violence, that is every power which manages to impose meanings and to impose them as legitimate by concealing the power relations which are the basis of its force, adds its own specifically symbolic force to these power relations.'[32] Despite its inelegance, the meaning of this statement is straightforward. By inculcating its values through education (as opposed, for example, to explicit political propaganda), Bourdieu claims that a superordinate class is able to avoid transparently coercive and manipulative strategies, thereby simultaneously concealing and consolidating its position. Hence Bourdieu urges us to regard the entire apparatus of education as a process of cultural reproduction, framed within power relationships that it legitimises, conceals and reinforces. Working class educational failure is considered explicable in terms of the pupils' greater distance from the middle class culture of the school, and the argument leads to the following exclamation.

'So it has to be asked whether the freedom the educational system is given to enforce its own standards and its own hierarchies, at the expense for example of the most evident demands of the economic system, is not the quid pro of the hidden services it renders to certain classes by concealing social selection under the guise of technical selection and legitimising the reproduction of the social hierarchies by transmuting them into academic hierarchies.'[33]

The class domination theory alleges that leisure consists of a series of arenas in which comparable transmutation occurs, and where analogous quid pros are transacted.

The whole of mass culture, from news reporting to sport, is seen as pervaded by the values of dominant groups and institutions. One result is the differences in prestige between different uses of leisure; a presentation of society that masks exploitation and domination, which gives the class structure a benign appearance, thereby defusing opposition to inequalities. Just as news reporting tends to disseminate a consensual world-view and favours the interests of a dominant class while suppressing contrary values and interpretations of events, so with education and other apparatuses sustaining mass culture. The values of the dominant class are not presented as such. News is presented as apparently neutral and apolitical as is the case with sport, which increases the likelihood of the latent values gaining general assent. This is why the processes of social control in question are effective. They are insidious. Members of the public are unlikely to recognise the conditioning to which they are subject. Hence the claim that the whole of leisure is most appropriately treated as an ideological domain, and its servicing institutions analysed as ideological apparatuses. This may not be the everyday, common-sense view of leisure, but it cannot be casually dismissed as ludicrous.

Working class youth culture

One group of writers, largely orchestrated from the Institute for Contemporary Cultural Studies at Birmingham University, has vehemently made the case for the class analysis of leisure in relation to working class youth culture.[34] These writers are sceptical of interpretations that attribute young people's behaviour to a generation gap, or to strains, turmoil and tension inherent in the process of growing up. They are particularly critical of talk of a classless youth culture. And they address unqualified hostility towards commentators who brandish labels such as 'hooligans' and 'mindless yobos'. Indeed, it is argued that far from being mindless, working class kids have a great deal of interest to say about their society in general, and its class structure in particular. These writers show that socio-cultural control is not accomplished in an uncomplicated, straightforward manner. Leisure offers ample evidence of the dialectics of class struggle even if, for the time being, the net outcome is class domination.

The myth of classless youth is exploded by showing that, beneath superficial façades, class differences are easily discerned. Murdock's research among secondary school pupils has shown how friendship groups tend to splinter along social class lines, and how different styles and tastes, in music for example, tend to be adopted by young people from different classes.[35] Elders who believe that young people all dress alike and enjoy the same kinds of music only prove how little they understand the young. Actually it is hardly necessary to distinguish young people according to their appreciation of Reggae in order to crack the classless façade. It is sufficient to compare the career and life-style of a university student with the adolescent experience of a 16-year-old entrant into factory work.

Advocates of class analysis dismiss the notion of adolescent rebellion triggered by a generation gap with similar ease. Rather than rejecting values emanating from adult society, they argue that young people's behaviour is more frequently explicable in terms of expressing these very values. Paul Willis studied 12 working class boys throughout the last two years of their academically undistinguished careers in a secondary modern school and during their early months in employment.[36] The immersion of these lads in a school counter-culture could have been read as a rejection of society's values, maybe provoked by their labelling as failures at school. Willis shows, however, that his lads' counter-culture shared many features in common with the shop-floor culture in industry such as an aggressive masculinity, attempts to control situations informally, and constant attempts to avoid boredom with jokes and laughter. Furthermore, the us–them division in industry was mirrored in the lads' attitudes towards 'ear 'oles' – conformist pupils who were always listening, never doing. The lads certainly rejected the values of their middle-class teachers, but how many working-class parents share these values?

Stan Cohen has gone beyond suggesting that the mods and rockers were expressing working class values, to argue that the wider society's reactions to these youth phenomena possessed a social class character.[37] Cohen's research into the incidents at Brighton and other seaside towns between 1964 and 1966 furnished illustrations, mentioned earlier, of the media's tendency to sensationalise. Scuffles were reported as riots and, paradoxically, this 'blowing up' amplified the behaviour that was being deplored. The media helped provoke a moral panic in which social control was heightened, scooterists were harassed, and teenage day-trippers turned away from railway stations. The public became so sensitised to a threat in its midst that sightings of these strange and novel creatures, the mods and rockers, began to be reported in all parts of the country. From vague ideas, mods and rockers were developed into types of people, thereby creating movements with which adolescents could vicariously identify, often merely in a quest for excitement. Cohen argues that the identification of mods and rockers as folk devils helped to conceal the working class character of the initial styles of behaviour and dress that the media subsequently amplified. Labelling those involved as mindless deviants or 'sawdust Caesars', justified the suppression of their culture. The manifest issue became law and order versus hooliganism, concealing a deeper underlying class conflict. According to the theory under discussion, the treatment of mods and rockers, then subsequently skinheads and recalcitrant pupils, illustrates a displacement of the class struggle onto a cultural ground that favours currently dominant interests.

A class analysis of leisure in general, and working class youth culture in particular, draws attention to the dialectical interplay between cultural forms that are nurtured and embedded in authentic working class experience, and the apparatuses of social control including the media that constantly tend to encapsulate these developments. Working class youth are culturally oppressed with labels such as 'mindless', 'hooligan' and 'delinquent' but they are not battered into meek acquiescence. Stan Cohen and Paul Willis are alert to an heroic quality in their response. The working class has its own heritage, its own cultural capital, which young people put to imaginative use in resolving the 'contradictions' in their situations. Murdock has argued that the transposition of class inequalities into cultural differences creates a new resource, the pop culture, through which adolescents can 'work out' the contradictions in their treatment at school and work.[38] For example, personal development is prized by the middle classes, but rarely available in education and occupational milieux. Hence the ability of pop culture to resolve this contradiction by offering an expressive level of experience. Comparably, for working class young-sters who are denied achievement at school and work, pop culture can offer scope to excel.

Phil Cohen's discussion of working class youth culture, which relates trends in adolescent styles to the impact of occupational and urban change upon the working class, is among the more impressive exam-ples of the type of class analysis under consideration.[39] Cohen's argu-ments are inspired mainly by his knowledge of London's East End, but possess a wider relevance. He writes about a traditional working class culture that was built around the three interwoven nexuses of family, locality and workplace. It was a complex culture containing various levels within itself. The 'respectable' working class comprised the backbone. Their life-styles were distinguishable from the 'lumpens' among whom criminality was concentrated. Then, at a higher level, stood the 'mobiles', often self-employed, who were enjoying social and economic success. East Enders were never bound into a single homogeneous working class way of life but, in Cohen's portrait, there was a unity between the levels for individuals, families and entire ethnic groups could move up the ladder through recognised strategies and stages. Cohen argues that, since the 1950s, this traditional working class culture has fallen apart under the impact of urban redevelopment and economic change. As a result, young people have become exposed to two sets of values that were once reconciled within the working class culture, but are now contradictory. On the one hand there is the puritan work ethic, while the ethic of consumption beckons in different directions. Cohen hypothesises that the youth cultures in which work-ing class kids have become involved are best understood as a series of attempts to create life-styles that can resolve the tensions. Successive styles swing in alternative directions. Rockers and skinheads revive puritan masculinity, while mods accentuate consumption-oriented values. In so far as the tensions are eased, Cohen argues that the solutions are 'magical', meaning that in the final analysis the contradic-tions to which young people are exposed are rooted in the class structure and can never be fully unwound on a purely cultural level.

Like other human beings, working class adolescents are imaginative. Hence their ability mentally to create and eventually act out styles which appear to cut through the uncertainties. Like orthodox writers on adolescence, class analysts stress the importance of ambiguities and the resultant tensions, and regard the youth culture as an 'acting out' process. The ambiguities, however, are seen not as inevitable conse-quences of growing up, but as reflecting society's class divisions. Young people are rarely more than vaguely aware of the sources of their problems. Indded, the political significance of the pop culture lies in blurring the class structure and giving the social hierarchy a more acceptable appearance. Through the media and other channels, dominant political and economic interests are seen as deflecting the class struggle to a cultural level where radical dissent can be contained.

Leisure and alienation

Class domination theorists do not argue that the public-at-leisure is left consciously dissatisfied. Such an outcome could undermine the political economy. It is recognised that leisure makes life more bearable. But contemporary uses of leisure are considered a poor substitute for life in a truly humane and liberated society. This sentiment runs through Wright-Mills's much quoted indictment: 'Each day men sell little pieces of themselves in order to try to buy them back each night and week-end with the coin of "fun". With amusement, with love, with movies and with vicarious intimacy, they pull themselves into some sort of whole again, and now they are different men.'[40] It is argued that the current social order limits possible uses of leisure, despite the human worth of alternatives. As Pearson puts it, 'The point needs to be made that individual leisure is the result of or even at the mercy of, the providers, whether they are the local council, or your friendly multinational.' As a result, Pearson concludes, 'Leisure itself is a bit of a compromise, the remains of the week after the effects of work have worn off. Leisure itself has no solutions for working people, but it does make life more enjoyable.'[41] While their current 'bread and circuses' might keep the masses quiescent, it is strongly hinted that leisure could be better.

Sport is considered flawed by the penetration of bourgeois values. Like the industrial worker, it is argued that the sportsman is alienated from his activity. Ingham insists that, '. . . only when sport is freed from the reality of the market place will the athlete be allowed to be himself rather than a manufactured public image. Then, and only then, will the athlete cease to sell his labour, to be treated as a commodity by those who appropriate it.'[42] These remarks focus upon the predicament of the professional sportsman, but it is argued that sport at all levels is distorted by the bourgeois values of competition and the market-place.

According to the class domination theory, leisure is not the home of true freedom, but a sop that stifles discontents that would otherwise simmer to consciousness. It is interpreted as a response to mankind's alienation, performing equivalent ideological functions to church-religion in earlier eras. Rather than the good life, leisure is portrayed as yet another lock that keeps men bound into an oppressive social system. An implication of this theory is that mainstream leisure research has missed the point by taking too narrow a view of its subject-matter. To understand leisure, do we not need to look well beyond the apparently self-determined activity that occurs in non-working life? The class domination perspective insists upon a broader political economy of leisure, and argues for treating alienation as the key concept with which to explore leisure problems. In a society where most people are denied the economic and political power to exert real control over their lives and futures, how can individuals simply 'be themselves' and engage in self-determined activity during their leisure? Could mainstream leisure research be acting as another ideological smokescreen?

This analysis points towards its own characteristic solutions in so far as present-day leisure fails to deliver the promised fulfilment. According to this theory, it is not the *mass* character of the media and other agencies servicing leisure that is the problem, so much as their role in a class society where they inevitably become instruments of social control. This theory disputes that ultimate solutions to leisure problems will ever be found within leisure itself. In the final analysis, it is claimed that leisure will only become genuinely free when class domination has been overthrown. However, it is not recommended that we simply sit back and await the revolution. The class domination theory can offer something more constructive. The 'new criminology' and its yet newer successors oppose the 'medical paradigm' with its reformist overtones that treat delinquency as a disease to be cured. It is argued that the teenage cultures which incorporate delinquency can only be properly understood through class analysis. Radical criminologists claim to show how both the life-styles in question and the societal reactions that are stimulated are related to class interests and circumstances, and proceed to celebrate instead of censuring and proposing to cure the cultures that harbour delinquency. It is argued that this celebration might politicise both criminology and delinquency itself.[43] Politicising delinquency means strengthening the working class values amid which it is rooted, and making their holders aware of the 'class' character of these values. This means fighting interpretations offered by teachers, police, courts and conventional criminology. The battle can be extended to education, again with the object of revealing the prevailing pattern of class cultural control, and likewise the struggle can be extended into the rest of leisure. As yet these intentions are encouraged by little more than fanciful imaginations. But given the analysis, the aim of transforming mass culture from an agency of social control into a force for social structural change is entirely credible. And leisure is treated as only one subsidiary theatre in which the class struggle can be waged. Leisure is not completely written off, but its genuine liberation is seen as requiring a broader political and economic transformation.

Chapter 6

The pluralist scenario

It is hardly realistic to treat the class domination theory as a set of hypotheses to be rigorously tested through a strategically-designed research project, since this level of theory rarely proves wholly right or entirely wrong. Many writers have already proved that modern societies are sufficiently complex to offer numerous illustrations both in support and opposition. As the previous chapter has demonstrated, it is not difficult to illustrate the processes to which the class domination theory draws attention. There are scores of advertisers attempting to shape public taste, and many examples of governments promoting uses of leisure conducive to 'upright' citizenship. It was not just a desire to give young people a good time, but the concern engendered by an apparently anti-social youth culture that led to the appointment of the Albermarle Committee on the Youth Service whose report in 1960 led to a substantial injection on finance.[1] Like the mass society analysis, the class domination theory spotlights genuine tendencies. Few would dispute that the theory also serves a purpose in sketching and alerting us to a scenario that *could* become a reality. But to exactly *what extent* does the theory explain leisure behaviour and provision in present-day society? While class domination theorists are mainly of left-wing persuasion, their theory is most readily reconciled with reality in the socialist world. In Western societies there are convincing grounds for insisting that the tendencies upon which the theory rivets attention remain, as yet, subservient to other processes. Furthermore, as we shall see, much of the evidence that the theory marshals is susceptible to alternative and, on balance, more convincing interpretation.

The functions of leisure

Some correspondence between uses of leisure and the wider social order is inevitable. Leisure may help to consolidate the social system, offering gratifications which act as safety valves reconciling men to an otherwise unacceptable society. Leisure may also carry the imprint of values consistent with existing economic and political practices, thereby legitimising the social order. But does it necessarily follow that these functions of leisure are manifestations of an oppressive capitalist infrastructure together with its state apparatuses of social control? The truth is that leisure, or the alternative forms in which play can be institutionalised, performs comparable functions in all societies.

In his discussion of sport and games in Samoa, Dunlop describes how play integrates the community, provides an outlet for feelings of rivalry, celebrates socially significant occasions such as weddings, and teaches skills that are useful in other social roles from warfare to fishing.[2] It is difficult to see how uses of leisure could ever remain uninfluenced by the broader social contexts within which they are developed, and the fact that such influence can be discerned in our own society is hardly a ground for criticism.

The comparative research undertaken by J. M. Roberts and B. Sutton-Smith has identified some of the processes through which the surrounding context can shape leisure behaviour.[3] These investigators collected information about the games played in a large number of relatively simple societies. They classified games according to whether physical skill, strategy or chance predominated, and found that each type of game tended to enjoy prominence within a particular type of culture. Games of physical skill proved most common in societies where mastery of the environment was a principal challenge. In contrast, games of strategy were prominent in more complex societies where child-training stressed obedience and following rules. Games of chance were most common in a different type of setting; where there existed a pervasive belief in an omnipotent, supernatural being. Roberts and Sutton-Smith interpret this evidence as suggesting that games perform an expressive function, relieving anxieties that broader patterns of social life generate. Hence the type of game that is popular depends upon the type of anxiety that a particular society engenders. When the emphasis is upon achievement and mastery of the environment, games of physical skill can offer a form of simulated achievement. In contemporary America, therefore, such games are most common among men in the higher socio-economic strata where childhood-training stresses individual achievement. In contrast, games of chance are prominent among women, reflecting the relative passivity of the female role.

In opposition to interpretations derived from conflict theory, functionalist sociologists have brought leisure within their own perspective. Whereas class analysts see leisure as reflecting and reinforcing broader patterns of conflict and domination, functionalists stress the contribution of leisure to the well-being of society as a whole. They draw attention to leisure as an arena in which individuals can develop and practice generally useful skills such as sociability, and how consorting with people who 'understand' enables life's tensions to be borne.[4] These are exactly the kinds of evidence to which the class domination theory draws attention, and the inescapable conclusion must be that this evidence is susceptible to alternative interpretation. Contemporary sport may display the imprint of the capitalist infrastructure. But so what? In a capitalist society enterprises are inevitably going to profit from leisure. Likewise the technology and styles of organisation in wider use are inevitably going to be incorporated into leisure industries. These extensions from the rest of life into leisure occur in all cultures. It is difficult to conceive of a society in which people will not use opportunities for play to release tensions, and to develop skills and personal attributes which are more generally rewarded. If such features of leisure can be discerned in our own society we should not be surprised, and neither should we rush to the conclusion that our leisure is particularly unfree. Gardner has illustrated the numerous ways in which American sport reflects the surrounding culture.[5] The commercialism and competitiveness that are valued in economic life spill over into sports, which are then prized for nurturing and rewarding these American values. To gain acceptance in America, it helps if sports can manifestly demonstrate their consistency with American values and character. Indeed, Gardner argues that the popularity of baseball can only be fully understood when account is taken of its advantage in being a peculiarly American game. These linkages between sport and the wider social order are not in dispute. But what do they prove? Do they reveal American sport as an apparatus of social control and domination? Or are we merely confronting interrelationships between leisure and other institutions that are inevitable in any society?

The role of the state

Without denying all credibility to the class domination theory we must recognise additional grounds for state involvement in recreation. It is possible to account for a great deal of state involvement in leisure without attributing any sinister motives. To begin with, it is difficult to imagine any society in which the state could adopt a completely *laissez-faire* approach to recreational tastes and behaviour. Rape and Paki-bashing might amuse sections of the contemporary British public, but the remainder surely have a right to protection. If we want to live in a society as opposed to anarchy, leisure activities must be contained within a framework of law. Until we have a totally consensual society, there will always be arguments about whether the public needs protecting from influences that some consider harmless. At the moment the availability of alcoholic drink, opportunities to gamble, and the right to witness sexual acts on screen and stage are cases in point. Government controls in these areas cannot be realistically interpreted as signs of a repressive state in action. That these issues are at all controversial simply reflects the fact that different sections of the public possess different tastes and values.

Second, if they attempt to plan the use of land, governments must inevitably become involved in planning for leisure activities that involve using large spaces in either urban or rural areas. If national parks and other places of 'natural beauty' are to be preserved as recreational resources and managed so as to cater for the visiting public with car parks, toilets and other facilities, is there any alternative to supervision by some public body? Similarly if land in urban areas and on the fringes of cities is to be kept available for sport and recreation, it is difficult to see how this can be guaranteed except by the state. Two-fifths of all the land in England and Wales is currently subject to some type of active conservation,[6] and it is impossible to believe that the public's scope for recreational choice would be enhanced by removing this control. Likewise with other resources where the supply is finite, including broadcasting wavelengths, it is difficult to imagine the public being adequately served by anything other than a system of government regulation.

Third, a great deal of local and central government involvement in the leisure field is the inevitable by-product of quite different concerns. Rightly or wrongly, depending upon the political philosophy, since the nineteenth century governments in Britain and other industrial societies have been assuming a widening responsibility for public welfare by promoting, for example, health and education. These concerns unavoidably spread into leisure. Although today they are increasingly recognised as recreational services, the libraries, parks and swimming baths administered by local authorities in Britain were not originally developed merely to allow people to enjoy themselves, and they retain important non-recreational purposes. Similarly in America, before the First World War, what can now be recognised as recreation provision normally had other principal objectives, particularly conservation, health, and preservation of historic landmarks.[7]

Finally, if recreation opportunities are to be made available to economically disadvantaged groups, public provision is a logical if not the only method. If the state did not subsidise sport and other forms of recreation that involve the use of land, the majority of children would be unable to participate. The state does promote sport, particularly through education, but it is surely naive to see this as a subtle plot to implant acquiescent values into the minds of the young, or as a strategy to stimulate a profitable demand for sports equipment. Local government departments responsible for recreation are increasingly paying attention to the needs of other disadvantaged groups including the disabled and the ageing. Some of the services provided remain little known. For example, it is not widely broadcast that in 1974–75 local authorities helped to provide 104,800 people with holidays.[8] As with all other social services, whether or not this provision is desirable must be accepted as open to debate, but the points raised by the class domination theory hardly seem the central issues.

The charge of being laden with middle class values is easily hurled, but it is more difficult to make the indictment stick. Which recreational tastes are shared by the majority of middle class citizens but interest only a working class minority? The most popular forms of recreation including television and holidays transcend class boundaries, while other interests, such as the traditional arts, attract small taste publics rather than entire social classes. Public bodies like the Sports and Arts Councils certainly lie open to the charge that the working class is under-represented among their beneficiaries, but who doubts that if any critics could explain how to attract more working class participants the authorities would be happy to respond? In all formally organised activity, including politics and religion, the working class tends to be under-represented.

The entire spectrum of state-supported recreation cannot be whitewashed so casually. It is impossible to contend that all government enterprise in the leisure field is explicable in one or another of the ways outlined above. Why does the state in Britain support opera, squash, ballet and golf? Answers to these questions would hardly be complete without some reference to the social class compositions of the respective taste publics. Why do we subsidise British competitors in the Olympic Games? The preceding discussion has certainly not exhausted the reasons for state involvement in leisure. What has been illustrated is that there are numerous grounds for this involvement, and accounts that see social control writ large across all these endeavours are refusing to acknowledge the complexity of the picture.

The leisure market

Listing the diverse explanations for government involvement is not strictly an adequate answer to less vulgar versions of the class domination theory which disclaim conspiratorial overtones and rest content with identifying the covert social structural consequences of leisure provision. These arguments challenge not so much the motives of politicians and bureaucrats as the effects of their actions. A more satisfactory reply, therefore, is to explain that its impact upon the public's uses of leisure cannot be as impressive as the scale of government involvement since, in the leisure industries, the suppliers remain subservient to market forces. Consumer sovereignty remains a reality in the leisure market and one reason is that, to date, neither central government nor the local authorities in Britain have developed anything resembling coherent policies for recreation. Practitioners in the public recreation services tramp from conference to conference waiting to be told what their objectives should be. As Smith has noted, '. . . the community has yet to develop its own consensus on the nature of the leisure problem, and the role of politicians in articulating that consensus has to precede administrative reorganisation.'[9] Public bodies deal with a series of youth, educational, arts and sports problems and have encountered little pressure to coordinate their efforts into a coherent leisure policy. Outside observers may note that local authority parks, baths, museums, schools and other services are all in some sense catering for leisure, and likewise at a national level we can observe that the Arts Council, the Sports Council and the Countryside Commission, together with the forestry, broadcasting and water authorities are all active in the leisure field. The fact is, however, that these various agencies have been established at different times with highly specific and sometimes completely non-recreational purposes in view, and the total leisure outcome is an entirely unplanned phenomenon.

Likewise in America it is impossible to identify any clear policy or goals in the public recreation services. In their discussion of public provision in the USA, Godbey and Parker rightly stress the multiplicity of bodies that make up the public sector, their diverse origins, and the absence of any clear objectives.[10] Economists who have examined the work of bodies such as the Arts Council in Britain have deplored the vagueness of its aims and the failure of the Council to evaluate the returns on its investments in a rational manner.[11] Consultants who favour management by clear objectives soon lose patience with the public leisure services.

Given the vagueness surrounding objectives together with the fact that leisure is rarely a matter for party political controversy, it becomes easy to understand how public bodies can become involved in ventures for almost fortuitous reasons. For example, when the head of the Arts Council favoured 'few but roses' the Council's policy was to concentrate its resources upon centres of excellence. The total size of the grants awarded to the Sports and Arts Councils appears highly dependent upon the skills of the recipients in lobbying and discovering sympathetic ears in Westminster and Whitehall, and the views of chief officers and individual councillors can be highly relevant in decisions such as whether and where to build a sports centre, and whether to support the arts. It is impossible to commend this looseness in distributing public largess, and, as will be argued in the concluding chapter, particularly with the continuing growth of leisure and consequent scale of provision, clearer policy guidelines than have operated in the past are now required. At the moment, however, the point at issue is that the unsystematised condition of public provision is hardly consistent with the view of the state either consciously or covertly controlling uses of leisure in order to achieve a desired result.

Equally important, the absence of any coherent leisure policy tends to place the providers at the mercy of the market, subject to rather than manipulators of public taste. No one who works in a public recreation service knows that his job is secure on account of the publicly recognised importance of his work. Personnel operating in different recreation fields have to compete for limited resources, and one way of justifying their claims is to demonstrate public interest and appeal. Meanwhile, members of the public can pick and choose. They do not have to use country parks, Forestry Commission nature trails, arts centres or sports halls. People only use the facilities that they find useful, and if the public sector does not satisfy their tastes, individuals can turn to commercial provision or self-help. Schemes to extend public participation in recreation policy-making and management owe as much to the professionals' interest in discovering the public's tastes as to the public rebelling against alienation in leisure.

In leisure as in other spheres, there is a complex interactive relationship between demand and supply. Demand for a facility such as camping sites may provoke a supply, but it is easy to quote examples of supply-led demand. Until ten-pin bowling was commercially promoted in Britain no one was demanding to play it, and the visible availability of camp sites may increase demand for camping holidays. The relative weight of the influence flowing in each direction between supply and demand depends upon the state of the market. In leisure, as in other markets, a movement towards monopoly increases the power of the suppliers. While pluralism reigns in leisure supply, however, with the existence not only of voluntary and commericial sectors, but an uncoordinated public sector as well, it is the suppliers who are at the mercy of the market forces. It is public taste that has determined how television and radio broadcasting will be used in Britain. Whatever its early aspirations towards educating the public and raising levels of taste, the BBC has found that it can only win a mass audience, thereby justifying its revenue from the government, by catering for existing public interests. Likewise suppliers of sports complexes, arts centres and country parks have to wait and see what uses the public makes of their offerings and respond accordingly. Public provision accounts for only a small part even of organised recreation activity.[12] The providers have no captive audience. It is the public that can pick and choose.

Needless to say, the above comments about consumer sovereignty apply even more forcibly to the commercial sector. It is easy to talk about advertisers foisting their goods and services upon a susceptible public, but things never look so simple from the suppliers' side of the market. Advertisers may often try to shape public demand, but they are more rarely successful. Nine out of every ten new brands launched are failures. During the last 30 years the British public has largely deserted the cinema, the large dance palais, gents' hairdressers, and the bowling-alleys that were built during a short wave of popularity. Anyone who knows the advertising secret to tempt the missing customers back can make a fortune. The recreation business can be profitable, but leisure is a notoriously risky market. Public taste is fickle. Demand for basic necessities is easier to predict. And to complicate the problems of private enterprise, competition from a subsidised public sector is never far from the foreground. A secure position as a leisure supplier requires either a wealthy patron or a spread of risks across a large number of leisure industries so as to be waiting wherever demand might flow.

Socio-cultural pluralism

As far as uses of leisure are concerned, the public remains far from a single, undifferentiated mass. Our understanding of leisure is aided, but to no more than a limited extent by the mass society theory. Likewise the class domination theory offers insights, but cannot accommodate the greater part of the evidence about uses of and provision for leisure. The models of society offered in these theories are too simple to do full justice to a more complex reality.

Life-styles vary in a host of ways that cannot be explained by reference to the interests of a single dominant class. To explain these variations, it is usually more fruitful to refer to the interests and circumstances of the sections of the public directly concerned. Uses of leisure are related to social class. Working class households view more television, while the middle classes predominate at live theatre. There are few forms of recreation where participation is not somehow related to individuals' social class positions, usually assessed in terms of occupation, and the nature of these relationships will be explored more thoroughly in Chapter 8. For the moment the point at issue is that while social class is certainly a useful predictor of leisure behaviour, the same applies to numerous other bases of social differentiation. We shall also see that age, sex, marital status and education are among the social determinants of leisure conduct. It is important to keep social class in perspective. Social class is important, but some sociologists of leisure display an unnecessary obsession with the subject.

Working class youth culture owes something to its working class foundations, but it also owes a great deal to the fact that its members are young and possess interests that differ from other age-groups. Class analysis never offers more than a partial explanation of leisure. Even with age and social class held constant, uses of leisure vary considerably between the sexes. The data in Table 6.1 derive from a study of 14- to 16-year-olds at one Dudley School,[13] and illustrate how sharply the life-styles of adolescent boys and girls differ. There are

Table 6.1 Adolescent boys' and girls' involvement in selected leisure activities (percentages)

Leisure activities	Boys	Girls
Have a hobby	54	25
Dances/discos	49	84
Own a bicycle	64	17
Team sports	30	8
Watch sport	51	23
Visit relations	37	73
Help parents	49	84

(Data from E. Derrick *et al.*, *Schoolchildren and Leisure: Interim Report,* Working paper 19, Centre for Urban and Regional Studies, University of Birmingham, 1973.)

inevitable points of contact, but girls' lives are considerably more home and family centred. When they 'go out', dances and discos are among the most popular venues. Boys are more involved in hobbies, sport, and other forms of active outdoor recreation. Social class is but one among many influences upon uses of leisure, and the sum of the evidence simply will not justify making it the central explanatory concept.

From exposing the limitations of the mass society and class domination theories we can begin to identify a more valid approach to understanding leisure, and the ˙senses in which its growth constitutes a problem. Both the mass society and class domination theories draw attention to tendencies that certainly operate but which are counterbalanced, in each case, largely by individuals and primary groups developing their own tastes and interests, and using the media and other facilities for their own purposes. The model of society that best enables us to understand contemporary leisure is a pluralist model – the unofficial ideology of Western society. Sociology has always been a debunking subject, but in this case the conventional wisdom is less out of tune with reality than its more vociferous critics. All grand theories necessarily simplify a more complex social reality, but the pluralist theory offers a better fit than its principal rivals, certainly as regards the analysis of leisure. In Britain and other Western societies there exists a variety of taste publics that possess contrasting interests generated by their different circumstances. The uses of leisure of these publics are certainly influenced by commercial and public provision, but the providers are at least as responsive to the public's tastes, and the public has a distinguished history of saying 'No'. In recreation and other spheres the public uses its leisure to nurture life-styles that supply experiences which the individuals concerned seek and value. 'Freedom from' is a condition for leisure. But there is also a positive side of the coin that involves individuals exploiting their 'freedom to' and leads logically to socio-cultural pluralism, meaning societies in which various taste publics are able to fashion life-styles reflecting their different interests and circumstances. This is the reality of modern leisure, and theories that fail to spotlight this aspect of reality prove only their own need of revision.

The pluralist theory incorporates a relatively complex model of society, but its explanations of leisure behaviour are characteristically economical. In contrast, the class domination theory with its more readily assimilated imagery of society consisting of dominant and oppressed strata, often has to resort to highly convoluted explanations when faced with the details of leisure conduct. For example, there are theories that purport to relate the appeal of competitive sport in general, and violence among both players and spectators in particular, to class structure and class struggle.[14] Some of these theories would benefit from a touch of Occam's razor. It is advisable to appraise more obvious explanations before embarking upon speculative class analysis. It is difficult not to sympathise with Petryszak's observation that, 'Unfortunately capitalism and its assumed agencies of manipulation including the media, all too often serve as the convenient scapegoats and explanatory catch-alls for sterile sociological thinking'.[15] Petryszak's own preferred 'bio-social' explanation of violence in sport is theoretically economical and simultaneously persuasive. He commences with the observation that human beings possess a need for group membership, notes that competitive sport can meet this need for both participants and spectators, and proceeds to hypothesise that violence whether on the field or among spectators can heighten collective feeling. Students of leisure are well advised to try relating behaviour to the interests of those directly involved before speculating about the significance of the class struggle.

There are numerous patterns of attempted domination and exploitation in leisure, as is the case in most areas of social life. Middle class interests are more diverse than theories which persistently deplore the oppression of the working class suggest. The self-employed complain about expanding government bureaucracies triggering escalating rates and tax burdens, while the salary expectations and career prospects of new middle class armies of executives and professionals including civil servants, teachers, social workers and medical practitioners depend upon the further growth of public expenditure.[16] Within the leisure industries expoloitation is not the prerogative of commercial and political élites. Recreation professionals have their own diverse and vested interests. They include holiday camp workers who use campers as easy sources of money, and sometimes sex as well.[17] Then there are the fairground gaff-lads who skilfully and systematically short-change customers.[18] In so far as exploitation is occurring it is not only the state and propertied classes that are the guilty parties.

It is difficult to see how capitalism could ever win the argument with its more determined critics. If workers are employed for 70 hours per week and receive only subsistence wages, the charge of exploitation is sure to follow. Then if hours of work are reduced and wages increased, we are told that this is to enable capitalism to stimulate a demand for its non-essential products. In a capitalist economy it must be possible to make profit from leisure, but the market-place can and does make this conditional upon members of the public receiving goods and services that they value.

One remaining argument in the class domination theory that has so far escaped challenge alleges that even if our leisure behaviour is relatively self-determined, individuals' own choices must be from among alternatives that have been pre-structured by government and commercial interests, which encourage certain uses of leisure while discouraging those associated with values liable to stimulate social dissent. As a result, it is argued, leisure may be a source of some satisfaction, but is less fulfilling than it could be if business and government agencies did not distort the public's appetites. It is easy to make this kind of assertion, but very difficult to supply convincing evidence. Critics who are wholly out of sympathy with modern Western-type societies seem to require no evidence to convince themselves that uses of leisure in these countries are less satisfying than could be the case. Those who find it distasteful to be employed in organisations where individuals sell their labour for the coin of fun are, of course, entitled to their point of view. But what is the alternative? What would leisure be like in a truly humane and liberated society? There are cross-cultural differences, but there are also remarkable similarities in uses of leisure between different countries. The number of hours that people work each week shows little variation between capitalist and communist regimes, while in urban areas throughout the world the amount of time devoted to television shows only modest variation.[19] It is not easy to specify the exact ways in which leisure in modern Britain, America and other Western societies is deformed.

There are romantics to whom formal organisation is anathema whether it is commercially or state sponsored and who insist that, to escape alienation, individuals and communities must organise their own leisure. However, there is already plenty of this communal organisation in our own society. This is the living proof of the pluralist case. There are participant-run dart and domino leagues, golf clubs and photography societies, while kids play street football and arrange their own informal games. We have this and more besides. And is anything lost when schools or recreation departments arrange regular football matches, erect goalposts and provide referees, and when supplies of kit can be purchased? The notion that technology and formal organisation along with their rational values are inherently alienating is surely a misconception. The study of leisure challenges such misconceptions, and the growth of leisure is rendering the broader theories of society from which these notions are derived increasingly suspect.

It is worth noting that despite their deep and often bitter differences, there is little disagreement on basic values between supporters of the class domination and pluralist theories. Both reveal a preference for societies in which members of the public can develop diverse lifestyles, supported but not controlled by business and political apparatuses. The disagreement concerns whether this is possible within the present political economy. The pluralist case rests on the claim that while they are certainly at play, class domination tendencies are currently held in check, and that the form of political economy that has developed within Western societies offers a better protection against class domination than any of the known alternatives.

The above paragraphs contain more assertion than systematic proof of the pluralist argument. The evidence directly relevant to the theory is presented mainly in the following chapters. The preliminary point now being argued is that pluralist thinking allows some credibility to be attached to the propositions in both the mass society and class domination theories without carrying these perspectives to extremes, and can accommodate a great deal of additional evidence besides. Needless to say, the pluralist theory is not only about leisure. Its propositions relate to the composition of the wider social system, as is also the case with the mass society and class domination theories. An examination of leisure, even if absolutely thorough, could cover no more than a tiny fraction of the relevant evidence. But the study of leisure cannot shirk contact with these theories. Leisure is as suitable an arena as any to test their claims. What is more, we can only make sense of the known facts of leisure behaviour by postulating a pluralist social system. Hence the value of this theory in explaining leisure phenomena. In addition, the theory enables us to recognise certain consequences of the growth of leisure, namely the strengthening of pluralist tendencies in society-at-large. The pluralist perspective is preferable to the alternative sociological theories that have been offered. It can incorporate but go beyond their valid contents. And it is superior to specifically recreation theory and research in that it allows us to appreciate how leisure influences and is influenced by the surrounding social context.

Leisure and anomie

Can the pluralist theory assist our understanding of leisure problems? Why is leisure often desultory rather than euphoric? Why does fashioning uses of the scope for choice that leisure unleashes fail to consistently enrich the quality of life? The principal answer, which is compatible with the pluralist scenario, is contained within anomie theory.

Leisure is intrinsically anomic. This is the crux of the leisure problem – how to play the options that the growth of leisure bestows. The term anomie is well known in sociology. It describes situations characterised by an absence of social norms, or where the norms are unclear, conflicting or unintegrated. Individuals are left without meaningful values to interpret and direct their lives, and are denied the security associated with clear moral guidelines. Anomie is a property of social situations. Its parallel psychological condition is called anomia. Individuals feel unable to direct their lives purposefully, that other people cannot be relied upon, and are uncertain or pessimistic as regards the future.[20] Emile Durkheim, who coined the concept of anomie, observed that human contentment depends upon the existence of norms to limit people's aspirations,[21] and subsequently sociologists have noted numerous ways in which normative orders can break down. Misfortunes such as economic collapse and defeat in war can leave whole communities uncertain of how to proceed. When individuals who have been motivated to strive for success, in education for example, are confronted by failure, their lives can be left without a sense of direction. Failure can produce anomie and so can success.[22] A rapid rise in standards of living can tender traditional norms of budgeting inappropriate, and the manner in which leisure nurtures anomie is directly analogous. Must not leisure be intrinsically anomic in so far as this sphere of life is, by definition, the home of relatively self-determined behaviour?

Anderson[23] has perceptively described leisure as an unintended and unwanted by-product of industrialism. An industrial society unavoidably generates leisure whether individuals welcome it or not. People cannot work all the time. In advanced industrial societies individuals must take time off to consume the 'non-essential' products of their labour. Furthermore, industrialism inevitably weakens the family, community and religious bonds that elsewhere impose a clearer morality upon non-working time. Industrialism's success necessarily generates leisure, but the values that stimulate industrialisation tend to devalue spare time, and offer little guidance as to how leisure should be spent.

Its anomic character does not mean that people will consciously dislike leisure any more than they consciously resent rising standards of living. Nor does it mean that leisure will be entirely devoid of satisfying experiences. It means simply that leisure is unlikely to be consistently satisfying. Surveys rarely find individuals complaining that they are damaged by their leisure. People are able to use their scope for choice to avoid negatively valued experiences. Yet at the same time, feelings about leisure often fail to rise above a blank indifference. In his analysis of *Permissive Britain*, Christie Davies argues that permissiveness may be an admirable formula for avoiding misery, but that it is less successful for maximising happiness.[24] A stable sense of well-being requires the security associated with clear moral guidelines. Where can man-at-leisure find such comfort?

Ralph Glasser has deplored the absence of any clear goals in leisure.[25] Hence, in his view, the condition of aimlessness that is enveloping contemporary man. Leisure, according to Glasser, has been held up as the prize towards which men strive and work, but when the prize is grasped it is found to contain not the promised fulfilment but 'robot's cramp' – extreme stress with no known cure. Glasser is critical of the new 'high priests' who control the modern persuasion industries. These are the authorities to whom contemporary anomic man turns for guidance. Yet their disparate messages and meanings lack the consistency, certainty and depth offered by traditional religious values. Glasser regards the leisure problem as urgent; the main challenge facing contemporary man. According to Glasser, the creeping moral anarchy could lead to social collapse, and he envisages only two solutions. The first would amount to state tyranny, as portrayed in the class domination theory, with governments promoting secular religions to define, among other things, approved uses of leisure. The communist world offers illustrations which Glasser finds unattractive. In his view, the only and preferable alternative is a religious revival restating traditional values, but Glasser offers no convincing agenda through which such a revival might be accomplished and his analysis, therefore, conveys an air of doom.

Is there no other alternative? Hitherto sociologists have deplored anomie and have associated its presence with virtually every malaise from suicide to crime. Observers who are less bound by sociology's conventions, however, have noted that anomic circumstances can sometimes be used to good effect. Jonathan Raban's enthusiasm for the 'soft city' is a prime example. He is alert to the dangers of social and personal disorganisation inherent in urban contexts. 'Cities are scary and impersonal, and the best most of us can manage is a fragile hold on our route through the streets. We cling to friends and institutions, fear being alone too much.'[26] Yet simultaneously Raban applauds the opportunities that cities afford.

'You're a balloonist adrift and you need anchors to tether you down. A sociologist, I suppose, would see these as classic symptoms of alienation, more evidence to add to the already full dossier on the evils of urban life. I feel more hospitable towards them. For in moments like this the city goes soft, it awaits the imprint of an identity. For better or worse, it invites you to remake it, to consolidate it into a shape you can live in.[27] *. . . The freedom of the city is enormous. Here one can choose and invent one's society and live more deliberately than anywhere else. Nothing is fixed, the possibility of personal change and renewal are endless and open.'*[28]

Leisure is Raban's soft city writ large. It is certainly possible for individuals to miss their way and descend to the vacuum where they can only cling to whatever friends and pastimes surface. But the enormous freedom makes it possible as never before for individuals to shape their lives with the imprint of their own identities. Uncertainty, unpredictability and diversity are not necessarily pathological. Like the city, leisure can be desultory, but can euphoria be other than a fleeting experience?

Sennett has attacked the hygienic ideal of the 'purified community', a vision that has figured in many areas of social policy.[29] Town planning in particular has been tantalised by the aim of creating environments where individuals can function with total coherence. Indeed, this is the standard approach to solving social problems. Poverty, crime and disease have been addressed by endeavouring to create conditions in which individuals cannot inflict mischief upon themselves. Leisure deserves a different approach. Jacobs expresses admiration for cities that retain their essential character, born of unplanned growth,[30] while Sennett approves an even wider though not total disorder which permits constant innovation and surprise. The existing literature on anomie alerts us to the dangers inherent in situations that are socially and normatively relaxed. But there are also advantages inherent in these same situations, and the challenge of leisure concerns how to avert the dangers without destroying the opportunities that have become available.

Leisure is not a modern calamity calling forth political or religious zealots, or even armies of recreation professionals to redirect history. The spectre of leisure leaving mankind stranded in a social wasteland can sound persuasive when well argued, but it has little empirical foundation. In so far as it is devoid of unambiguous socially defined aims, leisure certainly opens the danger of mankind floundering in a moral wilderness. But loosening traditional obligations need not leave a moral and social void. The absence of consensual leisure aims among the public does not necessarily leave individuals bemused and unhappy. Man-at-leisure does not characteristically flounder aimlessly. As noted in Chapter 2, rather than drowning in excess spare time, there are stronger grounds for alleging the arrival of a harried leisure class. The following chapters will explore how uses of leisure are influenced by the family, work and other statuses that people occupy, and how individuals use the relationships and interests formed in these milieux to construct preferred life-styles. There could be no greater mistake than interpreting the diversity that leisure permits as aimlessness or moral anarchy, and prescribing 'cures' that would suppress the heterogeneity that the growth of leisure allows.

Anomie is never an absolute condition, and likewise leisure can never be more than *relatively* self-determined behaviour. Give two people the opportunity to interact and before long their behaviour will be guided by mutually agreed norms. Modern leisure depends upon individuals being released from the traditional obligations of law, custom and morality, and this *could* leave them like balloonists adrift. Simultaneously, however, leisure creates opportunities for new social relationships to be forged, within which new experiences can be gained. Haworth has expressed the hope that through leisure more individuals will find the fulfilment associated with creating their own experiences and futures.[31] Raban uses his soft city to this effect, and the opportunity conferred by leisure is to make this experience more common for more people. The precondition is a correct appreciation of the nature of modern leisure, how its character and uses are fashioned by the surrounding society, and the reasons why it sometimes fails to fulfil its promise. Solutions to leisure problems based upon misinterpretations of leisure itself are unlikely to avoid mischievous consequences.

Chapter 7

Leisure and other social roles:
(1) The family and related influences

Social networks

The arguments about leisure and the wider society that have been pursued through Chapters 4 to 6, culminating in an affirmation of the pluralist theory, lay the basis for understanding how variations in uses of leisure are associated with the different roles that individuals play within the larger social system. With the pluralist theory in the background, it becomes possible to explain why some factors, such as the family, exert a more powerful influence upon leisure than certain others, such as education. Furthermore, it becomes possible to explain *how* this influence is communicated – the processes whereby the family, education and other aspects of individuals' present circumstances and histories shape their leisure behaviour.

A major theme in the earlier criticisms of the mass society and class domination theories insisted that members of the public are not merely puppets who respond willy-nilly to impersonal forces or dominant class interests. Previously one of the main limitations attributed to orthodox recreation theory and research lay in its preoccupation with facilities and activities. In opposition it was argued that adequate explanations of leisure behaviour must also talk about life-styles, experiences and social relationships. The importance of the social dimension in leisure was strongly emphasised. Recreation is typically group behaviour. People build life-styles that offer experiences they value upon the social relationships by which they are surrounded. These are the foundations from which members of the public incorporate products from the mass media and other leisure industries into their preferred life-styles, and it is by commencing analysis at this level that sociology can best clarify how social factors influence uses of leisure. The mass media are important, and the opportunities offered by commercial interests and public authorities are certainly not irrelevant. But an implication of the pluralist theory is that a more effective point of entry towards understanding variations in uses of leisure will focus upon the social circumstances and related interests characteristic among different sections of the public. The social relationships amid which members of the public are enmeshed are the key processes that link leisure to the wider social system, and it is at this level that we can best understand how the family, for example, exerts a major influence upon uses of leisure.

The Rapoports' study of *Leisure and the Family Life-Cycle*[1] is important for its insistence that specific uses of leisure are related to individuals' broader life-styles, and to the preoccupations and interests that characterise different social statuses. This is a sensible strategy in order to keep the 'experiencing' dimension in leisure analysis, and to capture the 'holistic' quality of people's systems of leisure behaviour. The meaning of any given leisure activity, whether listening to music, reading or watching sport can rarely be fully understood outside the broader life-style to which it contributes. The Rapoports move beyond palpable demand to explore preoccupations, interests and life-styles, and we can probe even further to relate individuals' life-styles to their personal social networks thereby recognising the importance of the people with whom leisure is spent.

This network concept refers to the total systems of social relationships by which individuals are surrounded; relationships that can have many bases including family, work, education and neighbourhood. Each individual's social network will possess unique characteristics, but as different types of work, family life and so on involve different patterns of social relationships, distinctive types of networks tend to arise among different sections of the public. Individuals' life-styles are built upon these networks, and it is within these frameworks that individuals express their interests and experience the various leisure activities in which they become involved.

To prove the value of this approach, the argument pursued in this and the following chapter draws extensively upon data from a survey investigation undertaken during 1972 involving interviews with 474 economically active males from a sample selected at random from the electoral registers covering a part of suburban Liverpool.[2] This Liverpool enquiry was not concerned exclusively with uses of leisure, but one of its objectives was to operationalise and test the value of the ideas outlined above. Information was collected about each respondent's uses of five evening and weekend occasions during the week prior to each interview, and also about participation in specific leisure activities such as church-going, membership of clubs and entertaining friends at home. In analysing responses to the diary-type, open-ended questions in which respondents were simply asked to describe their behaviour on certain evening and weekend occasions, having first eliminated uses such as sleeping and working that could not be described as leisure, four main types of leisure behaviour were distinguished. First, watching *television* was classified separately to confirm what is already known about the large proportion of all leisure time that it accounts for. The second use of leisure distinguished covered other forms of *mass entertainment* including the cinema, the theatre and concerts. With the remaining uses of leisure a division was made between where respondents explained their use of an occasion in terms of pursuing a particular *activity* which could be anything from reading to sport, and when the occasion was described in terms of being with, visiting or meeting other people. How occasions were classified depended basically upon how respondents themselves described what they had been doing, and approximately one-third of all answers fell into this *social* category, confirming the importance of this use of leisure time. There are many other possible ways of classifying uses of leisure, and it is not being claimed that the method described above is the only valid approach. However, the analysis in Table 7.1 will show that it is one useful way of probing beyond the information that can be derived by simply enumerating activities.

Table 7.1 Types of leisure activity undertaken with different associates (percentages)

Uses of Leisure	Associates				
	Alone	Household	Relations	Friends	Total
Television	8	51	9	3	32
Other entertainment	2	3	5	9	4
Activities	65	14	17	27	24
Social	11	15	58	55	25
Other	15	17	11	7	14
n (of occasions) =	317	1,215	127	425	2,084

In this table, and also in Table 7.2, respondents are reported as having been 'alone' on some occasions that are classified as having been spent 'socially'. This is not due to coding errors so much as to an almost inevitable degree of arbitrariness in allocating responses to a limited set of categories. For example, it is possible for a person to go out alone to meet friends in a public house.

The value of this classification is illustrated in Tables 7.1 and 7.2. Responses were analysed to seek relationships between leisure behaviour and variables such as age, income and marital status, and, as will become evident, many such relationships were established. However, in addition to asking respondents *what* they did on five occasions during the week preceding each interview, information was also sought concerning *who* each respondent was with at the time, and relationships between the types of participating groups and uses of leisure proved considerably stronger than connections between leisure behaviour and characteristics of individual respondents. Table 7.2 shows, for example, that television is primarily a household activity. Respondents rarely watched television when alone or in any other type of company. As many as 93 per cent of the occasions accounted for by television were family occasions, when respondents were at home and in the company only of other members of their households. Rather than simply expressing *individuals'* preferences, it is more useful to conceive recreation demand as arising from primary social networks. This is what the pluralist theory leads us to expect, and it is in these

Table 7.2   Types of associates with whom different leisure activities are undertaken (in percentages)

Associates	Uses of leisure				
	Television	Entertainment	Activities	Social	Total
Alone	4	6	40	7	15
Household	93	42	34	34	56
Relations	2	7	4	14	6
Friends	2	45	22	45	22
n (of occasions) =	669	86	510	517	1,782

terms that we can explain how and why the family exerts a powerful influence upon leisure behaviour.

The strength of this influence has been previously documented, and the following evidence offers confirmation. Uses of leisure vary according to the sex roles that individuals play within the family, the type of family concerned and its position in the life-cycle. All this is well known. The main interest in what follows, therefore, concerns the theoretical significance of the family's influence. How and why is the family so important in shaping uses of leisure? Answering these questions will illustrate and support the approach to leisure analysis proposed above, suggesting that particular uses of leisure are best understood by exploring their contributions to the broader life-styles of the persons concerned, and relating these life-styles to the types of social networks within which the individuals are located. As we shall see, the family's influence upon leisure derives from its pivotal position in structuring the public's social networks. The next chapter will endorse this theoretical position by showing that the influence of work upon leisure is less pronounced, for although the income, status and free time associated with different occupations must affect uses of leisure to some extent, work is normally a less potent influence in the construction of personal networks.

Gender

A point that cannot be overstressed in considering the influence of the family upon leisure is that we are not dealing with a source of minor variations. This area offers some sharp contrasts. To begin with there is the gender variable. In general leisure time is not evenly distributed between husbands and wives. Women are very much the second class citizens. Inequalities in the distribution of leisure time within families make the contrasts that can be drawn between social classes pale to insignificance.

Bell and Healey[3] have written about the decline of the traditional family and the emergence of new styles of marriage embodying joint conjugal roles with greater similarity of status between husbands and wives. As a result, they argue, leisure is gradually becoming available for women on the same terms as experienced by their husbands. An articulate body of opinion has certainly been urging the liberation of women, but if the trend that Bell and Healey discuss really is underway, recent findings do not suggest that it has progressed very far. The truly symmetrical family is still an only exceptionally realised ideal type. Trends towards jointness in the conjugal relationship have been uneven. During recent decades there has been a substantial movement of married women into the labour force, sharing out the breadwinner role. Housework, however, is rarely shared out equally. When housework is counted, the work-week of the contemporary wife frequently exceeds 60 hours. Despite the downward trend of hours worked in industry, it is doubtful whether the total work-week of married women has declined over the last generation.

In a sample of London couples each of whom was employed outside the home, Cullen found that the men spent only 36 per cent of the women's time on household chores.[4] Some women may regard cooking and shopping as leisure activities, but it is difficult to avoid concluding that women have substantially less leisure time than men, and this is one reason why men are the more active in virtually all types of out-of-home recreation.

Not only do women have less time free from household obligations, but their uses of the leisure time they do enjoy are relatively limited. This applies in all social classes but particularly for working class women. Following interviews with 48 working class wives with young children in North London during the early 1960s, Hannah Gavron[5] reported on the isolation of the 'captive wife'. These working class women experienced precious little social intercourse outside the nuclear family. The area of the enquiry was not a stable working-class community, and only 15 per cent saw their mothers daily, only 16 per cent their mothers-in-law, only 8 per cent a sister and only 29 per cent reported any contact with neighbours. As many as 79 per cent of these working class wives stated that they watched television every single evening. Times are supposed to be changing but, ten years later in the early 1970s, following a survey of 352 individuals aged 18 to 32 in Hatfield, Parry and Johnson[6] reported a situation little different from that portrayed by Gavron. Married women, especially working class wives, recorded exceptionally low rates of participation across nearly every form of out-of-home recreation, and in their homes they did little that could be described as leisure except watch television. When the women went outside their homes for recreation it was nearly always as a couple or as a family group; rarely alone or with friends. The trend towards sex equality has been less apparent in much of society-at-large than in the literature.

The source of these persistent inequalities in leisure opportunities lies in the woman's domestic role being of a more general, all-absorbing character than that of the man. Particularly when there are young children to care for, the family often becomes the only active base in a woman's social network. Studies in traditional working class districts have shown that a local extended kinship system can greatly enrich women's social lives. In the absence of kinfolk, however, a woman's home and family can bind her captive. The role of the husband/father makes less extensive demands. Men usually have jobs which act as a source of social relations, and as home and family continue to be treated primarily as the woman's responsibility, husbands are better able to maintain contact with friends during evenings and weekends. Males' social networks are spread over a larger number of bases supporting relatively diverse life-styles and leading to a wider range of leisure interests.

As children mature and parental responsibilities diminish, women become less tied to their homes but their life-styles continue to diverge from their husbands'. Booth surveyed 800 American adults all aged 45 and over, and discovered that the men in this age-group possessed more friends than the women, and belonged to more voluntary associations.[7] The women compensated in so far as their smaller number of friendships were affectively richer, and the total amount of time that they devoted to the smaller number of groups in which they did participate was no less than in the case of the men. However, these findings show that even when women enjoy similar amounts of leisure time, their social networks remain less extensive than their husbands', and their life-styles are accordingly narrow. It may not necessarily follow that women's life-styles are less satisfying than men's but they are certainly different.

The family life-cycle

Similarly impressive contrasts in uses of leisure are found between different stages in the family life-cycle. The changes in leisure behaviour that occur as individuals move from childhood, through adolescence, to marriage, parenthood, the post-parental stage and eventual retirement have been well documented. The Rapoports[8] have illustrated how the unfolding of this life-cycle is associated with shifts in basic preoccupations and interests, while Sillitoe[9] has coined the concept of 'domestic age' in portraying these developments. Data from the Liverpool investigation that was introduced earlier confirm the importance of the life-cycle, and, more importantly, enable the changes in uses of leisure that occur at particular junctures – with marriage, parenthood, and the later diminishing of parental responsibilities – to be examined in the depth necessary to clarify the underlying processes responsible for these changes.

The respondents interviewed were all economically active males and among this sample the group whose leisure was most emphatically 'different' comprised the unmarried under 30-year-olds. Compared with other informants, they were less occupied with television which accounted for only 20 per cent of the occasions examined. As Table 7.3 shows, in their uses of leisure time, the accent was upon social pastimes; meeting people in homes, pubs, cafés and other environments that support diffuse sociability. In addition to querying how occasions

Table 7.3 Uses of leisure and domestic age (percentages)

	Unmarried Aged <30	Married Aged <30	Unmarried aged 30–44	Married aged 30–44		Married aged 45+
				No children	Children	
Uses of occasions						
Non-leisure	9	19	5	11	17	10
Television	20	33	22	32	37	35
Entertainment	7	3	6	6	4	3
Activities	21	19	33	18	21	30
Social	43	26	33	32	21	22
	—	—	—	—	—	—
n =	245	173	119	87	750	841
Companions						
Alone	11	15	24	6	15	17
Household	23	63	30	77	65	66
Relatives	2	5	8	3	5	7
Friends	64	17	38	13	14	11
Others	—	—	—	1	1	—
	—	—	—	—	—	—
n =	249	160	142	88	737	880

were spent, each respondent was asked whom he had been with at the time, and the unmarried under 30-year-olds also differed from the remainder of the sample in terms of their leisure companions. Their life-styles were not family centred: leisure was spent mainly with friends rather than members of their households, and these friends were exceptionally likely to be persons met 'socially' rather than relatives and other individuals met through the family, a very prominent source of leisure-time associates among other age groups (see Table 7.4). Youth has long been recognised as a flowering period during which time and money are spent outside the home developing a style of life that is irrevocably lost upon marriage, and the results of our Liverpool enquiry confirm this impression.

Table 7.4 Sources of leisure-time associates from outside immediate households (percentages)

	Single	Married		
	aged under 30	aged under 30	30–44	45 and over
School	13	19	4	3
Work	28	30	25	19
Family/relatives	3	26	37	38
Neighbourhood	29	20	23	24
Social	27	6	11	17
$n =$	90	54	206	225

Upon marriage the uses of leisure of the under 30-year-olds changed radically. With the advent of domestic responsibilities, hours of work increased as individuals set about building careers and maximising their earning potential, and a greater proportion of married respondents' occasions could not, therefore, be classified as leisure. Within the sample, the demands of work were allowed to recede to adolescent proportions only following the child-rearing phase. Furthermore, uses of the leisure occasions that remained were adjusted following marriage. Leisure became centred upon the home and television which subsequently accounted for 33 per cent of all occasions, while time spent with friends and upon social pastimes declined sharply. Following marriage the proportion of leisure occasions spent with friends declined from 64 to 17 per cent, and parenthood gave these trends a further push. With the arrival of children, time spent watching television rose further to account for 37 per cent of the occasions and the decline of social pastimes was accentuated. However, especially in terms of the companions with whom leisure is spent, the data indicate that it is marriage rather than parenthood that heralds the main break with adolescent life-styles.

These trends will seem less dramatic to the persons experiencing them than they appear in our columns of figures. With marriage, the girlfriend becomes a wife and watching television becomes the most convenient way of passing leisure time. Nevertheless, irrespective of whether individuals feel that they are breaking with former styles of life, marriage does concentrate leisure within the home, increase the audience for television at the expense of out-of-home recreation, and focus social intercourse upon a single conjugal partner rather than a wider circle of friends.

One way of avoiding telecentred leisure is to stay single. Unmarried respondents in the 30-plus age group devoted hardly any greater proportion of their leisure to television than younger single respondents. Outside marriage, adults do not become involved in the family relationships that encourage televiewing. But adolescent life-styles are not easily preserved. As peers marry, opportunities for social uses of leisure decline. So even for individuals who personally avoid matrimony, its prevalence leaves a gap in their former life-styles. Instead of being drawn to television, however, they tend to fill the vacuum with activities; doing things rather than socialising.

As explained in Chapter 3, recreation researchers normally conceptualise leisure in terms of 'doing things', and furthermore, in folk philosophies of leisure 'doing something' with one's time tends to be regarded as meritorious. In contrast, doing 'nothing in particular' is often considered a reprehensible waste of time. Having a hobby, developing an interest, and playing a sport are commonly regarded as worthwhile uses of free time that deserve public patronage, and the tasks of educating and catering for leisure are often seen in terms of offering so attractive an array of things to do that none need succumb to idleness and boredom. Sitting around, being entertained, drinking and watching television are less likely to be commended as arts deserving sponsorship and cultivation. This whole approach to leisure with its accent on purposeful activity has already been questioned, and the evidence now being presented reinforces the theoretical points made earlier. Rather than the essence of leisure, this evidence suggests that participating in specifically chosen activities is better regarded as a residual use of leisure time.

Of all the occasions about which information was collected 56 per cent of time was spent with other members of respondents' households. Unmarried adults, therefore, particularly those who do not live as members of families, are left with considerable 'spare' time. Furthermore, being involved in their own households, most married persons are not 'free' to associate with the single. Hence the void in the lives of the unmarried which is largely filled with activities, pursuing hobbies and other specific interests that either do not require companionship or generate their own interest groups. Among the uses of leisure distinguished in the Liverpool investigation, participation in specific activities was the most likely to occur when respondents were alone, and the proportion of individuals' leisure devoted to activities depended principally upon how much leisure time was spent in solitude. Only 24 per cent of all the occasions surveyed were devoted to activities, yet this use of leisure prevailed on 65 per cent of occasions when respondents were alone. Likewise in Hatfield, Parry and Johnson found that crafts and hobbies were most likely to be pursued when individuals had time on their own.[10] This accounts for the popularity of activities among unmarried over 30-year-olds. Life-styles centred upon pursuing specific interests become pronounced only in the absence of the social relationships that otherwise fill leisure, and this constitutes the case for regarding activity-centred leisure as a residual type.

Contrasts between the uses of leisure of older and younger unmarried individuals, and between both of these and married persons are best explained in terms of the social networks that typically surround these statuses. As suggested in Chapter 3, to understand leisure we need to push activities from the centre of the analysis. Relating life-styles to social networks is a more effective approach towards clarifying variations in uses of leisure between different sections of the population, and its effectiveness is demonstrated in explaining the changes that occur during the family life-cycle.

Life-styles may be reshaped following the child-rearing phase. Diminishing domestic responsibilities can leave individuals less tied to their homes creating opportunities for more outgoing life-styles, and for some people middle age appears to be a leisure renaissance. It is known, for example, that activists in local political life and religious organisations are often drawn from this age-group and there was evidence of renewed interest in 'activities' among the Liverpool sample. Partly because family responsibilities were lighter, the 45-plus age group was able to relax the demands of work. With less need than in previous years to maximise earnings through overtime and shift-work, there were relatively few occasions about which the sample was questioned when this age-group was not at leisure. In view of the apparently greatly increased scope for choice, uses of leisure changed less than could possibly have been expected. For example, there was no trend whatsoever towards spending more time socially with friends, nor towards out-of-home entertainment, and television retained its appeal. The sole change compared with the previous stage in the life-cycle was the devotion of the greater quantity of time freed from work to activities. Children may depart but the conjugal relationship persists and usually continues to dominate leisure. At an earlier period in the life-cycle it is marriage rather than the arrival of children that decisively centres leisure upon home and television, and this is where leisure normally remains centred in middle-age. For married persons, irrespective of whether they are responsible for dependent children, their families are usually the central elements in their social networks and uses of leisure are shaped accordingly. It is possible to talk of opportunities being missed and of the life-styles of the middle-aged having fallen into ruts that resist recasting. Such judgements, however, overlook the fact that for married persons simply being with their families can be a major and valued aspect of leisure. Just spending time socially with people among whom one feels comfortable is not peripheral but a normal use of leisure time, and for many people the nexus of home, family and television is the most comfortable milieu available.

Style of marriage

The data from the Liverpool study indicate that, in addition to sex roles and stages in the life-cycle, the style of marriage and the conjugal relationship that it incorporates act as a further family-based source of variation in uses of leisure. Among married respondents, a high level of jointness across certain aspects of the conjugal relationship was associated with leisure being exceptionally centred around home and television, the term 'joint' being used in opposition to 'segregated' in reference to the extent to which the same tasks are performed by both conjugal partners.

Some writers[11] have attributed contemporary trends in leisure behaviour to a decline of the traditional family with its segregated roles, in which the male 'breadwinner's' spare time would be spent with his 'mates' while his wife remained tied to 'her' responsibilities in the home. The emergence of a non-traditional family embodying greater jointness in the conjugal relationship has been held responsible for producing greater similarity in the sexes' uses of leisure, with women becoming more likely to venture out for leisure either with or as well as their husbands, while men accept more responsibility in the home and, therefore, spend more of their leisure within it. The extent to which women are achieving sex equality in the distribution of leisure opportunities has already been queried, but the Liverpool study supports the view that insofar as the traditional family is in decline the effects upon leisure will be in the suggested directions.

The Liverpool sample was entirely male and no part of it was drawn from a 'traditional' city area. Hence the results cannot comprehensively test the above propositions. However, among the husbands interviewed, certain types of jointness in the conjugal relationship were associated with home-centred leisure, which is in line with previous interpretations of the significance of the traditional family's demise. The data also suggest, however, that it may be misleading to talk about one non-traditional type of family.

Questions probing three aspects of jointness drew answers which, when aggregated, proved associated with clear variations in uses of leisure. The relevant questions all concerned specifically familial tasks and decisions; namely, the extent to which the male respondents assisted with housework, and whether the family's annual holiday and how to decorate the lounge were decided jointly or by only one of the domestic partners. When responses to these questions were pooled (as Table 7.5 shows) the lowest scorers along the resulting jointness scale were found to spend less leisure than the highest scorers watching television and in the company only of other members of the households concerned, while a greater proportion of the occasions were spent with friends and engaged in social pursuits.

Table 7.5 Style of marriage and leisure behaviour (percentages)
Married respondents: aggregated scores for jointness in the performance of selected family tasks

	High	Low
Uses of occasions		
Non-leisure	13	13
Television	37	23
Entertainment	5	3
Activities	27	28
Social	18	32
n =	443	94
Companions		
Alone	15	16
Household	67	59
Relatives	7	8
Friends	10	16
Other	1	–
n =	445	98

Other indices of jointness, however, displayed different associations with leisure behaviour. As found in an earlier enquiry in Luton,[12] the Liverpool study discovered weak and sometimes negative correlations between some measures of jointness, suggesting that jointness is not necessarily an unidimensional and generalised feature of domestic roles. For example, the measures of jointness detailed above were unrelated to the ways in which household income was distributed and managed, and the lowest rather than the highest scorers along the jointness scale were the more likely to have been out socially with their wives during the week prior to each interview (63 per cent and 51 per cent).

Any trend towards jointness and away from traditionally segregated sex roles can be expected to increase the domesticity of the male, but as a result of such movements various combinations of jointness and segregation can occur across different aspects of family life so as to produce contrasting non-traditional styles of marriage. One combination produces a *companionate* style where the emphasis is upon domestic togetherness, and home-centred leisure among the Liverpool respondents was most pronounced in this type of family. Another combination produces a *colleague* style, where spouses treat each other as equal partners, venturing jointly for leisure outside the home relatively often, but 'share out' rather than 'share in' the range of domestic tasks. Respondents whose conjugal relationships approximated towards this latter type retained a wider circle of friends outside the family than where the conjugal relationship was more companionate, and their wider networks appeared to draw these individuals into social uses of leisure outside their homes, sometimes with but often without the company of their spouses.

Is this relatively outgoing life-style the cause or the effect of the style of marriage with which it is associated? Individuals' broader life-styles and their conjugal relationships probably exert a reciprocal influence upon each other. Irrespective of the direction in which causality runs, however, these relationships confirm the importance of social networks in accounting for variations in uses of leisure, and the importance of the family as a determinant of leisure behaviour derives from the pivotal position it occupies in the social networks of most adults.

Education, social networks and leisure

The proportion of leisure time spent in the home depends upon the nature of the family roles that individuals play and also upon the presence or absence of other bases in their social networks that are liable to draw individuals into a wider range of pastimes. Employment can act as one such base and the significance of this influence will be examined in the next chapter, while another base can be constructed in education. Table 7.6 presents the relevant information from the Liverpool enquiry, holding occupational status constant and subdividing the sample into three educational categories; early secondary or elementary school leavers who had received no further education, 'stayers on' who had received some full-time post-secondary education, and an intermediate group. The figures show that, particularly within the white-collar strata, the more education respondents had received, the lower the proportion of their leisure time that was subsequently spent watching television and in the household, and the greater the proportion that was devoted to social pastimes with friends. These differences are unlikely to result from any formal programmes

Table 7.6 Education and leisure (percentages) –
Registrar-General's social class 1–3a and 1–3b.

	1–3a		
	Left school 16 or later: some full time further education	Intermediate	Left school 14 or 15: no further education
Uses of occasions			
Non-leisure	14	9	19
Television	22	29	34
Entertainment	4	6	4
Activities	22	32	21
Social	38	23	22
	—	—	—
n =	138	681	211
Associates			
Alone	14	16	13
Household	54	54	59
Relatives	5	4	8
Friends	26	24	18
Others	1	1	2
	—	—	—
n =	146	731	196
Sources of Leisure Associates from outside immediate households			
Education	13	7	3
Work	19	17	17
Family	15	17	32
Neighbourhood	17	27	15
Social	37	32	33
	—	—	—
n =	47	219	65

to educate for leisure. In the past, when the respondents were in education, such programmes were virtually non-existent. The underlying process appears to concern the manner in which education until late adolescence enlarges the active bases in individuals' personal social networks. A prolonged education helps to develop the social skills and contacts which mean that, in later life, individuals are less dependent upon the family for social intercourse and are more likely to

3b–5

Intermediate	Left school 14–15: no further education
10	13
34	37
3	3
25	23
27	23
—	—
440	546
13	17
56	65
8	5
22	13
1	–
—	—
454	560
6	3
24	26
29	39
17	23
25	9
—	—
159	180

maintain and develop friendships based upon a wider range of sources.

However, compared with the changes in uses of leisure that occur during the family life-cycle, the variations that education explains are marginal. The family occupies a central position in most adults' social networks, and hence the sensitivity of life-styles to variations in family circumstances.

These findings have implications for leisure policy which will be explored more extensively in the final chapter. Basically, however, the analysis challenges the view that catering for the growth of leisure is principally a matter of providing more opportunities for out-of-home recreation. In drawing attention to the importance of the family, the above discussion suggests that the quality of leisure depends much more upon the quality of domestic life than the availability of parks, sports centres and similar facilities. Furthermore, the importance of social networks suggests that demand for leisure facilities outside the home is as much a demand for environments that will support sociability as a demand from individual enthusiasts to pursue specific interests. Recreation managers often recognise that a subsidiary function of sports halls and swimming pools is to offer opportunities for social intercourse. Hence the designs that include cafeteria and seating for spectators. Rather than subsidiary, however, the implication of the above analysis is that its social dimensions are primary aspects of leisure behaviour.

Chapter 8

Leisure and other social roles: (2) Work and its corollaries

Work centrality

Work is another influence upon leisure, and an intention in this chapter is to explore how occupational differences account for variations in leisure behaviour. At the same time, the following argument warns against exaggerating the significance of work. The influence of work upon leisure is much less powerful than the familial variables examined in the last chapter, and just as analysis in terms of social networks and life-styles allows us to understand the family's importance, so it also reveals why the impact of work upon leisure should be relatively marginal; much less dramatic than suggested in some previous accounts.

In the past sociologists have tended to treat leisure as a subsidiary sphere of life with a character derived from more pivotal institutions, particularly work. As Giddens has noted, 'Leisure has in general been regarded as merely ancillary to those systems of economy, power and prestige which have been taken in sociology as crucial to the explication of social behaviour.' Historically, sociological research into leisure developed largely as an adjunct to the sociology of occupations. This was probably to be expected given that contemporary leisure owes its character to industrialism, coupled with sociology's continuing 'obsession' with social class. Nothing has seemed more obvious to many sociologists than that variations in uses of leisure will be attributable to individuals' occupations. Hence the volumes charting the significance of various aspects of work including income, prestige, career patterns and whether work is a source of interest and friendships. Literally scores of enquiries have sought to identify how work can affect leisure, conveying the impression that work is the central determining factor in individuals' life-styles.

In his book on the mass media, Golding reflects this presumption of work centrality, stating that, '. . . work experience is a central determinant of the amount and type of leisure demands an individual will make'.[2] No evidence is marshalled in support of this proposition; the statement is clearly not intended to arouse controversy. Golding simply refers to the volumes of research on the influence of work, and the many previous writers who have made similar remarks. Sociologists have reiterated work centrality so frequently that requests for evidence seem superfluous. It is standard practice in survey investigations to categorise respondents according to their occupations. Whatever the main object of enquiry – educational achievement, religion, family life or theatre going – failure to explore the influence of occupational status would be considered utterly naive.

Even when they admit that work accounts for a smaller proportion of lifetime than a century ago, many sociologists nevertheless insist that values rooted in the economy continue to pervade the entire culture. In considering the class domination theory we have already encountered the view that hopes of leisure offering scope for freedom and choice remain illusory while society as a whole is still governed by the logic of industrial capitalism, its privileged strata's interests, and their supporting state apparatuses. Parallel arguments are encountered at a micro-level. It is alleged that individuals' roles in the economy, their occupations, are so important as sources of identity and self-consciousness, that their influence inevitably spreads into non-working life. Everett Hughes writes,

'A man's work is one of the things by which he is judged, and certainly one of the more significant things by which he judges himself. . . . A man's work is one of the more important parts of his social identity, of his self; indeed, of his fate in the one life he has to live, for there is something almost as irrevocable about choice of occupation as there is about choice of a mate.'[3]

The frequency with which it has been approvingly quoted by sociologists testifies to the widespread agreement with this statement. We are reminded that the getting acquainted question, 'What do you do?' is still ordinarily taken to mean 'What work?' We place and identify each other with reference to our occupations. Hence the social and psychological in addition to purely economic problems that accompany involuntary unemployment and enforced retirement.

Observing the role of work in identity formation and maintenance has prompted discussion of the 'hidden injuries of class' – the ways in which work that devalues the individual can inflict psychological damage with crippling implications for the rest of life.[4] Peter Berger claims that a technological rationality invades every corner of everyday life.

'Elements of consciousness that are intrinsic to technological production are transposed to areas of social life that are not directly concerned with such production (for example, problem-solving ingenuity). Everyday life in just about every one of its sectors is ongoingly bombarded, not only with material objects and processes derived from technological production, but with clusters of consciousness originated in the latter.'[5]

Elsewhere Berger has discussed how part of the contemporary social malaise results from the division of labour with its specialised and meaningless jobs which deny the worker a meaningful identity.[6] He regards professionalisation as a strategy, available only to some, through which valued occupational identities can be protected and projected. Other workers are obliged to express their true 'selves' in private, non-working life, which cannot be entirely satisfactory for, in Berger's view, it goes against the prevailing expectation that people will express themselves through their work, and conflicts with the manner in which we continue to 'type' each other according to our occupations. Wilenski argues in similar vein that boring work so stultifies the personality as to produce passivity during leisure.[7] Individuals in the more interesting and intellectually demanding types of empolyment participate most extensively in the more active leisure pursuits. Friedman echoes this argument, suggesting that enforced passivity at work is associated with 'voluntary' passivity during leisure.[8] Others have hypothesised that individuals whose creativity is frustrated at work might attempt to compensate during leisure with handicrafts and do-it-yourself hobbies. Whichever argument is correct, the presumption of work centrality in which the character of leisure is seen as following from individuals' occupations is endorsed.

One of the most systematic and influential assertions of the pivotal role of work has been offered by Stanley Parker, inspired by his own research among social workers and bank clerks.[9] Parker identifies a work–leisure relationship that he calls the *extension* pattern, where work extends into and pervades leisure. Individuals devote a great deal of their 'non-working' time to activities which can include meeting colleagues, talking shop, reading professional literature and attending conferences. This extension pattern was common among the social workers that Parker investigated, and he hypothesises that it may well be typical in other occupations where individuals are highly involved and identify positively with their work. Parker contrasts this extension relationship with an *opposition* pattern, which is attributed to occupational groups such as coal-miners and trawlermen whose work is dangerous and disagreeable. This type of work, Parker claims, encourages individuals sharply to demarcate working from non-working time, and to use their leisure to seek opportunities for distinctly non-worklike behaviour, such as during working class 'binges' when freedom is overtly flaunted. Parker completes his typology with a midway *complementary* pattern, which he considered characteristic among the bank clerks that he studied. Their work was neither intensely alienating nor emphatically rewarding. Attitudes towards work were better described as indifferent, and work and leisure were regarded as simply different spheres of life, complementary sources of different experiences and satisfactions.

Salaman's research among architects and railwaymen illustrates and clarifies the processes that produce what Parker terms the extension pattern. Albeit in rather different ways, both architecture and railway work supply the foundations for occupational communities. Shared viewpoints, attitudes, values and social relationships develop among practitioners and tend to spill into leisure. Salaman recognises that not all workers are bound into occupational communities. Such communities arise only in especially favourable circumstances such as when work is intrinsically satisfying and emotionally rewarding, or when an occupation's geographical isolation or 'unsocial hours' isolate individuals from other companions. However, when occupational communities do develop, Salaman believes that they make a considerable impact upon leisure. He alleges that members tend to be 'affected by their work in such a way that their non-work lives are liable to be permeated by their work relationships, interests and values'.[10]

Attributing such central importance to individuals' occupations implies that leisure cannot hope genuinely to compensate for deprivations encountered at work; that individuals cannot so easily escape from work's over-arching influence. It is maintained that the quality of leisure depends upon the quality of working life. Rather than being solved, problems of alienation and monotony at work are seen as transposed into leisure. It is argued that the character of work experience is always liable to penetrate life in general, and that while some individuals might attempt to compensate, their leisure can be no more than a palliative which at best makes life more bearable, but only by blinding those involved to the real sources of their troubles.

So far little reference has been made to the ways in which the hours of work and income levels that are associated with different jobs must influence the rest of life. Their likely influence is probably too obvious to need spelling out. Beyond these 'constraints', however, sociologists have emphasised the 'spill-over' effects which operate through social relationships, attitudes, interests and values generated in the workplace. Hence the portrait of work centrality in which leisure is sketched as a dependent shadow. When placed together, the numerous ways in which work is alleged to influence leisure convey an impression of work as the powerful and central force structuring individuals' total life-styles.

The compartmentalisation argument

No one would wish to deny that leisure is influenced by work. As indicated above, investigators who have probed this area have uncovered many relationships. In social research, however, statistically significant connections are rarely difficult to unearth. Social life is an interconnecting web in which everything tends to be related to everything else in some way or another. The really important questions, therefore, concern exactly how powerful an influence work exerts, and the sum of the available evidence indicates that today this influence is rather weak – sufficiently so to justify talk of the compartmentalisation of leisure from the influence of individuals' work roles.

Although work certainly influences leisure, it creates a false impression to dwell solely upon the positive relationships that can be discerned while ignoring other data. Scrutinising *all* the evidence leads

Dumazedier to the conclusion that on balance the sociology of leisure has been '. . . hampered by its derivation from the sociology of work'.[11] In a survey designed to examine the interconnections between work and leisure, Dumazedier found that '. . . out of some two hundred theoretically possible correlations twenty are significant (x^2 at 0.10)',[12] and such findings are not untypical. The truth, Dumazedier rightly insists, is that 'the division of labour (in industry) is not reflected by leisure differentials as sharp as the contrast between the job of a semi-skilled worker and that of a manager.'[13] There are wide variations in uses of leisure among individuals practising the same occupations, while some leisure activities are popular among people in diverse types of employment. Knowledge of an individual's work-role is of only marginal value in predicting his leisure behaviour. Age, sex and marital status are more discriminating variables.

The data from the Liverpool enquiry fully support Dumazedier's argument. It is tantalisingly easy to discover leisure differences because there are so many hundreds of specific leisure interests and alternative ways of measuring them upon which attention can be focused and, needless to say, the greater the discrimination with which any phenomenon is examined, the greater the likelihood of differences becoming evident. Hence the importance of not searching out differences too vigorously. We need to pay equivalent attention to constant features of leisure across different populations, and when this is done, the extent to which leisure is compartmentalised from the influence of work appears as impressive as the job-related variations that admittedly can be discovered.

Constraints: time and income

Many of the influences of work upon leisure are permissive rather than deterministic, meaning that a pay rise, for example, may widen an individual's leisure choices, but it will not determine exactly how he uses the extra money. Many work-based 'causes' are translated into specific leisure effects only through independent mediating processes. Besides being workers, individuals are involved in other social relationships and immersed in other sources of values. Family, neighbourhood, educational and religious contexts translate opportunites such as accompany rising wage levels into particular uses of leisure. Likewise the additional free time offered by shorter hours of work is used in contrasting ways depending upon the life-styles towards which individuals are independently oriented.

In the Liverpool investigation, throughout the sample as a whole, shorter hours of work were associated with increased involvement across virtually all the uses of leisure that were distinguished, reflecting the greater amount of time available. However, as evident in Table 8.1, this extra time was used in different ways among the blue- as against the white-collar strata. Within the non-manual strata shorter hours of work increased participation in activities; more leisure time was spent doing more things. Among the blue-collar sample, in contrast, the additional time gained as hours of work fell was accounted for by television and social uses of leisure.

Table 8.1   Hours of work and leisure (percentages)

Uses of occasions	White-collar				Blue-collar		
	Hours worked per week				Hours worked per week		
	51+	*42–50*	*38–41*	*Under 38*	*51+*	*42–50*	*38–41*
Non-leisure	22	13	8	7	19	10	11
Television	26	35	28	29	32	37	37
Entertainment	2	6	6	6	4	3	3
Activities	21	27	29	35	21	23	23
Social	28	20	30	23	23	27	27
n (of occasions) =	212	271	281	275	181	358	413

Parallel findings emerge when the relationship between income levels and uses of leisure is examined. In Table 8.2 respondents are divided into more and less affluent groups depending upon whether or not they were earning in excess of £2,000 per year at the time of the investigation, and within the white-collar strata affluence is shown to be associated with a shift in leisure behaviour away from social intercourse and towards activities. As the constraints associated with both income and hours of work are gradually relaxed, white-collar life-styles accord more prominence to the activities that more generally distinguish middle from working class uses of leisure. Within the blue-collar sample, in contrast, affluence was associated with a decline in time devoted to activities, while the emphasis switched towards social uses of leisure. Rather than promoting the embourgeoisement often anticipated, blue-collar affluence and shorter hours of work appear more likely to accentuate distinctly working class uses of free time. One obvious inference suggests scepticism towards predictions of trends in leisure behaviour based upon assumptions such as that if and when income levels rise throughout the population, the life-styles currently confined to the affluent will become increasingly widespread. Predictions derived from this type of reasoning could prove very wide of the mark.

Apart from the details of how changes in income and hours of work affect leisure being less than fully determined by these independent

Table 8.2 Income and leisure (percentages)

Uses of occasions	White-collar		Blue-collar	
	Annual income		Annual income	
	Up to £2,000	Over £2,000	Up to £2,000	Over £2,000
Non-leisure	14	10	12	13
Television	29	31	36	36
Entertainment	5	5	3	3
Activities	23	32	25	18
Social	29	22	24	30
n (of occasions) =	363	546	674	264

variables, it must also be stressed that the variations in uses of leisure associated with these changes are not dramatic. They hardly compare, for example, with the changes that occur during the family life-cycle, or the divergences between the sexes' leisure behaviour. In the light of this evidence, how can we explain the findings and conclusions of sociologists who have stressed work centrality? The snap answer is they have mostly 'cooked the books', albeit in highly conventional ways. They have spotlighted differences while ignoring apparently less interesting statistics that imply similarities between the uses of leisure of different occupational groups, and have accentuated the available contrasts by using the social class concept as a deceptive 'umbrella'.

Surveys that compare rates of involvement in certain specific leisure activities between social classes can uncover some sharp contrasts. For example, while only 29 per cent of the working class wives interviewed by Hannah Gavron reported contact with neighbours, 69 per cent of a comparison group of middle class wives did so.[14] The label 'captive wife' was less appropriate in the white-collar strata where 67 per cent claimed lots of friends, 84 per cent entertained regularly, and only 17 per cent watched television every night as against 79 per cent among the working class sample. Such figures offer impressive contrasts and might appear to support the view of work as an extremely important influence upon leisure. This appearance, however, is misleading. The 'social class' variable covers a large number of influences, only some of which are products of individuals' occupations. For example, social class is associated with education which, as we have seen in the previous chapter, is itself related to variations in uses of leisure within social strata. As Musgrove[15] has argued, middle class styles of education at non-local grammar schools and colleges are important in developing the social skills and contacts that subsequently widen individuals' social networks. The educational, family, neighbourhood and occupational differences that lie behind the blanket label of social class interact to produce contrasting life-styles, and the explanation of these contrasts lies in the processes of interaction rather than any single independent variable or work-based factors alone. The ways in which the effects of rising income levels and shorter hours of work depend upon social class context are just two examples.

Another consideration that deflates otherwise impressive illustrations of the effects of work concerns the status of comparisons in terms of participation in selected, specific activities. When total life-styles are compared, as in the above tables, the contrasts are less dramatic. The most popular forms of recreation in Britain show only modest variation between occupational groups. In all social strata, television accounts for the largest single block of leisure time, while alcohol and tobacco are consistently important objects of recreational expenditure. The popularity of gambling and sex transcends class boundaries, and although there are numerous subtle variations in exactly *how* these interests are pursued, the similarities are at least equally impressive. Occupational differences colour in the details, but do not write the overall pattern of leisure behaviour.

Querying the importance of work's effects upon leisure might appear to be quarrelling with common sense. Many leisure goods and services cost money, so surely income, for example, must make a big difference. Working class families simply cannot afford round-the-world cruises, private stables and paddocks for their horses, or regular weekends in luxury hotels. Focus upon such specific uses of leisure, and clear contrasts will be apparent between groups with different levels of income. What must be borne in mind, however, is that at all income levels a great deal of leisure is spent at home, doing nothing in particular, or watching television. Theatre-going is a mainly middle class pastime and rates of working class participation lag far behind.[16] But theatre attendances account for only a minute proportion of all middle class leisure. A far greater volume of middle class leisure time is spent watching television which is also popular among the working class. Examining total life-styles enables some of the sharper social class contrasts that can be drawn to be kept in perspective. Although the majority of families cannot afford weekends at luxury hotels, they can usually devise uses of leisure time to perform similar functions in their life-styles, such as taking trips to the coast or countryside. Similarly, although the type of holiday must depend upon income, most families in Britain can afford a holiday away from home, and likewise most individuals can afford to participate in some sport. There are social class variations to uses of leisure, but these are by no means as clear cut as, for example, in politics, where the majority of middle class electors vote Conservative, while Labour is easily the most popular working class choice.

Work-related variables constrain some groups' uses of leisure more than others, but as constraints are eased, the opportunities created are mostly used to modify details within the basically unchanged life-styles that the individuals in question continue to prefer. Shorter hours of work, therefore, allow manual workers to spend slightly more leisure engaged in the social intercourse that, in any case, tends to be a prominent feature of their life-styles. Variations in hours of work and income levels do not produce really dramatic shifts in life-styles since in themselves they do not reshape the social networks upon which, as argued and illustrated earlier, uses of leisure are constructed.

Occupational communities: the spill-over from work

This latter point is again illustrated when considering the effects of occupational communities. To examine these effects, two extreme sets of respondents were separated within the larger sample covered in the Liverpool enquiry. The first set comprised individuals who were highly integrated into occupational communities. In response to the relevant questions they stated that they were completely satisfied with their jobs, described two or more people from work as 'close friends', and were in the habit of meeting at least two such friends socially outside their workplaces. The second group met none of these criteria, and

Table 8.3 Occupational community and leisure (percentages)

Uses of occasions	Integration into occupational committee			
	White-collar		Blue-collar	
	Weak	*High*	*Weak*	*High*
Non-leisure	10	7	11	13
Television	33	30	39	24
Entertainment	3	6	1	2
Activities	27	29	25	22
Social	28	28	25	40
	—	—	—	—
Attended church during previous week	22	52	25	3
Been out with wife during previous week	39	62	46	58
Entertained friends to a meal at home during previous week	24	41	7	30
Member of sports and/or social club	45	55	49	77
	—	—	—	—
n (of respondents)	53	33	55	30

focusing upon these extreme types allows the consequences that follow from membership of occupational communities to be thrown into sharp relief.

The findings in Table 8.3 confirm that membership of an occupational community makes a difference to uses of leisure. Membership was related to relatively high levels of participation across virtually all areas of out-of-home recreation. In addition to the diary-type questions, respondents were asked about their involvement in more occasional specific leisure activities, and with the solitary exception of church-going among blue-collar workers, on all the relevant items those who were the more highly integrated into occupational communities were the more active. The detailed effects of an occupational community must obviously depend upon the individual character of the community in question. However, the findings of this enquiry indicate that membership *per se* has consequences that distinguish the leisure of those involved from other workers' life-styles, and in general these consequences involve drawing individuals away from preoccupation with home and television, and boosting participation in out-of-home recreation. These are the consequences that social network theory leads us to anticipate. An occupational community widens its members' networks thereby drawing their life-styles away from exclusive preoccupation with home, family and television.

It should be noted, however, that despite the 'extreme' character of the sets of respondents compared, the differences between their day-to-day life-styles proved by no means as sharp as the contrasts that occur with the unfolding of the family life-cycle. This is because, among married persons, the family normally remains the central element in their social networks irrespective of the strength of work-based social relationships which, therefore, play no more than a subsidiary role in the life-styles of those concerned. Work relationships produce modulations upon a dominant pattern, but do not dictate it.

Furthermore, as in unravelling the consequences of hours of work and income levels, the evidence suggests a need to relinquish attempts to explain the implications of occupational communities in simple cause–effect terms. It is more appropriate to think of relatively complex processes of interaction and to recognise the existence of contextual processes that independently incline various sections of the population towards different uses of leisure. For example, the Liverpool data show that the consequences of membership of an occupational community differ between blue- and white-collar workers. Membership of an occupational community is a more discriminating influence within the blue-collar strata. Among white-collar respondents, marked contrasts between the highly and weakly integrated groups only become evident when attention is focused upon occasional specific activities such as church-going and entertaining friends to a meal at home. Day-to-day uses of leisure varied little between the two non-manual groups. Furthermore, paralleling the cases of hours of work and income levels, whereas among blue-collar workers membership of an occupational community tended to boost 'social' uses of leisure time, among the white-collar sample it was mainly entertainment and other activities that compensated for the decline in televiewing. Once again we see that *how* work affects leisure depends upon the life-styles to which individuals are independently oriented.

Table 8.4 Occupational community and sources of friends (in percentages)

Sources of spare-time associates (other than members of household)	Integration into occupational communities			
	White-collar		Blue-collar	
	Weak	*High*	*Weak*	*High*
Education	14	5	12	–
Work	12	14	22	42
Family	23	32	29	23
Neighbourhood	32	30	28	13
Leisure	20	20	9	23
n (of associates) =	53	33	55	30

Occupational communities make the greater difference to blue- as opposed to white-collar life-styles, and this is because non-manual workers' social networks are the more broadly based. Table 8.4 summarises the answers received when respondents were asked to name the two people, other than members of their households, with whom they were most likely to spend leisure time, and further information was then sought about these associates including where they were originally met. Given the nature of the question, persons in all subsections of the sample had to name the same number of friends, and this should be borne in mind when interpreting Table 8.4. Manual respondents could not name a smaller number of friends, and the evidence that their social networks were relatively narrow is of a different kind. The important findings are, first, that when white-collar workers are closely integrated into occupational communities, their friends are only slightly more likely to be drawn from work than otherwise. This can only be because other sources of friends are so productive that membership of an occupational community makes little difference to an individual's social network. A middle class background tends to involve experiences such as an education beyond the compulsory minimum, and geographical mobility between various neighbourhoods where individuals become accustomed to forming friendships and developing related interests. When white-collar occupational communities are influential, therefore, they become only one among several active centres within their members' social networks, and in their absence individuals can simply make greater use of other associates.

The second important finding is that even when blue-collar employees are only weakly integrated into occupational communities, work is a source of a higher proportion of their friends than in the case of highly integrated white-collar workers. This can only be because, among manual workers, other sources of friends do not operate prominently. Numerous surveys of working class communities have drawn attention to the prominence of the family, which can be the base for a rich pattern of day-to-day living in areas characterised by close-knit and well-populated extended kinship systems. In such districts the family can offer introductions to a wide range of associates among whom individuals learn to mingle with effortless sociability. However, the Liverpool investigation was not conducted in this type of traditional working class neighbourhood. It was undertaken in the type of suburban area, mainly owner-occupied but also containing a large council estate, in which working class families are increasingly being rehoused. In such milieux, the working class family tends to become a privatised nuclear family, and other parts of individuals' social networks wither. Given these circumstances, membership of an occupational community can furnish otherwise non-existent opportunities for social interaction outside the home. The addition of an occupational community makes a major difference to the otherwise limited social networks of the individuals concerned, and working class life-styles are receptive to this influence.

The receptivity of life-styles to the effects of an occupational community is an important variable. As Table 8.5 demonstrates, the older respondents in the Liverpool enquiry reported the greater number of close friends at work, reflecting the manner in which relationships mature with passing time. Yet unmarried respondents aged under 30 were more likely than married persons in the 45-plus age group to be in

Table 8.5 Stage in life-cycle, work relationships and leisure (percentages)

	Single, aged under 30	Married, aged over 45
Three or more close friends at work	22	29
Three or more workmates met socially outside the workplace	33	24
$n =$	55	197

the habit of meeting colleagues from work socially outside the work-place. This paradox is resolved by intersecting the life-styles and social networks of the groups concerned into the equation. The life-styles of young single persons are ordinarily less home and family based than among any other section of the population. Such individuals, there-fore, are exceptionally likely to draw upon all non-familial sources of leisure time associates. It is possible to talk about work spilling into and influencing leisure, but in this instance, rather than work permeating leisure, it is as appropriate to speak of receptive life-styles drawing upon work as a source of social relationships.

The autonomy of modern leisure

While work and leisure do not coexist in absolutely unconnected compartments of life, the sum of the evidence does not justify treating leisure purely as a dependent variable. Uses of leisure are certainly influenced by the nature of individuals' occupations. But when we ask how and to what extent, we see that rather than treating work as a determinant, it is often more appropriate to regard individuals as accommodating to the constraints that their working lives impose and using the resources that their occupations offer to cultivate whatever life-styles they prefer as a result of their personal tastes and the social relationships in which they are involved in their non-working lives. The effects of work frequently amount to no more than modulations upon constant themes. Work differences tend to produce deviations around but do not submerge independently recurrent patterns, and these patterns can rarely be explained principally in terms of work-related factors.

Workers are also people who are influenced by the other roles that they play, particularly their family roles, and can manage their leisure to sustain the life-styles they seek by accommodating to whatever distinctive constraints and opportunities accompany their types of employment. In the absence of friendly relationships at work, white-collar employees in particular draw upon kin, neighbours or other friends for social intercourse. Income may rule out expensive activities such as polo, but substitute forms of recreation can be discovered without exceptional ingenuity. Human beings are innovative creatures and are capable of building upon the opportunities that accompany their work to pursue their independently formulated preferences. In contemporary pluralist societies 'man at leisure' is subject to heterogeneous influences and opportunities within which the effects that in isolation would follow from work can be managed and assimi-lated into life-styles to which individuals are independently commit-ted.

Of course, there are some individuals whose leisure is strongly influenced by their work, and in these cases treating leisure purely as a dependent variable can be appropriate. There are people who remain strongly motivated by a work ethic and for whom work is a central life interest that patterns their uses of leisure time. Today, however, such work–leisure relationships are exceptional. It may be wrong to regard the instrumentally oriented worker for whom leisure gives meaning to life as an exclusive product of the twentieth century. Clayre offers ample evidence that instrumental approaches towards work were common in nineteenth century Britain.[17] However, the growth of leisure during the twentieth century has enlarged the opportunities for such individuals to free their lives outside the workplace from the imprint of their occupational roles. In addition to charting the influence of work, therefore, the analysis of leisure must also stress the autonomy that this sphere of life has attained. Historically contemporary leisure may have been shaped by industrialism, but it is no longer just a minor by-product. This is the substantive conclusion towards which this chapter points, and uses of leisure have been released from the influence of work because individuals' social networks contain other and usually more potent bases.

Work is important, but even its claims upon lifetime must be kept in perspective. At any point in time, one-half of the population is economically inactive. Without taking any account of the involuntary unemployed, the young and the retired plus full-time housewives account for approximately one-half of the total population. For individuals who are currently part of the labour force, work consumes less than a quarter of their time in any one year. In Chapter 2 we dismissed prophecies of work diminishing to become a trivial, almost incidental pastime. Work remains an important activity, but it is less domineering than sometimes imagined. In his survey of work ideologies during the industrial era, Anthony has drawn attention to features that radical and conservative viewpoints have normally shared in common.[18] Both have seen work as a duty – something that must be done, and have urged that it should be fulfilling. Conservatives have called for these values to be implemented within existing types of work, while radicals have sought changes in work to enable the values to be realised. Anthony suggests that we may have reached the point where a reappraisal of work is required, and the above evidence endorses this sentiment. Treating work as *the* sphere of life containing men's major social obligations and hopes for self-expression discords with the autonomy that leisure has attained in the lives of most present-day citizens.

To say this is not to belittle work, which continues to account for a substantial block, even if not the greater part of lifetime. But work today is less than the central force still postulated in many tests. The value of a sociological perspective in a proper understanding of leisure is one of the recurrent themes in this book. Yet it is necessary to repeatedly protest the inadequacy of some favourite sociological perspectives when faced with the leisure phenomenon. Sociology's texts, journals and conferences stress politics, the economy and stratification as casting the macro-social structure, The family, neighbourhood communities, and leisure as well, are often dismissed as incidental and trivial – easy stuff suitable for those who fight shy from major theoretical and social controversies. Capitalism, fascism, socialism and industrial democracy are issues that quicken sociology's pulse, and of course, these matters *are* important. Nevertheless, there is now a wealth of evidence that the quality of life, individuals' well-being and happiness, depend mainly upon the quality of the primary social relationships by which they are surrounded. Self-rated happiness depends more upon social participation than income. When asked what *they* consider the main determinants of the quality of life, members of the public are more likely to talk about homes, friends and families than social class, the economy and politics. The macro-structure *does* impinge upon primary social relationships – to an extent. But contemporary societies are sufficiently loosely-knit systems to make the primary relationships amid which individuals experience life substantially independent of the larger political economy. Work centrality still reigns in much of sociology, but contemporary society is different.

While it may be one crucial element, work is not the only source of contemporary man's consciousness and identity. It is conventional in sociology to think in terms of *the* social system, so functionalists and Marxists offer their opposing interpretations of the logic that governs present-day life. Daniel Bell is one of the few sociologists to display a persistent capacity for freeing himself from the orthodox theoretical tramlines, as a result of which his admittedly controversial conclusions constantly promise to add to our understanding of the world around. In thinking about modern Western societies, rather than attempting to conceive one social system, Bell argues the value of conceptualising three overlapping but largely independent and increasingly estranged realms, each ruled by its own logic.[19] First Bell distinguishes a techno-economic social structure – the economy, governed by norms of rationality and efficiency. Second he identifies the political system, which is ruled by principles of equity. Third he discusses an increasingly anti-rational cultural realm, in which the effects of experiences upon the 'self' are regarded as the touchstones of worth. At one time, Bell argues, in bourgeois society, a protestant ethic and religion overarched these realms and maintained a consistency which is now evaporating. Rising standards of living alongside consumer credit, motor cars and suchlike have permitted the emergence of a hedonistic culture stressing the desirability of fun, consumption, play and instant pleasure as ends in themselves. 'To assume, as some social critics do, that the technocratic mentality dominates the cultural order is to fly in the face of every bit of evidence at hand.'[20] This is one of the cultural contradictions that, in Bell's view, the development of capitalism poses. 'On the one hand, the business corporation wants an individual to work hard, accept delayed gratification – to be, in the crude sense, an organisation man. And yet, in its products and advertisements, the corporation promotes pleasure, instant joy, relaxing and letting go. One is to be "straight" by day and a "swinger" by night.'[21]

Individuals' occupations remain important elements in their self-identities. Men in particular, but women also to an increasing extent, require a work-role in order to enjoy a creditable social status. Take the work-role away through unemployment or compulsory retirement, and individuals' entire personality structures can begin to topple. In itself the growth of leisure contains no solutions to the problems traditionally associated with unemployment and retirement. Yet while it may be a basic prop, we do not need to regard work as the only source of identity for contemporary man. It is surely more realistic to regard individuals' work-roles as bases – essential bases, that people can add to and build upon in the course of developing preferred life-styles outside their workplaces. And in these life-styles it is possible for individuals to cultivate qualities and self-images that differ from and, as Bell points out, are sometimes inconsistent with the demands of their jobs. Presuming work centrality neglects these aspects of social reality.

In addition to asking how uses of leisure vary alongside work-based differences, we also need to question how individuals accommodate to the constraints and exploit the opportunities associated with their particular occupations to construct and defend life-styles to which they are independently committed as a result of their family circumstances, other social relationships and resultant personal tastes. We need to explore how individuals manage and rationalise the sometimes contradictory pressures to which they are exposed in their working and non-working lives. To understand leisure we certainly need to recognise the implications of work, but without remaining transfixed within an assumption of work centrality.

Chapter 9

The society with leisure

How important is leisure? We have discussed its growth, aspects of its content, how its uses are greatly influenced by individuals' family circumstances and, to lesser extents, by their education and occupations. To explain uses of leisure we need to look outside its boundaries, which is one justification for sociological study. Another is the need to enquire whether leisure has a reciprocal influence upon other spheres of life, and a message of this book is that it most certainly does. Leisure is too important to remain the exclusive concern of recreation specialists. To understand developments in the family, the life-styles of young people, education and the shape of working life, the impact of leisure has to be considered. To equate the growth of leisure with increased demand for television, squash and car trips to the countryside takes too narrow a view of the subject. Leisure certainly includes recreation and its growth stimulates recreational demand, but there are other consequences of equal if not greater importance.

In Britain from the beginning of this century to the end of the 1960s, the proportion of all consumer expenditure devoted to specifically 'leisure goods and services' remained virtually static at around 16 per cent.[1] The emphasis shifted from alcohol and towards other forms of recreation and the total amount grew, but no faster than other expenditures, which may seem inconsistent with earlier arguments about the containment of work and the growth of time and money available for discretionary spending. The puzzle is solved once leisure is distinguished from recreation. Leisure is the relatively freely chosen non-work area of life. Individuals can use their leisure for recreation. Alternatively, however, they can spend their time and money in their families, on their homes, in education and other mainstream institutions. Just as the pluralist theory enables us to understand how uses of leisure are influenced by individuals' other social roles, so it allows us to recognise the ways in which leisure itself has wider repercussions. The social relationships within which leisure is spent are acquiring a leisurely quality, and through these relationships leisure's influence is filtering into numerous areas of life. What do we mean by a leisurely quality? Leisure means scope for variety and choice in non-working life. Its growth is liberating diverse subcultures, harbouring life-styles that reflect the various interests of different sections of the public, and recreation itself is best understood in terms of its contributions to the

126   *The society with leisure*

life-styles in question. The course of change is making it inappropriate to conceive leisure *merely* as a part of life and more appropriate to treat it as a quality pervading multiple spheres of activity. The growth of leisure has not only boosted recreation, but is helping to change other institutions. Hence, in addition to leisure *and* the family, it is necessary to discuss leisure *in* the family.

Leisure in and around the family

We have noted that the family is a milieu within which considerable leisure time is spent. This is why uses of leisure so greatly depend upon the types of families to which individuals belong, and the roles they play within them. It also means that acting as a framework for recreation is now among the family's major functions. Previous writers have explained how shared recreation contributes to family cohesion,[2] and how the growth of leisure is magnifying the playful character of family life. It has been alleged, for example, that rather than a moral or religious duty, sex has become principally a form of play, indulged in for pleasure. Largely inspired by Kinsey's findings, Nelson Foote was among the first to draw attention to the equalisation of sex norms between men and women and the increasing frequency of orgasm among females as indicating a widening acceptance of sex as play.[3]

Improvements in contraceptive techniques and knowledge have substantially dissociated intercourse and conception, but the extent to which sex has been released from traditional inhibitions should not be exaggerated. Gorer's interviews with 1,987 under 45-year-olds revealed that 40 per cent of the women believed that females do not have a physical climax[4] and while not more than 48 per cent of the women and 26 per cent of the men were wholly against *pre*marital sex, only 22 per cent reported kissing someone else seriously during their own marriages, and only 5 per cent admitted extramarital intercourse. Responses to survey questions about sex are often and rightly held in suspicion. Will people tell the truth? We cannot be sure, but it is interesting that Michael Schofield's[5] findings among 376 under 25-year-olds were remarkably similar to Gorer's. Only 7 per cent of Schofield's married respondents reported that they had been 'unfaithful' to their spouses, and although 71 per cent had intercourse before marriage, 56 per cent of the married sample had experienced intercourse with only one partner, the person (sometimes subsequently) married.

Sex is not being swept into an anarchy of permissiveness. Nevertheless, the selection of marital partners is now based upon personal choice and attraction rather than prescribed by elders, economic necessity or religious duty. Couples' main aspirations concern the affective quality of the conjugal relationship[6] and in Britain disappointment with the quality of this relationship is now accepted, in practice, as sufficient grounds for divorce.

Divorce has not only become more common but, if the law and the attitudes of churches to the re-marriage of divorcees are reliable guides, has become increasingly acceptable. The status of divorcee is now less of a stigma than among previous generations. The 1969 Divorce Reform Act indicates this shift in attitudes. Divorce no longer requires the identification of a guilty party. Since the Act came into force in 1971, the irresolvable breakdown of a marriage has been the sole ground for divorce, the former matrimonial offences including adultery being relegated to proof of such a breakdown and additional indicators are recognised; namely, the fact that the spouses have lived separately for stipulated periods. When the Act first came into operation the number of divorce petitions per year immediately rose from approximately 71,000 to 110,000, and subsequently the divorce rate has remained at this 'high' level, disproving suspicions that the 1971 figures would be a peak after the 'backlog' of cases for whom divorce first became available in 1971 had been processed. In 1976 there were half as many divorces as marriages, and it was estimated that one-fifth of all marriages were destined to end in divorce.

It has been argued that the rising divorce figures, which previously climbed to new heights when the grounds for divorce were extended in 1936, and when legal aid became available after 1948, do not indicate a growing instability of the family, but merely that family breakdowns are more frequently formalised by divorce proceedings. It has also been pointed out that lower mortality rates combined with younger marriages have been placing unions at risk for longer periods. Furthermore, the majority of divorcees re-marry, suggesting that divorce is only exceptionally a retreat from family living, and that the availability of divorce can strengthen rather than weaken the family by allowing the victims of unsatisfactory marriages to form more healthy unions.

It is certainly correct to resist equating the growing frequency of divorce with a decline of the family. In any case, the termination of marriage by divorce remains the exception. In the USA, where for a long time divorce has been more common than in Britain, over three-quarters of first marriages do not end in divorce. There are no signs in either America or Britain of lifelong monogamy ceasing to be the cultural norm. Talk of the family's decline misreads the trends, which are more appropriately summarised as a growing acceptance of diversity. Traditional monogamy is still entirely acceptable and widely practised, but today new types of family career sometimes involving several consecutive marriages are also accepted in law and public opinion; one example of a new diversity in family behaviour.

When birth- and death-rates ran at higher levels, and when children were regarded as an automatic and early sequel to marriage heralding a career in motherhood often terminated only by death, there was little scope for diversity. Women were bound in wedlock if not by love then by economic necessity and for a lifetime. In contrast, the age of planned parenthood and lower birth-rates coupled with wider job opportunities for married women opens new possibilities. It is possible for couples who so desire to postpone parenthood and maybe marriage, if not permanently, until both are established in careers, and to dissolve their relationship if it ceases to be satisfying. There is no need for relationships to follow this pattern. Many develop otherwise. But it is an example of the options now available. Although their standards of living usually decline, it is now possible for single parents to cope with the predicaments following separation and divorce, and during the postparental phase there is often no overwhelming need for couples to remain imprisoned in stale relationships. The growth of leisure does not so much generate any one new pattern of family life as permit greater variety.

The term 'women's liberation' draws attention to a number of interrelated examples of this diversity, all of which, in one way or another, involve abandoning traditionally stereotyped sex roles. Unisex fashions are just symptoms of this broader trend. Official statistics show that a growing proportion of married women work outside their homes, while researchers tell us that husbands are being introduced to housework and childcare.[7] The Rapoports have described the dual career families in which both husband and wife pursue uninterrupted occupational careers.[8] These families are still uncommon, but the Rapoports argue that the pattern could become increasingly widespread. During the last decade women have won new legal rights as a result of the Equal Pay and Sex Discrimination Acts, giving equal access to education, employment and other services. Not very long ago it was a matter for debate whether female newscasters on television would be taken seriously. Today it would be illegal for television companies to entertain any such doubts in their selection procedures. Women's liberation is no longer just a radical idea.

The ideas and arguments inspiring the contemporary women's movements are not new. They have been rehearsed for centuries, and well over a generation ago, Margaret Mead was offering convincing evidence that sex roles are prescribed by societies rather than biology.[9] The recent catalyst has been the intersection between the evidence, arguments and social structural changes. The decline in fertility and mortality, and the acceptance of contraception have relaxed the traditional female role. Employing a broad historical perspective, Collins[10] has identified a series of cumulative changes favouring sex equality. Noting that human beings possess strong aggressive and sexual drives, and that men are physically stronger than women, Collins suggests that these crude facts of life produce the basic feature of sexual stratification; women become men's sexual property. Collins argues that when governments monopolise force, women's disadvantages are somewhat reduced. When women can free themselves from motherhood to earn their own livings and cannot be driven into sexual liaisons by economic compulsion, the scene is set not only for women's lib, but for the companion ideal of male sexual attractiveness.

As with other changes in family life, the evidence is easily misread. Liberation means different things to different women, and it is wrong to imagine that all females are going to use their scope for choice, freedom and bargaining power to the same effect. While it is valid to comment upon the emergence of dual career families, it is more debatable whether the current instances are pioneering a future norm. Lifelong occupational careers do not attract all women, including the majority of the 571 wives in the Chicago area that Lopata studied.[11] In her investigation Lopata discovered a type of housewife for whom this 'occupation' was the basis for a thoroughly satisfying way of life. *Occupation Housewife* introduces us to a competent, multidimentional, modern housewife, usually highly educated and enjoying an affluent life-style, financed by her middle class spouse. Rather than seeking paid employment for herself, this housewife involves herself in her home, the surrounding community and the social life of her husband. Many feminists are critical of this life-style. But if liberation means freedom to choose, who is entitled to judge? Lopata's study shows that being a housewife can offer a satisfying and many-faceted life-style, while studies of assembly lines demonstrate that employment is not necessarily liberating. Some advocates of women's liberation are clearly too adamant for the majority of their own sex. In her examination of housework, Oakley attempts to show that this really is work, boring work, and advocates the complete eradiction of gender as a basis for social discrimination.[12] Yet she has to report that most of the 40 housewives she interviewed expressed contentment and spoke disparagingly about womens' lib. When aggressively marketed, the role of the liberated women can appear as constraining as the traditional female role.

Leisure totally explains neither the state of the family nor everything that is happening to the gender variable. What it explains is just one feature of the scene, the variety, that, as we shall see, reappears across many areas of contemporary life. Leisure means relatively self-determined behaviour – scope for choice. Once we understand leisure we can see why sex roles are not merely changing but are becoming looser and less stereotyped. For some time pundits have debated issues such as whether the proper place for a mother of young children is in the home. Half a century ago most citizens would almost certainly have answered in the affirmative. Today the difference is not only that more women would dissent, but that the issue has been defused. We are ceasing to believe that a woman has any one proper place.

The role of kinship in modern societies is a complex topic and it is not the aim of this discussion to address all the issues. For present purposes it is sufficient to note that in industrial societies the extended family loses some of its former functions including economic production, which is taken over by industrial organisations, and the provision of many welfare services, which become the responsibility of the state. Yet despite its curtailed role, the extended family survives both in working class communities and among the middle classes, and continues to play an important role in its members' lives; a role that can include offering sociability, recognising major occasions in the life-cycle, and providing economic support in times of difficulty.[13] In this discussion the main point at issue does not involve identifying exactly which functions the extended family still performs, or whether its changed role amounts to a decline from its former importance. The crucial point concerns some qualitative differences between tradi-tional and modern kinship systems. In researching kinship systems in contemporary societies social anthropologists have discovered that they cannot be charted in the same terms that are employed when investigating primitive peoples. Modern kinship is different, not only in performing fewer functions, but in that its social relationships pos-sess a permissive rather than an obligatory character.

In their study of 90 middle class households in north London, Firth and his colleagues[14] found it impossible to chart any precise rights and responsibilities recognised in the extended family. Relationships be-tween kinfolk were individualised. People were treated as persons rather than according to kinship status. Which kin were recognised and interacted with varied from family to family. Each conjugal unit had a range of kin available, and decisions on which relationships to imple-ment were matters of mutual adjustment on the basis of personal preference. This investigation concluded that rather than a structured set of positions, the form in which kinship can be analysed in most pre-industrial societies, contemporary kinship is better conceptualised as a 'flow of social behaviour'.

Needless to say, this is just one among many attributes of modern kinship systems, but it is particularly relevant for this discussion since it parallels other characteristics of modern family life, all involving a tolerance of diversity and an absence of definite rules prescribing how relationships should be conducted. These developments within the family are the exact consequences that we should anticipate from the growth of leisure. One of the contemporary family's functions involves acting as a leisure milieu. As shown in an earlier chapter, simply being with the family is an important use of leisure and, therefore, the growth of leisure is among the developments responsible for changing styles of family life. It is not just that families now possess the time and money to take more holidays and motoring trips, and to watch television together. Leisure is invading the family in a deeper sense. Family relationships are becoming increasingly leisurely, meaning, in this instance, relatively self-determined. Bemoaning permissiveness misunderstands what is occurring. The growth of leisure loosens the social structure and widens the limits within which diversity can be tolerated, and members of the public are begining to explore the new options.

The youth culture

Young people are touched by the growth of leisure to a greater extent than most other sections of the population. To begin with, the young enjoy exceptional quantities of leisure time. Those in education 'work' shorter hours and have longer holidays than are normal among the labour force, while for workers under age 18 there are legal restrictions on their availability for shift-work and overtime. Even more important, prior to marriage domestic responsibilities are minimal, particularly for males, which releases otherwise committed time and money. Young people enjoy not only unusually ample leisure time, but also have a great deal of cash for discretionary spending. Since the 1930s the gap between adolescent and adult earnings has narrowed, and at home it is now normal for young workers to go 'on board' from the outset of their working lives, often paying only nominal sums.[15] Many who remain in education find part-time work, and, in any case, it is common for parents to 'spoil' their adolescent children, agreeing that 'you're only young once'.[16] Hence the appearance of the modern affluent teenager whose circumstances contrast sharply with the situation of school-leavers 40 years ago who faced unemployment or juvenile wages, and whose families usually required the income that all their members could earn. Young people today spend considerable sums on clothing, transport and entertainment, cultivating adolescent styles of life that can leave older generations gasping in amazement. Elders may suspect contemporary youth of having it too easy, but the youth culture is no aberration; it is a manifestation of leisure.

As pointed out in an earlier chapter, young people's lives contain less fun and excitement than sometimes imagined. If the youth culture offered a really great time, it is reasonable to suppose that fewer individuals would opt out in favour of marriage and parenthood so quickly. The irony of the situation is that even sympathetic adults can offer little assistance. Having observed that despite their renowned willingness to experiment in search of 'kicks', many young people are far from fully satisfied with their leisure, the orthodox well-meaning response is to establish working parties and committees to consider youth's recreational needs and to vote more money into the Youth Service. The real facts of the situation, however, are that no one, even adults with all their collective wisdom, knows the answers.

There is a sense in which young people are ahead of older generations who often find themselves learning from the young. We live in a changing society and one thing that social change leaves in its wake is a generation gap. There is some truth in the folk wisdom maintaining that people become more conservative with age. In terms of political allegiances, modes of domestic life and leisure pursuits, individuals tend to sink into ruts as they move through adulthood. Young people, in contrast, are receptive to new ideas and behaviour. Individuals' first political loyalties are normally 'inherited' from their parents, but many young people change their ideas before moving into careers as citizens and voters during which party attachments become increasingly firmly anchored. If fashion blows in a particular direction whether in hair-styles or politics, young people are receptive simply because they are young and have not become rigidly set in their ways with a weight of tradition around them.

It is unlikely that adult society has yet recognised all the options that leisure opens. Young people are beginning to explore some of the possibilities and can they be criticised for trying out alternatives to television? In recreation adults now learn from young people. Until the 1940s, fashions in dress were developed in 'fashionable' adult society and young people emulated whatever was 'in'. Today it is more common for fads and fashions to spread from young people to the rest of society. Tastes in music are nurtured among young people and subsequently evolve into family entertainment, while fashions in hair-styles and clothing spread up the age ranges.

Despite impressions to the contrary, there is no single monolithic youth culture but a variety of adolescent subcultures that splinter along sex, age, educational and social class lines.[17] Many adolescent trends that provoke condemnation of the entire younger generation involve only minorities of young people. Most teenagers remain perhaps sur-prisingly conventional. Fogelman[18] found that only 3 per cent of his national sample of 16-year-olds rejected the idea of marriage, while 86 per cent reported that they 'got on well' with their mothers and 80 per cent with their fathers. Few young people are totally alienated from adult society. As Barker has observed, both adolescents and their parents mostly stress the virtue of 'keeping close'.[19]

Exploring the new freedom is easily mistaken for rebellion. Some young people have pioneered new styles of communal living creating what have been termed counter-cultures and alternative societies.[20] One school of thought portrays these communities of the young as signs of rebellion against an oppressive society which constrains and alienates in education and employment. For example, Charles Reich[21] claims to have detected a new consciousness among American youth. Rather than adapting to the system, Reich sees the younger generation as inspired by a belief in self-expression and ultimately ushering in a revolution, a greening of America, leading to a better, happier society.

In Britain, having systematically investigated the 'counter-culture' Musgrove has offered a relatively sober but more convincing interpre-tation.[22] Musgrove notes the trends in the youth culture that Reich discusses; rather than fighting to get in, today many young people are fighting to get out, and privileged middle class students rather than the deprived are at the centre of the action. As Reich also observes, this counter-culture is no longer a purely teenage phenomenon but has spread to the young adult age-group. But Musgrove's research under-mines accounts that view the counter-culture as a rebellion against oppressive institutions. A university is the most oppressive institution that many participants in the commune culture have ever encountered, and they are more likely to originate from liberal than authoritarian families. Musgrove's evidence suggests that the counter-culture is a response to anomie rather than oppression. Young people who opt out of orthodox careers and into communes are the most uprooted, socially isolated and lonely of their generation. 'The counter-culture is a revolt of the unoppressed. It is a response not to constraint, but to openness.'[23] Musgrove agrees that the counter-culture nurtures distinctive values. It is suspicious of work while dedicated to service, favours sincerity, nature, open and free communication, artistic creativity and a sense of community. 'For the lonely the commune is the millenium.'[24] Yet rather than sweeping an entire generation and eventually society along, Musgrove's data suggest that only 2 per cent of all young people are becoming fully involved in this counter-culture, though up to a third of all males and a sixth of females are more loosely sympathetic to its values.

Intergenerational differences do not necessarily mean conflict, and some of the youth culture's most bizarre effervescences indicate not rebellion but imaginative use of the scope for self-determined behaviour that is possible in a society with leisure. Scope for choice means variety, and while some young people are using their new freedom to form communal families, many more are becoming teenage brides and grooms. The growth of leisure is the underlying condition permitting this diversity.

Just as the recreational interests of adults amount to bewildering variety, so young people use their leisure in diverse ways. Teenage drinkers attract understandable concern, and a study of 14- to 16-year-olds in a Dudley school[25] found that over a fifth of both boys and girls visited pubs regularly. Adults use alcohol extensively in their own life-styles and it is not surprising that some teenagers find uses for it. It is important to remember, however, that many young people, both under and over age 18, rarely or never visit public houses. Scope for choice can be used in various ways, and to conform as well as to rebel. In itself the growth of leisure neither favours nor wholly explains any specific trends in adolescent behaviour. The significance of leisure lies in permitting the variety of life-styles that are evident among contemporary youth.

Education

It is important to recognise manifestations of leisure for what they are, otherwise young people are liable to be misunderstood as rebellious, trends in family life misinterpreted as a collapse of the institution, and likewise in education. Americans have grown accustomed to contemplating college students in their hundreds of thousands and asking whatever the eventual graduates will do with their diplomas. Can the economy absorb so many trained people? Can they all hope to find jobs commensurate with their qualifications? In Britain, particularly since the post-Robbins expansion, the public has begun to ask similar questions. Higher education is no longer synonymous with university

education. In addition to universities there are now the new poly-
technics, while former teacher training colleges are gradually resurfac-
ing retitled as colleges or institutes of higher education, and as this has
happened the optimism that surrounded the Robbins Report has
evaporated. Critics have become increasingly sceptical of whether this
investment in higher education will ever yield an economic return.

Drawing attention to the growth of leisure makes us realise that this
entire perspective on education deserves less pre-eminence than in
earlier eras when resources were relatively scarce, when the majority
of children could be offered no more than elementary schooling, and
when higher education was a route only to a few prestigious professions and scholarly vocations. In such times, before committing
resources, it was only sensible to ask whether any economic returns
would follow and this question retains some relevance. But the
advanced industrial societies can now afford education for other purposes.

Some types of education can be directly likened to recreational
pursuits; components of preferred life-styles before, during or after
occupational careers. In an essay on adult education, Jary[26] has noted
how evenings in the ivory tower are best understood as leisure occa-
ions. In some parts of Britain as many as 80 per cent of evening class
students are women. The 'night school' has been one of the few
respectable 'nights-out' for women unaccompanied by husbands and
boyfriends, and it is short-sighted to condemn this as a misuse of
educational resources.[27] Whether the finance is raised through taxes or
fees, as a society we can now choose to provide classes for adults who
wish to paint, learn basketry, discuss Shakespeare, or simply enjoy
each other's company and conversation. Likewise, if we consider it
desirable, we can support young people in college until many have
ceased to be young. There is scope for choice in the allocation of
educational resources.

In their survey of education's contribution to social and economic
inequality in America, Jencks and his colleagues have drawn attention
to how little difference education itself makes.[28] In a society where the
vast majority of the population is illiterate, access to secondary education can hardly avoid enhancing the skills and life-chances of a
favoured few. Given universal elementary and secondary education, in
contrast, the remaining scope for variation makes relatively little difference to individuals' prospects when set in the context of other
factors such as family backgrounds and personal qualities that continue to make a difference. Hence Jencks's advice that we judge
educational programmes against other criteria, such as the intrinsic
satisfactions that are yielded. Jencks had elementary and secondary
schooling principally in mind, but his advice is equally appropriate in
other sectors of contemporary education.

All modern societies continue to use education as an agent of
occupational selection. It is doubtful whether many students enter

higher education purely to taste the lifestyle. For most students, education remains principally a competition for credentials. Individuals who want to 'get on' have little choice but to press through the 'rat race'. But as a society we do not *have* to extend the mass competition for credentials into the college sector. This is just one among several ways in which educational resources can now be employed. Occupational requirements need not be decisive.

College can mean many things. In the past in Britain it has nearly always meant a three year degree course prior to work entry. In the USA it is still possible to complete a bachelor's degree in three years, to top it with a master's degree twelve months later and embark upon a career, but it is also possible to spend four, five, six or even more years reading for a first degree and to follow this with several years in graduate school. Summers can be spent abroad or surfing rather than studying. This is one of the ways in which society can use the resources that are being unleashed. When the majority of young people proceed to college as in the USA, a first degree ceases to carry much weight in the job market, and it makes less sense than previously to discuss college purely in terms of its vocational relevance. The cases for and against mass higher education have to be debated on other grounds. Students can travel, widen their social and intellectual horizons, and, being free from the discipline associated with careers, can experiment with alternative life-styles. The commune culture, as described by Musgrove,[29] is one of the life-styles that higher education today is helping to support, and in considering the value of a mass college system this type of product must be accounted alongside its occupational relevance.

The growth of leisure means that education can be extended beyond its formerly more limited uses and we need to recognise this new status of education in order to plan its future realistically. Different sections of the public will no doubt want to use education in different ways for, as in family life, in education the growth of leisure favours diversity.

Work and leisure time

The more leisure grows, the greater the variety of forms it can assume, and perhaps the clearest illustration lies in its relationship with working time. In Britain the take-off into industrialism required long hours of work from the labour force. Subsequently industry's demands have been contained, and work now accounts for a smaller proportion of lifetime than a century ago. Non-working time has grown, which means not only that people have more leisure, but also that greater variety is possible in its distribution.

As argued in Chapter 2, rather than excess free time the trends are towards a harried leisure class. Non-working time remains a scarce resource. Hence the need to query the advantages of a shorter work-day with more leisure every evening. Is a four day work-week with a longer weekend preferable? Or is it more desirable to aggregate additional free time in annual vacations, the main form in which time released from work during the last 30 years has been taken? Then there is the case for sabbaticals. From time to time during their careers individuals could take several months or a year free from work to be used, for example, for travel or study, or to become full-time homemakers. Should we ease the demands of work upon any particular sections of the population? How about making the hours and holidays conventionally considered part-time available for more female workers. Do we want to enlarge the ends of the life-cycle that are free from work, providing more education for the young and/or a longer retirement for the ageing? These are all among the options created by the growth of leisure. As in education, few people may be fully aware that the above choices are open, but the point remains that the economy's requirements no longer dictate the answers.

One of the advantages of a society with leisure is its ability to tolerate diversity. Hence we need not answer the above questions with a single collective voice. Just as individuals can choose whether to play squash or golf so is it possible, in principle, for different sections of the labour force to arrange their work and leisure in different ways. Flexibility is one of the options. The shape of working life no longer needs to be common throughout the entire population. During the early years of industrialism, the requirements of work imposed one dominant rhythm of life and leisure, whereas today there is greater scope for several overlapping rhythms. Flexitime, which allows workers to decide exactly when they will clock on and off, is one example of the possibility of allowing individuals to arrange the demands of work and leisure to suit their varying domestic needs and personal tastes.[30]

There are additional ways in which flexibility is spreading, often so stealthily that it is not recognised for what it is, and the sources of this trend are often so misunderstood that it is regarded as a problem requiring treatment rather than a welcome development. For example, it is surely mistaken to imagine that ending sex discrimination in employment means that working women in general must pursue the types of careers and obtain equal earnings to men. Many working women, and working men as well in dual career families, desire a shorter work-week than the 'breadwinners' who seek whatever overtime is available to maximise earnings. There are currently wide variations in the hours worked by individuals in the same occupations, and rather than deploring overtime and moonlighting, this diversity can be applauded. Is there any reason why everyone should work the same number of hours? The possibility of retiring before age 65 is welcomed by some men. It is not difficult to find examples of middle aged drop-outs forsaking the 'rat race' in preference for semi-retirement in less demanding occupations.[31] At the same time, it is equally easy to unearth complaints from men who resent being retired solely because they have grown 65 years old. One of the options in a society with leisure is to move away from a fixed retirement age. Present levels of training allowances and redundancy pay enable some workers to take 'sabbaticals' while they retrain or refresh. Statutory maternity leave is another form in which the sabbatical is spreading. These opportunities can be consolidated, without expecting everyone to take advantage. Thousands of workers are also students but only some have sympathetic employers, though there is no reason why sympathetic support should not be progressively extended to all who wish to study, spend more time with their families, conserve their health, or even pursue a recreational interest.

Society is increasingly able to allow individuals the scope to decide how many hours to work each week, how many weeks' holiday to take each year, and how many years' work their lifetimes will contain. Work is not receding to a point of unimportance, but it is being contained to an extent requiring that we re-evaluate what have previously been abnormal patterns of work such as overtime and short-time, and liable to be labelled as problems.

The impact of leisure

Leisure has not become the sole basis for family life, the youth culture or education, and the above discussion has not attempted a comprehensive analysis of any of these areas. Rather has the intention been to illustrate how leisure has become a facet of these spheres. The growth of leisure has made an impact beyond recreation. Leisure has become a broader quality of social life. This is why a sociological perspective is necessary fully to grasp the significance of leisure and it is equally the reason why sociologists are unwise to dismiss leisure to the periphery of their subject.

It is worth repeating that leisure is *relatively* self-determined behaviour. Unmitigated individualism is a sociological impossibility. The very existence of a society means that freedom to choose cannot be absolute. The growth of leisure is not leading towards every individual doing his own private thing. Leisure means that the social system can tolerate more 'play' or 'looseness', and accommodate cultural diversity that was impossible in previous eras.

In his survey of *Permissive Britain*[32] Christie Davies observes that any trend towards permissiveness has not been total. The breathalyser law, restrictions on tobacco advertising, limitations on individuals' freedom to discriminate on racial and sexual grounds, and the control of 'hard' drugs are all examples of society becoming less permissive. Changes in the law towards divorce, abortion, censorship, gambling and homosexuality may be subsumed under the permissive label, but when all the evidence is presented it is difficult to allege an all-round drift towards a libertarian's paradise. If there is any one underlying trend, consistent with the above examples of both advances towards and retreats from permissiveness, Davies is surely right in identifying a decline of moralism and a rise of causalism, meaning that issues are no longer judged against absolute moral standards but pragmatically, in terms of whether, on balance, the effects of proposed changes in the law will enhance or diminish well-being. The supporters of the relevant changes in the law have not necessarily favoured divorce, abortion or homosexuality, and similarly supporters of the breathalyser law are not necessarily advocates of temperance. To claim any trend towards causalism as a consequence of leisure would oversimplify a more complex development, but this trend illustrates the type of change made possible by the growth of leisure. New forms of cultural diversity can be tolerated and, simultaneously, new checks become necessary when innovations such as the widespread use of motor cars threaten other groups' well-being.

We are not approaching an age in which individuals can be given a continuously open choice to decide, for example, the number of hours per week to work. It is hardly practical for commercial organisations to allow managers sabbaticals as and whenever they find the prospect attractive. Such opportunities need to be programmed. Likewise it will remain difficult for teachers to opt for night-work since few children are available for education other than during daytime. Many of the options that the growth of leisure creates are open to groups rather than solitary persons. Peer groups of all ages, families and work organisations rather than individuals benefit from the additional room to manoeuvre. Every individual's decisions affect the situations of other decision makers. Lifelong monogamy can only be a real option if both parties desire it. In so far as they can decide who to marry and which jobs to enter, individuals can extend control over their own destinies, but once they have been made choices cannot be wiped clean. There is no possible society in which individuals can be permitted to undo the consequences of their previous decisions. For a person who has been divorced, a lifetime with a single partner is no longer an option. Individuals can only make mutually consistent choices. It is difficult to envisage even a society with leisure allowing some individuals to opt for life in a counter-culture which devalues work and simultaneously to enjoy relatively high incomes.

Neither leisure nor anything else can offer mankind total individual freedom. This spectre is an illusion. Nevertheless, leisure is opening new types of choice, scope for diversity and opportunities to develop new life-styles, and it is important to recognise these implications of leisure in order to explain changes in education, the youth culture and patterns of family life. It is important to appreciate the real source of these changes lest they be misconstrued as deviance, signs of decay or other types of problems requiring treatment. One of the reasons for studying leisure is to stimulate awareness of the new possibilities that it creates, and these extend beyond more orthodox forms of recreation.

Chapter 10

A post-industrial society of leisure ?

Writers on leisure have sometimes treated their subject with holiday flamboyance and arrived at diversely colourful conclusions. Some portray leisure as just another sphere of life where men are oppressed by the ramifications of capitalist ideology and market forces. In contrast, other writers have argued that we are moving towards a society of leisure in which men will find true fulfilment. To dismiss leisure as trivial is to ignore the changes, discussed in the previous chapter, that have vastly affected the lives of most ordinary people during the twentieth century. But just how important has leisure become? Important enough to justify talk of a 'society of leisure'? Proclaiming a society of leisure may indicate the general direction of change, but could overstate the immensity of the developments it seeks to describe. While the growth of leisure has affected the quality of family life, education, the youth culture and traditional sex roles, these do not encompass the whole social system. What about work and politics?

Leisure in work

As argued in Chapter 8, although leisure is influenced by work, the strength of this influence is usually sufficiently weak to merit talk of a compartmentalisation of leisure from the effects of individuals' work-roles. Could causality flow principally in the opposite direction? Does leisure affect work?

Proclamations of a society of leisure mostly begin by charting the decline of the work ethic, a system of values in which work is defined as intrinsically virtuous, maybe a route to eternal salvation, and which requires that other spheres of life be subordinated to its demands. Under the imprint of such an ethic, leisure is valued principally in so far as it serves the worker by, for example, facilitating recuperation or even training in occupationally desirable attitudes and skills, and work values such as industriousness are liable to permeate leisure time. No one claims that at some point in the past everyone subscribed to this work ethic. Nevertheless, during the first half of the nineteenth century in Britain such an ethic became dominant in that public holidays were curtailed and factory discipline was imposed upon the working population, while the same era saw the rise of the temperance movement, church missions, and support for elementary education as an aid to discipline and morality.

A number of writers have argued that, subsequently, not only have daily, weekly and annual hours of work declined, but also that the values which helped stimulate the take-off into industrialism have become less influential.[1] Other commentators have suggested a need to rid ourselves of remnants of the work ethic in order to appreciate the leisure we now possess.[2] Kaplan is among those who argue a need to develop new values in order to undertake leisure life-styles in a more natural way thereby creating a 'cultivated order'. Among other questions Kaplan asks, 'What happens to parent–child relationships when the father works four hours a day, or for a "normal" day of eight hours but for only half the year?'[3] The implication behind this rhetoric is that values which were appropriate in the past have lapsed and need replacing to cope with a changed predicament.

The counterpart to the decline of the work ethic thesis is to proclaim the advent of what has been termed a 'leisure ethic' or 'fun morality'. Dumazedier is probably the most renowned exponent of this argument. According to Dumazedier, the growth of leisure has nurtured 'a new social need for the individual to be his own master and to please himself'.[4] Leisure values stress self-expression, being free to choose, and doing things for their own sake. In Dumazedier's view, these values are beginning to permeate all areas of life. The result is that, 'What used to be considered idleness when confronted with the requirements of the firm is now defined as dignity, what used to be called selfishness when confronted with the requirements of the family is now perceived as respect for the personality of one of its members. Part of what used to be considered sinful by religious institutions is now recognised as the art of living.'[5] Otto Newman echoes this conclusion arguing that today leisure has replaced work as the main source of meaning and self-identity.

'Undeniably the significance of work has universally receded into the background and centrality in the formulation of self-definition has passed within the compass of the non-occupational sphere, with leisure outstandingly the single most dominant element. It is in his leisure activity that late-industrial man satisfies his need to feel adequate, derives his ego-definition and achieves skills instrumental towards social integration, possibly to the extent of even infusing meaningful content to his objectively overwhelmingly dull and monotonous work.'[6]

Rather than the meaning of leisure being derived from work-based values, it is suggested that already in the present and increasingly in the future work will be judged and accorded meaning through leisure values.

This society of leisure viewpoint has received quite widespread endorsement, though less frequently as a result of its rigorous examination than from scholars who find it a convenient backcloth to their more specific interests. For example Turner and Ash introduce their study of tourism with the declarations that, 'What we are in fact seeing is the transformation of "Play" into one of the stronger roles in our culture',[7] and that 'we are starting to be judged on our leisure *persona* rather than our work role'.[8] In the course of examining the drug culture, Jock Young remarks that, '. . . it is during leisure and through the expression of subterranean values that modern man seeks his identity',[9] while in an essay on education Richmond asserts that, 'We are entering an era in which leisure, not work, will be the central element'.[10]

Is leisure really displacing work as the pivotal process? It is important to distinguish aspiration from actuality. Many people would like to believe that work is becoming more humane and leisurely. While Dumazedier acknowledges that this process is as yet little advanced, he is optimistic that it will continue. But is this optimism justified? It is not difficult to observe elements of leisure in work including piped music, the lunch hour card game and diffuse sociability.[11] It is probably true that man-management relations have become less authoritarian and, as Dumazedier illustrates, there are people who make career decisions mindful of where a job will involve living and its significance for leisure opportunities. In Britain the 'quality of working life' has recently become an issue of government as well as academic concern,[12] a number of firms have promoted job enrichment and job enlargement, while industrial democracy and workers' participation in management have become fashionable causes. Do these pointers indicate an imminent humanisation of work? One of the processes held responsible by those answering in the affirmative concerns workers who carry leisure values into their workplaces and demand satisfying working lives, combined with the possibility in advanced and relatively affluent societies, of sacrificing maximum efficiency in preference for satisfying jobs.

The problem with the above pointers is that counterparts have been observed for over a century without ever leading to a transformation of work. In the nineteenth century a series of thinkers including not only Marx but also Morris and Ruskin argued the possibility of ushering in a new golden age in which work could become meaningful and a major source of satisfaction. Are we at last on the verge of this golden age? Or are the contemporary pointers as misleading as their predecessors? The opposing argument maintains that, in reality, jobs are becoming increasingly systematised and 'work-like' due to the spread of bureaucratic rationality and advanced technology which make individuals' jobs meaningless while subjecting them to remote control.[13] For most people for most of the time, work remains work rather than an interest pursued for its intrinsic satisfaction, a key reward is financial, and in employment individuals do not please themselves but function within hierarchical authority structures. Leisure values might find some expression in work, but are there any trends suggesting that these values are likely to become a dominant influence?

It is impossible to address this problem with systematically-assembled empirical data, since the relevant evidence is simply not available. There are no surveys repeated at intervals since the early stages of industrialism enabling us to identify trends in the quality of working life. However, the issue can be approached theoretically, which does not mean in a purely speculative way. In a market economy, work has to be organised in ways that maximise efficiency and profitability. This need not entail that all jobs are boring. In some cases market pressures and humanistic considerations coincide. It does mean, however, that industry cannot be organised to maximise job satisfaction. Whatever politicians, employers and trade union leaders say cannot ease the pressures of the market. Some observers have noted that managements tend to become interested in job enrichment and other humane innovations only when they become profitable, either because the division of labour has been pushed so far as to reduce efficiency by increasing labour turnover and making recruitment difficult, or because unsatisfying jobs have lowered morale to a level where effort sags and disputes increase.[14] Legislation and trade union pressure can place limits on how far employers are allowed to push the drive for profitability. In Britain there is a long history of protective legislation placing restrictions on the employment of children, young people and women, and insisting upon standards consistent with health and safety. Trades unions have experienced considerable success in holding back the pressures of work as in car assembly plants, where today the speed of the track is normally subject to collective agreement, preventing the speed-ups for which Henry Ford became infamous.[15] In the future it is entirely possible that the quest for profit and efficiency will be subjected to further restrictions. Nevertheless, within whatever limits are in force, the logic of the market will continue to insist that industry is organised not to maximise job satisfaction but to yield profit.

Of course, the market could be replaced. Capitalism might be superseded by socialism throughout the Western world, and the market replaced by a command economy. In themselves, however, these changes carry no guarantee of improvements in the quality of working life. Socialist regimes could free industry from market pressures, institute workers' control, and allow production to be organised in whatever ways the producers found congenial. We know, however, that socialist regimes do not always use their power to this effect. Socialist governments are quite capable of valuing output in preference to worker satisfaction. In the Soviet Union bonuses are paid to plant directors who exceed production targets, and experience in Britain's nationalised industries confirms that governments are as willing as private employers to demand that enterprises maximise efficiency.

'True' socialists might deplore 'state capitalism' and insist that things will be different when 'real' worker power arrives. Can we be sure? In addition to being producers, workers are also consumers, and they may attach the greater priority to the latter role, insisting that industry is organised to support high levels of consumption. Although not designed for the purpose, the labour market is a quasi-experimental situation which measures the relative importance that workers attach to satisfying jobs and spending power. If job satisfaction were the stronger demand, it would be profitable for capitalist employers to organise production in the most intrinsically satisfying ways since labour would be attracted to the resultant jobs at a sufficiently low cost to outweigh the advantages of more conventional forms of organisational and technological rationality. We know, however, that men will work for high wages on monotonous car assembly lines, while vehicle production using craft techniques has been driven from the mass market.

The nineteenth-century sociological theorists said little about leisure. For them it was not a major issue. However, Marx, Comte, Spencer and their contemporaries did share a conviction that work could be genuinely humanised. Impressed by the productive power of industrialism, many nineteenth-century thinkers envisaged an age of abundance in which inequality and strife could disappear. Apart from time freed from work being used to cultivate interests in philosophy and poetry, they believed that in an age of abundance work could be humanised, freely undertaken, and organised to make it intrinsically satisfying. These dreams remain unfulfilled. The nineteenth-century theorists were not aware of all the impediments, and one thing that lay unforeseen was the ability of human beings to develop further wants once their basic needs have been satisfied. Some commentators deplore the values that make men willing to sell their labour if the price is right and accept monotonous jobs in order to acquire colour televisions and holidays abroad. Similarly there are critics who deplore workers' preference for fatter pay packets rather than shorter hours of work. But writers who condemn this 'materialism' usually enjoy comfortable living standards themselves.

If given the simple choice, everyone will vote against alienation in favour of job satisfaction, but in real life, whether socialist or capitalist, the choice cannot be so simple. Work could be made more fulfilling if this was what people valued above all else, but it is wish-fulfilment rather than rational argument to infer that the contemporary development of leisure will automatically bring this about.

It is mistaken to imagine that work and leisure are locked in a zero-sum equation, so that if leisure has grown in importance work must have undergone an equivalent decline. As argued in Chapter 2, historically there has been a growth of leisure, but through the containment rather than a decline of work. Even in the most advanced industrial societies, there is no justification for dismissing work as an incidental pastime. And as recognised in Chapter 8, work-roles are still an important source of identity. We continue to 'place' people by reference to their occupations. Studies of the implications of unemployment and retirement continue to report how, for men in particular, loss of work-role means loss of status and self-respect. Hence the cases where redundant executives conceal their predicaments from neighbours and, sometimes, even from members of their own households. In rejecting the presumption of work centrality, it was argued that leisure also can be a source of identity and status. Many individuals feel that they reveal their authentic 'selves' in their non-working lives, and the orientations nurtured outside that individuals take with them to work can affect their behaviour there.[16] For many employees in industry, work is not a central life interest, and leisure gives meaning to life as a whole. Notwithstanding this, work remains an important prop in the social *personas* of most adult males, and for many women as well. There are leisure milieux in which individuals can also express and confirm their 'selves', but without a work-role the remaining edifice begins to collapse. Being a competent amateur golfer or gardener is no compensation for lacking a work-role. Leisure has developed alongside work, and functions alongside it in identity formation and maintenance. It has joined rather than replaced work as a cultural force. Work is no more being taken over by leisure values than uses of leisure are conditioned by individuals' occupations.

Leisure and political participation

Politics is another area where the growth of leisure has made perhaps surprisingly little impact. Explaining a negative is always difficult. How do you explain why something has *not* happened? Whatever the difficulties, the failure of leisure to have certain political consequences is worthy of comment. Participation in most forms of recreation has been growing, but not in politics. Government provision for leisure has become very evident, but politics as a leisure activity remains undeveloped, except as a spectacle. Galbraith has likened contemporary politics to a spectator sport which the public follows, mainly through the media: '. . . politics in the United States has become a spectator sport. Unlike football or hockey, it's an all-season show. . . . As in football, it is form that counts, not substance. Points are awarded not for wisdom on issues but for performance in the game. Winning is, of course, the only test of achievement.'[17]

It might seem reasonable to suppose that as people acquire more leisure time, participation in civic organisations such as political parties should rise, but this has not been the trend. Indeed, in Britain over the last 30 years the actual trend has been in the opposite direction. Voter turnout at elections and memberships of the two main parties have fallen. There has been talk of an upsurge in community action and participation in pressure groups campaigning for causes ranging from racial equality to gay lib, but most of this talk has proved hollow. In New York City a 'school war' was fought for local community control, but turnout at elections for the resulting school boards is now running at around 10 per cent.[18] Elections to allow parental representatives on school management bodies in parts of Britain, including Sheffield, are being greeted with similar apathy.[19] Community pressure groups often turn out to have surprisingly shallow roots. Similarly in industry trade union activists remain very much exceptions to the rule. To judge from the interest they display in their own organisations, the majority of trades unionists have little inclination to exercise workers' control.

Such apathy could at one time be plausibly attributed to the impoverished condition of the working class, its lack of time, education and so on. One might have expected that as these constraints were lifted the ranks of activists in trades unions and political parties would swell, but this has not occurred. Leisure has not unleashed a flood of effort and commitment into civic organisations. It is impossible to furnish empirical evidence explaining why this, or anything else, has not happened, but a convincing theoretical explanation is available if we assume that rates of civic participation will depend upon the balance of costs and benefits to the individual. With mass participation to achieve collective gains, the additional benefit likely to accrue to any person is rarely significantly influenced depending on whether or not the single individual participates. For example, no one elector's vote in a general election is likely to make a crucial difference at Westminster, and the situation surrounding voting for trade union representatives and attending branch meetings is similar. Equally to the point, participation carries few intrinsic rewards. Handfuls of activists can derive immense satisfaction from running pressure groups, party ward organisations, trade union branches and strike committees. But no system of organisation has yet been devised enabling these rewards to be dispersed among large memberships. For the ordinary rank and file member, an evening at the trade union branch is unlikely to offer exhilaration, relaxation or whatever other experience the person values. Although it is widely applauded by political theorists, civic participation is not among the most rewarding leisure activities for the mass of the people. While the rewards are slight, the costs to the individual of participating can be immediate and significant, particularly in a society where individuals value their leisure pastimes. Why miss a favourite television programme, a sports event or an evening in the pub? Why incur the opportunity costs that participation requires? By making the opportunity costs heavier, the growth of leisure dampens rather than fuels civic participation.

Wippler[20] has argued that civic participation could be boosted by deliberately rewarding individuals for their contributions. But what currency could such rewards take? Esteem seems insufficient, so we are left with proposals for paying local councillors, school managers and 'lay' trade union officials, and the result is to make the culture of civic organisations resemble work rather than leisure. In socialist societies political participation runs at higher levels than in Western democracies, a difference explicable in terms of the one-party state's ability to reward activists with privileged access to education and job opportunities.[21] It is difficult to envisage this type of reward system being extended into multi-party politics, and in the Western world, therefore, the growth of leisure has not produced and remains unlikely to produce a new type of participant democracy.

Life and leisure

The growth of leisure is affecting the quality of life, but leisure is not becoming the whole of it. Talk of a leisure civilisation or a society of leisure is misconceived. There is more to the growth of leisure than increased demand for sports, the countryside and other forms of recreation, but the spin-off from leisure stops at the gates of work, and also stops short of revitalising political processes. Just as it is important to note the extent to which their jobs do not influence individuals' lives outside their workplaces, so it is important to recognise the parts of society that remain little affected by the growth of leisure.

It exaggerates the importance of the subject to suggest that educating and catering for leisure now hold the solution to all the main problems of human well-being and that recreation professionals are becoming society's new high priests. It is wrong to imply that we can begin to forget old problems such as boring jobs and pay relativities, while focusing upon television, sport and the state of the arts as the new issues of real importance. Leisure has grown but it is still only a part of life, and far from resolving mankind's longer established problems, the emergence of leisure is making the human predicament increasingly complex. All the problems of an industrial civilisation remain live issues. Few people now believe that we stand on the threshold of an age of abundance in which all our material wants will be satisfied. Hopes that economic growth might lift the whole of mankind to the standards of living enjoyed by America's middle classes have been abandoned. It has become more fashionable to predict ecological disaster.[22] Galloping world population growth, profligate waste of limited energy resources, and the blind exploitation of land and sea are seen as stretching existing economic and political institutions to breaking point. Instead of automation freeing civilisation from both work and want, contemporary futurologists insist that Western man must learn to accept a simpler life-style. The growth of leisure does not indicate that the old 'industrial' problems of how to produce the amounts that people desire to consume have been relegated to history.

Likewise with the familiar problems of distribution, inequality and their resultant political tensions. Hirsch has distinguished 'material' goods which we can all possess without interfering with each other's enjoyment, from 'positional' goods whose enjoyment is spoilt when others also possess them.[23] Education is an example of a positional good. A five-year secondary school course ceases to confer its former benefits when it becomes a universal right. Quiet beaches and road-space are further examples. Hirsch argues that in the economically advanced societies, the balance of consumer demand tends to swing from material to positional goods. Hence the predicament where we are all striving to better ourselves, but only succeed in remaining in the same relative positions, with the result that the total sum of human enjoyment is not increased. Hirsch's advice is that we cultivate collective instead of individualistic enjoyments and pursuits. In the meantime, however, socio-economic inequalities remain sources of tension and conflict. Leisure brings new opportunities and problems that are not replacing but resting alongside longer-standing economic and political concerns.

The new opportunities concern how to use and cater for leisure. These are increasingly important issues both for individuals and for society-at-large. How we address these problems affects the quality of life. Leisure is no longer a shadowy, residual substance that only becomes a matter of public concern if used in harmful ways. But leisure has not become and is not becoming synonymous with or the basis of modern life in general.

Rather than pacifying the human predicament, there are ways in which leisure makes it increasingly tense, as Bell illustrates with his 'cultural contradictions' of capitalism. Is it possible for an individual to be 'straight' by day and a 'swinger' by night?[24] The arguments developed in this and the preceding chapters agree with Bell's analysis: neither work nor leisure values are engulfing the other's territory. Hence the contradiction; the split in the social order and in the lives of ordinary citizens which aggravates the task of keeping the broader social framework intact and giving meaning to life as a whole.

Although they can claim to stand in its line of descent, students of leisure overestimate the significance of their subject when they adopt the idiom of nineteenth-century sociology wholesale, perceive their society to be on the verge of a new epoch and proceed to identify its character. Sociology's founding fathers lived through an age when traditional social orders were collapsing. They stood on the threshold of an industrial civilisation and their theories were attempts to sketch the dynamics and contours of the emergent order. If the contemporary growth of leisure were heralding a comparable movement into a new epoch, its study would be sufficient excuse for reverting to sociology in the grand style, but this treatment exaggerates the significance of modern leisure. As we know it today, leisure could only have developed within an industrial society, and it is difficult to accept its recent growth as sufficient excuse for labelling the epoch post-industrial. Bell gives this phrase a plausible meaning, characterising changes in the economy and occupational structure.[25] Industrialism is in decline in so far as there is a shift from manufacturing to tertiary employment and from manual to white-collar occupations, but Bell's post-industrial society heralds the demise of neither business rationality nor work. No doubt the business civilisation will eventually prove finite but, at present, we are unable to see beyond its lifespan. This territory remains a topic for speculation. Maybe during the twenty-first century a new social order will begin to evolve and grand theory will regain its nineteenth-century relevance. Claiming such historical significance for the growth of leisure during the twentieth century overestimates its importance. There are limits to how widely the influence of leisure is spreading throughout the social structure. Work and politics are two areas of life where its impact is slight and, while this remains so, talk of a society of leisure is ill-advised.

Chapter 11

Leisure and social policy

This chapter differs from its predecessors; it is less dispassionate and even more of a personal credo. There is a case for recognising the inevitable rather than trying to avoid the intrusion of personal beliefs and values into discussions of social policy. In any case, when debating leisure it is hardly possible to extract clear policy implications while sticking close to the known facts. Policies rarely flow from research in a direct and immediate manner. Critics who argue that social scientists should conduct useful rather than purely academic exercises rarely appreciate the difficulties in generating useful knowledge. When researchers simply address practitioners' problems their findings can be immediately useful. How many inhabitants in a given town will use a proposed swimming pool? If they resist so obvious a handmaiden role, it is not because researchers prefer to be useless, but to help practitioners eventually to ask more penetrating questions.

Leisure researchers begin with the problem of describing and explaining how people actually behave. As knowledge advances we can envisage the outcomes of different policies with increasing precision, but the present state of leisure research leaves a credibility gap. It offers a less than complete agenda for 'What to do on Monday?' Despite this, it is not necessary for researchers to leave policy issues entirely to practitioners. Like other citizens, even sociologists are entitled to a point of view, and one interim service that researchers can perform is to debunk implications that do not follow from the already known facts.

Having observed the growth of leisure, common sense beckons some writers to infer that here we have a problem whose solution requires purposive action. More often than not, the cry is raised for governments to initiate the action, and meet the challenge of leisure by ensuring that recreation provision is made available on a hitherto unprecedented scale. Enlarged budgets for the Arts and Sports Councils, local authority recreation departments and the Countryside Commission leading to more swimming pools, golf courses, nature trails, country parks and arts centres is the 'recreation lobby's' standard response to the growth of leisure. Before grasping this banner it is useful to recapitulate the so-called leisure problem, for the previous chapters have hardly pointed towards such implications.

Leisure is growing, but does this necessarily mean that we face a *problem* of leisure? Among the public it is possible to discern a variety of leisure problems. Depending on their tastes, people demand more comedy shows or documentaries on television, while others resent the price of petrol restricting their motoring habits. For folk whose livelihoods depend upon others' leisure, the public's lack of interest in their paintings, massage parlours, cricket matches and other services can be a problem. It is necessary to distinguish the frustration of specific interests from *the* problem of leisure. All parties tend to associate the furtherance of their own interests with the common good. It is not difficult to persuade artists that support for the arts serves the public interest. Likewise the sporting lobby is easily convinced that more sport for all will enhance well-being. It is important to be clear about the senses in which we face a general problem of leisure.

What is the nature of this problem? Mass society theorists deplore the seduction of the public to passivity by the irresistible but mediocre output of the media, and call for responsible élites – political, religious and artistic, to organise a rescue. Class domination theorists complain of how genuine freedom is inhibited by a logic of industrial capitalism whose values infiltrate the leisure industries which, therefore, operate as apparatuses of social control rather than aids to self-fulfilment. Other analysts who accept that modern leisure confers genuine freedom warn of the aimlessness and anomie that can leave men floundering in a moral wasteland of spare time. All these appraisals of leisure have been considered systematically – and rejected. One firm conclusion towards which this volume points is that leisure *per se* is *not* a problem from which mankind needs to be rescued. The public should beware unholy alliances of leisure researchers and practitioners who proclaim and offer their services to address a growing problem.

Sections of the public certainly find their leisure interests often frustrated, but this is inevitable given a universe of finite resources. Not even governments can resolve the age-old economic problem of scarcity. Nor are governments the most appropriate agents to decide which leisure interests shall be satisfied. This is another firm implication of the arguments in earlier chapters. The conventional approach to social problems, which looks to governments to marshal the necessary knowledge and resources, is ill-equipped to handle the issues that leisure poses. What is more, it pre-empts the options to assume that the growth of leisure necessarily requires a specifically recreational response. Do people want to devote to recreation the resources that accompany leisure? As explained in Chapter 9, past history suggests that the public prefers to devote a considerable part of its leisure to other uses.

The real issues and opportunities that leisure presents have too often been obscured by mistaken theories and special pleading. From what is known about the nature and consequences of leisure, there are no grounds for insisting that its growth be treated principally as a problem. Presuming that public authorities should play a central role in catering for leisure is unwarranted. And it is equally mistaken to assume that leisure must be filled with recreational activities and facilities. Sociology has always been a debunking discipline, and leisure today offers plentiful scope for this role. Once the myths have been exposed, however, we are still left with the question of 'What to do next?' Exactly where do the above arguments lead as regards social policy and public recreation provision?

The state of the art

Growing recreation provision by government bodies has been a common experience throughout Western societies since the Second World War.[1] In part this reflects the more general development of welfare states and government spending, but it has also been advocated as a 'natural' response to the growth of leisure itself. While they have strenuously debated the merits of different forms of intervention, leisure researchers and professionals have rarely questioned the need for public provision to match the growth of leisure. Providers' worries have centred on the classic economic problem, the scarcity of resources, and consequently upon their lack of clear standards against which to judge the merits of possible ventures.

In Britain, as in most other countries, public provision for recreation developed piecemeal, and rarely for the sake solely of recreation itself. Art has been supported for art's sake, and sport for its own merits. Particular forms of recreation have been promoted on grounds of their educational value, or because of their contributions to health and fitness. A desire to conserve the heritage has underlain the maintenance of other recreational resources, while the authorities administering forests and waterways have been thrust into the leisure business by public demand. It is the historical growth of leisure itself that has prompted our assortment of public providers increasingly to conceive their role in terms of catering for recreation.

In England and Wales the reorganisation of local government in 1974 created an opportunity for the relevant services' recreation function to be given institutional expression. Throughout the country the administration of various combinations of local authority parks, libraries, museums, sports, community and arts centres began to be amalgamated in leisure, recreation and similarly-titled departments. While many of the services encompassed have long histories, this administrative shuffle has created a new situation in so far as there is now an apparent need for the various types of provision to be judged and justified in terms of specifically recreational criteria. In Britain this catalyst has left many recreation personnel searching for objectives. Parks and libraries are no longer justified as worthy in their own right by having committees and departments exclusively charged with their maintenance. Support for sport and the arts can no longer be slipped

through education and public health budgets. Recreation departments
have to assess the merits of parks against museums and libraries, sports
centres against arts centres. This requirement that services be justified
in terms of leisure criteria is rather novel, and inevitably provokes a
great deal of soul-searching.

Demands that recreation departments justify their patterns of
expenditure tend to be embarrassing. As a result of its historical
piecemeal development, the contemporary pattern of public provision
seems to elude coherent justification. Lewes and Mennell's research in
Exeter illustrates the predicament.[2] These investigators found a widespread desire for a coherent policy among council officials, but in
practice decisions were taken on an *ad hoc* basis, and several illustrations are offered of the almost 'accidental' origins of particular initiatives. Exeter's spending on recreation and culture amounted to £6 per
head of population in 1973–74 and totalled 5 per cent of the authority's budget. Of this 40 per cent was devoted to libraries and a similar
amount to parks and sport, but there were no principles behind this
breakdown; it simply expressed how affairs had developed. In Exeter
only the local authority's golf course 'broke even' and as part of their
research Lewes and Mennell calculated the subsidy per user-occasion
on different types of provision. The costs of museums and field sports
proved exceptionally high, a finding that aroused considerable interest
among council officials who had never attempted such estimates. On
the council the leisure issues that aroused most heated debate were
those involving financial support for voluntary associations such as
orchestras and theatre groups, though Lewes and Mennell show this to
be an exceptionally cheap way of supporting recreation, and the
amounts involved were always minute compared with spending on
libraries and parks.

Such features of local government activity in recreation may or may
not amuse the public-at-large, but they certainly concern the personnel
directly involved. It is not only in local authority recreation departments that decisions are taken on an *ad hoc* basis. The same criticism
can be directed against all the public recreation services. With the
growth of expenditure, public recreation has begun to attract the
attention of economists, and the vague objectives of bodies such as the
Arts Council, their failure to manage by objectives, to relate means to
ends systematically, and to mount cost-benefit analyses has led to a
welter of criticism.[3] Hence the current search for rational standards.
To recreation personnel the absence of such standards is more than an
academic problem. To acquire resources recreation departments have
to convince their authorities, and ultimately the tax- and rate-payers
that their services are of value, and recreation staffs are aware of how
thin their cases invariably look when set alongside claims for hospitals,
schools and retirement pensions. Few recreation practitioners are
confident of what the public wants let alone needs. Will there still be a
demand for squash courts in 10 years time? Will a community use a

proposed community centre? Will the public be better seved by country parks on the perimeters of cities or by investing in usually more
distant national parks? One thing of which recreation departments can
be certain is that all their initiatives will attract criticism. The sports
centre that will cater for the interests of every local sportsman is still
awaited, and likewise the community centre whose design fits the
needs of every local organisation. Then there are the tax- and rate-
payers, some of whom can be relied upon to feel outraged at having to
finance other people's pleasures. Recreation personnel need answers
with which to confront their critics.

Muddling through in recreation is not a British peculiarity. In Mennell's study of cultural policy-making in 14 European towns,[4] phrases
such as *'ad hoc'* and 'serendipity' litter the discussion, but there are
different views on the urgency of this situation. Mennell's talk of
serendipity suggests that despite the manifest irrationality of cultural
policy-making, a latent common sense usually conspires to produce a
happy outcome. But is the outcome particularly happy? There is now a
growing body of evidence, much of which has been referred to in
earlier chapters, raising questions as to whether the public-at-large
really gets value from the public leisure services. Diana Dunn's
research has already been mentioned, revealing no causal relationship
between public recreation provision and other indices of the quality of
life in American cities.[5] Reference has also been made to Hall and
Perry's research in Stoke and Sunderland which discovered that recreation facilities were not generally regarded as important contributors
to either well-being or dissatisfaction with life.[6] Time-budget and
similar studies have revealed the limited role that public facilities play
in most people's life-styles, particularly in working class communities.[7]
Even when only out-of-home and group-based recreation are counted,
the commercial and voluntary sectors greatly outdistance public provision in popularity.[8] Economic geographers who have developed indirect measures of the public's willingness to pay for facilities normally
provided free of charge to the user, such as urban parks, have concluded that the types of provision in question can rarely be justified
purely in terms of market criteria.[9] In so far as the leisure market
measures utility, this raises further doubts as to whether the public is
currently obtaining value for money from the activities of government
agencies.

Recreation professionals react in diverse ways to the above evidence
and arguments. One response is to abandon guesswork about people's
needs and give the public what it manifestly wants. Gil Swift has argued
that especially when public expenditure is subject to severe restraint,
local authority ventures in recreation should be judged in terms of
participant or audience appeal plus financial viability.[10] He describes
his own experience with one urban park where pay roundabouts were
introduced into the children's play area, charges for golf were raised
and crazy golf installed, a pets' corner was transformed into a pay zoo,

catering was upgraded, and plants offered for sale as well as display. Not only did revenue increase, but during the period when these changes were introduced attendances at the park grew tenfold. Needless to say, there are difficulties with the 'give the public what it will pay for' approach. Pushed to extremes it could turn sports centres into middle class enclaves. We already support such enclaves at the National Theatre and Covent Garden. Do we really want to encourage more? Equally fundamentally, if the object is simply to satisfy manifest demand, why not leave all recreation provision to commercial enterprise and voluntary effort? Mecca and Blackpool together with the tobacco and brewing industries already have plenty of experience and expertise at giving people what they want. The wants versus needs argument impels a return to first principles. What is it about leisure that requires government involvement?

Let it be repeated that our ability to measure the quality of life remains far from perfect. The quality of the evidence certainly does not justify wholesale closure of parks, arts centres, playing fields and museums. But this does not defuse demands for rationality in policy-making, meaning the development of clear objectives, and the systematic appraisal of means against ends. Once we admit that rational standards are desirable we have to ask, 'What kind of standards?' and at this point the arguments pursued in earlier chapters assume relevance. One favoured route towards rationality would involve collating the existing evidence and commissioning new research to discover the public's needs, wants and tastes. The Rapoports' enquiry into leisure and the family life-cycle[11] was undertaken with this objective. This approach also favours public participation in leisure policy-making and management thereby assisting the political process to articulate public preferences. Upon the basis of the knowledge derived, it is envisaged that an overall policy for leisure could be formulated, and resources marshalled systematically so as to maximise satisfaction. Would this be as rational as it can be made to sound? Before succumbing to this logic we need to query the implications of such an open mandate to cater for leisure.

Earlier chapters defended a pluralist interpretation of leisure on a theoretical level against mass society and class domination theorists who deny that talk of socio-cultural pluralism fits the society in which we live. On a more practical, political level, pluralism is in equal need of defence against (usually unwitting) enemies who propose to rise to the challenge of leisure in ways that could warp its essential character. A threat to pluralism, though rarely intended as such, comes from those seeking to impose the above type of rationality upon the public leisure services. Discussion of public recreation provision invariably triggers ambivalent sentiments. Even if the evidence is less than convincing, experience persuades most observers that this provision contributes to the quality of life. Simultaneously it opens obvious dangers of political and professional élites appropriating the scope for choice that leisure permits. The problem, therefore, concerns how to fashion a role for public bodies that will safeguard rather than threaten pluralism.

Do we need a leisure policy?

In our bureaucratised and technological age, there tends to be a presumption favouring coherence not only in intellectual life, but also in administrative affairs. To many commentators it appears self-evident that governments who become involved in the supply of leisure goods and services should formulate coherent leisure policies. Coherent thinking, it is widely believed, is a condition for efficient and effective practice. In fact, however, an overall government policy for leisure or even recreation is unnecessary. Despite its untidiness, the present state of decision-making and administration in the public leisure services need not be deplored.

Attempts to develop comprehensive policies for leisure can be criticised, first, because it is simply impractical for the Welfare State to take even recreation within its total embrace. The public's tastes and interests are so numerous and capable of such indefinite extension that the state cannot realistically undertake to satisfy them. A commitment to service the public's recreational interests is too open-ended to be practical. In principle this same point could be applied to education and health. In reality, however, current social practice maps the contours of reasonable demand. With recreation existing interests are too diverse to make their satisfaction into rights of citizenship. In practice the state taxes many objects of recreational expenditure including alcohol, tobacco and gambling, and the national economy could hardly be managed otherwise. Governments appear to favour certain forms of recreation like opera which is subsidised over others including cigarette smoking which is taxed. It may be possible to defend these biases on health, fiscal and other grounds, but it is difficult to see how they could be justified purely in terms of recreational merit. Fiscal requirements inevitably lead to the pleasures that the public values most highly being subject to the strongest penalties. Having one's recreational interests serviced cannot be made into a right of citizenship, even in a society with leisure.

Second, there is no objective way of deciding which recreational tastes are particularly worthy and deserve support. In education and health the costs and benefits from alternative programmes can be at least roughly calculated, but this is not true in recreation. There is no inter-subjective consensus throughout the public as to which uses of leisure are especially meritorious. Nor is it possible to distinguish basic needs from other less essential objects of recreational provision. Precise measurement is admittedly difficult, but there are minimum levels of shelter, food and clothing that people 'need'. In contrast, although the term is sometimes used, it is doubtful whether human beings or societies possess 'leisure needs'. People develop leisure interests and wants, and some of mankind's physical, psychological and social needs such as for health and self-expression may be satisfied through recreation. But it is difficult to envisage any recreational equivalents to the minimum standards of food and shelter that can be agreed as necessary.

Third and perhaps most fundamentally, the very nature of leisure as self-determined behaviour implies that it cannot be stipulated and forecast by any authority. Developing and implementing a policy which decreed the life-styles to be encouraged among the public could become the antithesis of leisure. A comprehensive stipulative policy could turn leisure into the apparatus of social control envisaged in the class domination theory.

Guidelines

It is the criteria that should guide public provision rather than the very principle that is now under debate. Leisure has become a major factor in the quality of life, and there are ways of enhancing the quality of leisure that can only be organised by governments. The intention in the above discussion has simply been to rebut the view that, at government level, we need a comprehensive and stipulative policy for leisure. On the contrary, the absence of such a policy should be grounds for applause rather than concern.

Leisure is so interwoven with the rest of life, and government intervention in this rest of life is so extensive, that public authorities inevitably become involved in leisure provision. There is no alternative. If modern governments find it necessary to engage in land-use planning, as they invariably do, then irrespective of whether they wish to cater for leisure, they necessarily become enmeshed in the allocation of resources for recreation. Determining which tracts of land will be available for housing, industry and agriculture necessarily involves declaring which land will be safeguarded for recreation. When local authorities build housing estates they necessarily become suppliers or at least planners of community facilities such as meeting rooms and public houses. When governments decide that they must regulate the use of broadcasting, maybe on account of the medium's potential ideological and political importance, this entails control over a recreational resource. Governments cannot disclaim all responsibility for recreation. But this does not mean that they must attempt comprehensively to service the public's recreational interests.

Citizens and governments alike inhabit a world of scarce resources. It is therefore unrealistic for citizens to expect governments comprehensively to service their recreational wants, and it is equally inadequate for politicians and public bodies to justify provision solely on this basis. Surveying the public to discover its true desires, and inviting participation so that recreation departments can satisfy citizens' authentic interests promise more than they can hope to deliver. There is a touch of irony when local authorities survey their constituencies to discover what the public really wants. No doubt there is a huge potential demand for international cabaret and world cruises. The criteria against which recreation policies can be developed rationally must be sought elsewhere. To develop guidelines for public provision in a pluralist society we need to ask what the state is uniquely placed to add to commercial and voluntary effort, and three clear answers can be delivered.

First, when the supply of resources is finite beyond the short term the state can defend the public interest against, for example, the alternative of commercial monopoly. This is why the *principles* of government regulation of energy resources and land-use planning have become politically non-controversial. Land is the classic finite resource, and only the state can safeguard the countryside for leisure, and designate both land and buildings in and around urban areas for recreational use. Another resource in finite supply is the broadcasting wavelengths. Then there is the 'heritage' ranging through artistic skills to historic buildings which, once destroyed, could not be recreated. Only governments are in a realistic position to invite the present generation to bear the cost of maintaining opportunities for citizens yet unborn.

A second ground for public provision arises when recreation is an expedient means to a non-recreational objective. For example, few governments are totally disinterested in national prestige, and this political objective may justify state sponsorship of sport. Concern for public health may be a legitimate ground for encouraging participant sport. In so far as the state offers a comprehensive educational service, this must include recreation provision. Play-groups and nurseries are financed partly from educational motives, and also, sometimes, to free mothers for employment outside their homes. The maintenance of a transport network inevitably places governments in the leisure business. The greater part of public recreation provision has such 'incidental' origins, which is why the patchwork of leisure services is so uneven. What must be recognised is that despite surface appearances this state of affairs is *not* non-rational and therefore a ground for criticism. The fact that education incorporates leisure facilities does not require that schools be designed so that they can function as multi-purpose centres offering comprehensive recreation services to the entire public.

A third ground for state involvement is the pursuit of distributive justice. Opportunities for recreation are among the goods and services that public authorities can distribute to enhance the standards and quality of life among otherwise disadvantaged groups including the ageing, children, young people and the handicapped, who are less able than other citizens to pursue their interests through the market and

158 *Leisure and social policy*

voluntary effort. Why dispense any services in kind? Why not eschew paternalism and simply redistribute money for recipients to spend as they please? The answer is that paternalism may sometimes be justified, as when the beneficiaries are children, while in other cases it is a cost that must be borne for the sake of parsimony. It costs little to allow the unemployed access to sports centres and to offer the use of meeting rooms to ageing citizens when these facilities are otherwise underused. Also resources whose basic cost of production is nil, namely land, can be opened to all irrespective of means at minimal expense. If governments seek to correct the otherwise 'natural' distribution of resources there is no good reason why recreation should be excluded from their strategies.

Once recognised, the above grounds for public provision can be employed to assess the merits of existing and proposed ventures. The public has a right to ask why more is spent on sport than the arts. Likewise rate- and tax-payers have a right to query the value of municipal record libraries and squash courts, and if adequate justifications cannot be given in terms of the above guidelines, the implication is that the authorities should reconsider their priorities. The one defensible loophole is that existing public tastes and life-styles are respected. There is a complex interactive relationship between the supply and demand for leisure goods and services. Tastes in participant sport and the arts, for example, have both stimulated and been nurtured by the facilities that public bodies have offered in the past. It is reasonable, therefore, to ask public authorities to respect life-styles that they have helped to shape. It would be painfully doctrinaire to do otherwise. This loophole is inherently conservative, but entirely humane.

The practical implications of the above guidelines are anything but revolutionary. They do little more than explicate the grounds for state intervention that have operated implicitly in the past. Explication has become necessary as the scale and organisation of public provision have reached the point where formal criteria are required to prevent arbitrariness and to legitimise decisions. The above guidelines satisfy demands for rationality in a way that remains consistent with the maintenance of socio-cultural pluralism since they do not involve political agents in the dubious exercise of judging the recreational merits of alternative pastimes, intruding into areas that can be served adequately by commercial and voluntary enterprise, or coordinating provision to an extent that would oligopolise the leisure market. Socio-cultural pluralism requires plentiful scope for commercial and voluntary effort. The best safeguard against *dirigisme* in the public sector is to prevent the balance of power swinging from the consumers' side of the market. Despite its imperfections, the market remains one of the most effective participatory mechanisms devised for modern societies. Leaving consumers with money in their pockets is an excellent recipe for participation.

The above guidelines may appear to be fettering public enterprise, but government activity needs to be contained within clear parameters. Recreation has become big business and we must question the extent to which we wish this to lead to even bigger government. There are architects awaiting commissions to design park environments with up to 250 acres covered in a single span, and neighbourhood centres where everything from sport and the arts to bingo and evening classes can be offered.[12] It is not unknown for local authorities to be tempted to collaborate by the prestige that can follow such projects.[13] In July 1977 the Arts Council came to the aid of certain provincial theatres. Equity, the actors' union, responded with a demand for full public ownership. Arts cinemas subsequently joined the queue requesting public support. At some point we have to decide where the state's responsibilities are to end.

We should not be surprised when the analysis of leisure raises issues of political philosophy. If leisure is as important as earlier chapters have argued, its growth is bound to raise fundamental questions about the type of society we desire. Do governments know best? Is collective wisdom as articulated through state apparatuses superior to the sum of the wisdoms of individuals and smaller groups? It implies no opposition to the principle of Welfare State to point out that leisure, as defined in this and most other volumes on the subject, can exist only in so far as individuals and groups within society possess scope for choice. Using the resources unleashed by the containment of work and other developments that increase leisure to expand the power of the state might enlarge some opportunities for play and recreation but could the end product be meaningfully described as leisure?

The strengths and limitations of participation

All writers who have contemplated the issue claim to favour public participation in leisure policy-making. This is to be expected. No one who welcomes leisure could oppose the principle. But we need to be clear about how participation can be maximised, and the ends it can hope to achieve. On these matters opinions differ. In the light of the above arguments on policy and provision it is necessary to insist that participation is not synonymous with democratising the public leisure services. Consulting users and taking their opinions into account, which is what participation means in the public sector, can work to everyone's advantage. Yet over-reliance upon this variety of institutionalised participation could be counterproductive. Earlier chapters have shown that there are other ways in which individuals can actively participate in constructing their own life-styles.

As explained in Chapter 4, public participation in recreation policy-making and management has been urged as a remedy for massification, and if this were the sole ground for participation the case would be less than convincing. Participation is also advocated as a means of clarifying objectives and establishing an order of priority among possible ventures in public recreation. Advocates of a comprehensive leisure policy see participation as complementing academic research in laying the knowledge base from which such a policy could be rationally extracted. As argued above, this presumes so broad a role for the public sector as to threaten pluralism and unnecessarily limit citizens' real scope for choice. Maximising participation requires a more modest role for the public services. Yet in so far as there must be a public sector, and no one envisages its disappearance, there is everything to be said for building responsiveness into its operations. Many recreation personnel suspect that orthodox, bureaucratic administrative styles, in which objectives are declared at the top and executed through subordinate layers of officialdom, are inappropriate in the leisure field, and these suspicions are entirely justified.

Organisational research indicates that 'mechanical' styles of bureaucracy are most appropriate in stable and predicatable environments where objectives are clear-cut; conditions which do not apply in recreation. Objectives are typically vague. Public authorities frequently become involved in recreation as by-products of other concerns. Administrators find themselves supervising tracts of countryside, urban parks, art galleries, libraries, museums and sports facilities, but have few precise ideas about the recreational uses to which these resources should be put. Furthermore, tastes and interests in recreation are notoriously fickle. Twenty years ago no one was predicting the future popularity of indoor five-a-side soccer. Recreation personnel who wish to sensitise themselves and their organisations to developments in public taste find the orthodox political channels less than satisfactory. Recreation is rarely a party political issue and, therefore, elections and the representatives they produce do not necessarily articulate grassroots opinion.

Advocates of user involvement see dangers not only in the predominant bureaucratic style of government administration, but also in professionalism among recreation personnel, many of whom express genuine fears that their services could become over-professionalised. In America recreation has advanced a considerable distance down the professional road, generating an esoteric vocabulary that bristles with references to 'leisure services' and the design of effective 'delivery systems'. Experts in 'recreology' assess the 'leisurability' of proposed ventures. Sceptics point to the danger of inhibiting meaningful dialogue with the wider public. While simple to advocate, user participation is rarely easy to achieve. A variety of strategies are available, all possess limitations, and the issue is not to decide which one approach is best, but which are appropriate under different circumstances. Conventional strategies include appointing representatives of community interests to the management committees of sports centres, recreation complexes and other facilities, and sometimes organising open meetings to facilitate exchange of opinion between professionals and the public. These strategies are most likely to prove effective when potential users and uses can be defined in advance, as in the case of a sports centre with an existing clientele. The danger concerns these 'democratic' channels being manipulated by unrepresentative interest groups.[14]

Surveys can be commissioned to tap a wider spectrum of opinion, and can be useful when the issues are well known and understood among the respondents. For example, in Skelmersdale New Town the authority balloted residents on a housing estate to discover whether support for a proposed community centre outweighed opposition. The difficulty with surveys concerns the difference between what people say and their actual behaviour. When questions tap non-salient issues, that is matters that individuals have not necessarily thought about prior to being questioned, their responses can amount to little more than verbal nonsense. People may express interest in an arts centre, but this is no guarantee that they would actually use such a facility. The only thoroughly convincing way to establish whether there is a demand for a centre might be to build it and see what happens.[15]

Another strategy advocates building responsiveness and open-ness into both organisations and their staffs. In America Murphy and his colleagues have advised recreation personnel to define their role as enablers and encouragers rather than mere dispensers of services, and recommend decentralised management in which clients' viewpoints can be constantly fed into organisations. They argue that,

'The isolationist perspective commonly associated with facility management is no longer valid for the leisure service manager. He must function more as a dynamic, community catalyst — encourager of human development.[16] *. . . The effective delivery system is one which recognises the needs, interests and characteristics of the public it seeks to serve. Typically, it is developed on the basis of some initial and tentative assumptions about potential participants, defined largely on a group basis. It then moves towards individualisation and modification of the service as participants, and their uniqueness, are actually encountered.'*[17]

Such proposals read admirably. The problem is that, for the present, their practicality remains unproven. It is difficult to institutionalise qualities such as responsiveness. This is not to say that the attempt is undesirable; merely that its advocates must prove that their proposals can work.

Another approach to participation is to work through existing commercial and voluntary organisations. In Britain the Arts and Sports Councils normally channel support in this manner and, quite apart from the participation issue, it can be a spectacular cost-saving exercise. Local authorities can provide holidays for disadvantaged groups without establishing a public holiday industry. Drama groups and golf clubs are often only too willing to manage facilities free of charge. One drawback with working through other organisations is the lack of detailed accountability in the use of public funds, but however it is accomplished participation will relax bureaucratic accountability. Another problem involves the 'unfair' favouring of some organisations and sections of the public at the expense of others. Dispensers of patronage must stay alert to this danger. Yet despite the problems, the advantages of indirect support are considerable if only because thriving voluntary and commerical sectors are such highly effective participatory mechanisms in their own right. Participatory procedures within public recreation are admirable, but the maintenance of consumer choice is the best guarantee against the suppliers of leisure goods and services, whether public or private, dictating what the public will enjoy.

While impossible to argue against, it is important to recognise that participation is no solve-all. There are technical problems in implementing participation. How do we allow the thousands of potential users of a sports centre, for example, to participate in its management? Social science has yet to answer this basic question of social engineering, though it is a matter of no minor concern in societies that value democracy. In addition to the technical difficulties, there are issues at stake that are simply not susceptible to solution through user participation. Once a recreational facility is in existence, or when the decision to provide a facility has been taken, participation has something to offer. Why not pay every possible heed to the intended beneficiaries? But as argued earlier, public authorities cannot simply give the people what they want. Decisions about the scale and direction of government support for recreation often have to be taken with non-recreational criteria in mind. The politicians and officials involved in public recreation are responsible to a wider public than the users of whatever facilities they are managing.

Probably the most radical proposals for extending participation have arisen in Europe alongside the concept of *animation,* a term for which there is no satisfactory English equivalent.

'*Animation is a new term applied to an age-old process. It is a process in which individuals, small groups or larger communities are activated or animated to create for themselves or their neighbours improved social, physical, cultural or emotional settings. Sometimes described as "socio-cultural community development", animation refers to purposeful activity on the part of the community itself to bring about change or improvement rather than passive acceptance of the "status quo" or reliance on outside agents or agencies.*[18] *The role of the animateur involves actively encouraging and indeed cajoling those who make little use of existing facilities to express their "needs" so that they can be catered for. With this idea goes the suggestion that leisure should not be mere idleness but a positive process of learning, expressing oneself or participating in some way as part of the community.'* [19]

Animation has been debated most extensively in relation to the arts. Whereas the 'establishment' has sought a democratisation of culture, diffusing appreciation of the traditional arts, advocates of cultural democracy seek to recognise and awaken the artistic creativity of the millions and have embraced the strategy of animation. As Baldry has argued, cultural democracy and the democratisation of culture are not necessarily alternative and incompatible objectives,[20] but in a world of scarce resources the case for grassroots community art must inevitably be argued against competitive claims.

Needless to say, animation's relevance is not confined to the arts. The concept is close to what in Britain are referred to as community work and development. Community workers encourage residents in particular neighbourhoods to articulate their aspirations and bring consequent pressure upon the authorities. Critics have noted that both community work and animation can be politically subversive, but this is not necessarily an objection. As regards leisure, animation is a highly relevant concept for it acknowledges that the preferences of particular groups cannot be known in advance and that, once articulated, they might stretch beyond the bounds of recreation as conventionally defined. In serving minority and other disadvantaged groups, whose interests may differ from tastes in mainstream culture, animation appears a particularly appropriate strategy.

Sceptics may query whether citizens equipped with their own purchasing power might not be a better guarantee of participation than subsidised animateurs, but this mistakes the intentions of animation. Improvisation and creativity are naturally-occurring processes. We have previously seen how evident they are in family life and the youth culture, and the aim of animation is not to supply an artificial stimulus but to relate these natural processes to public provision.

While acknowledging its value, however, it is necessary to appreciate that animation is not always relevant. Sometimes the facilities available for public use are predetermined, as in the case of sports resources provided primarily for the use of schools. And once any facility is in existence it requires competent management. Animation may be commendable, but it is not the sole route to participation, nor can participation be the sole consideration in administering recreational resources. Furthermore, while encouraging people to articulate their interests and wants may be desirable, it is misleading to create the impression that the public authorities will always deliver the goods. Once animated, interests must often be expressed through the commercial sector or voluntary effort. Government bodies cannot guarantee to service whatever recreational interests the public happens to express. Animation and other schemes to enlarge participation are admirable strategies in implementing public policy, but in themselves they cannot set the parameters within which public enterprise must operate. In so far as it involves scope for choice and allows the development of life-styles reflecting the public's varied interests, participation is inherent in leisure. Democratising public provision is therefore desirable, but participation cannot be limited to implementing whatever leisure services are furnished by government bodies.

If public provision remains close to the guidelines suggested earlier, and if initiatives within these guidelines make use of the appropriate participatory strategies, the public-at-large will not only reap good value, but the services provided will remain compatible with the nature of leisure. If pursued too strenuously, catering for leisure could become a potent threat to the very area of life it seeks to serve. Leisure means scope for choice, which means that public services and personnel must play enabling rather than prophetic roles, and that leisure policy, if it deserves the term, must be passive rather than indicative. The society with leisure can offer choice and variety to its component publics, and this scope can be left in the hands of ordinary people. This objective is compatible with public provision, but only if its limits and strategies are appropriately tailored.

Education for leisure

As with participation, it is difficult to envisage anyone quarrelling with the idea of education for leisure. Once again, however, it is vital that the objective is not construed too narrowly. There could be no greater mistake than limiting our thinking to school education. Just as observations of leisure's growth often provoke blind calls for more provision, so they excite proposals to educate for leisure in order that individuals shall be made aware of the opportunities that are available, enabled to discriminate, and make satisfying choices in their leisure time. Talk about educating for leisure invariably sounds benign, but as with simple-minded calls for more government provision, it usually deserves a sceptical reception. There are numerous interest groups prepared to leap on to the leisure bandwagon. Many teachers of art, literature, sport and music suspect that they have found a new justification for their traditional fare; they now tell us that they are educating for leisure. No one would oppose the principle of education for leisure. But exactly what is to be taught? Who will decree which activities are worthy of educational endorsement? One can profess agnosticism about which uses of leisure are particularly good, and simply urge that young people be made aware of all the possibilities. This is a satisfying liberal posture, but the idea of introducing schoolchildren to every possible use of leisure is hopelessly impractical.

Whether or not we follow the deschooling proposals, it is difficult to dismiss the deschoolers' arguments that we already ask too much from formal education. We should hesitate before asking the schools to educate for leisure. Formal education has proved less potent in shaping pupils' values and life-styles than many of its supporters originally hoped. If the architects of the 1870 Education Act in Britain had been invited to envisage a time when all young people would receive at least ten years' schooling, and when secondary as well as elementary education would be universal, it is doubtful whether they would have believed that in such a society 'tabloids' would continue to outsell 'quality' newspapers, and that soap operas would be among the most popular television programmes. In Britain there are just two subjects, physical education and religious instruction, that by law must be taught in every state school, and for most young people regular participation in both sport and worship cease the moment their school lives end.[21] Would the schools be more successful if they broadened the recreational curriculum? Some pupils hold their schools in such negative regard that the official promotion of approved recreation could act as a negative recommendation. Moreover, we know from experience that when recreation is assimilated into school education it tends to be in forms that are convenient for the schools irrespective of whether they are likely to prove permanently interesting to the pupils, a case in point being the team games in which an entire class can be occupied under the supervision of a single teacher.

At the moment most recreational skills are learnt outside the schools; at home, in peer groups and local communities. This is where authentic education for leisure occurs – in leisure time, among leisure associates, who are pursuing leisure interests. Education for leisure is best conceived as one aspect of participation in all recreation provision rather than a process that occurs within educational institutions.

Genuine solutions to the challenge of leisure require genuine self-education, and the case argued in Chapters 6 and 9 implies that this is already occurring informally within the youth culture, in families and other places. A previous chapter noted the relationship between social participation and self-rated happiness. The quality of leisure depends at least partly upon individuals' ability to interact with a range of associates, collectively constructing life-styles that they find satisfying. The society with leisure makes this type of interaction possible, and in so far as formal education contributes, it is not so much as a result of what is taught in classrooms as what is learnt in the informal relationships that can be nurtured within schools and colleges which can widen individuals' future social networks and interests. Collective self-education is the only authentic education for leisure because there are no authorities with valid solutions to impose. If there are answers to the challenge of leisure they lie with ordinary people who are endowed with the ability to think and who can relate to each other in novel ways, thereby developing satisfying uses of the opportunities that the growth of leisure affords. Both provision and education for leisure need to be rooted in this interaction.

Leisure values

Thoughts on policy and provision need to keep pace with the manner
in which leisure itself is changing. The opening chapter explained how
the industrial revolution shaped a new type of leisure. By the end of the
nineteenth century, the meaning of leisure had been recast. Rather
than a quality of life as a whole, leisure had become a part of life, and in
the early phases of industrialism it was a compressed and subsidiary
sphere which aroused fears that it might be mis-spent. Fashionable
leisure philosophies of that age stressed the need to fill free time with
worthwhile or at least harmless activities. The devil was believed to
make work for idle hands, and opportunities for recreation were often
confined to the streets and public houses which were widely felt, in
respectable circles, to be full of temptations for vice and delinquency.
Mass leisure was seen as a potential threat to well-being, and this
thinking was enshrined in the early youth movements with their
uniformed and regimented styles. In such deliberate provision for
leisure as was instituted, the emphasis was upon self-discipline,
character-training and controlled competitiveness.

This view of leisure is not yet dead. Sports centres are still justified in
terms of keeping young people off the streets and out of trouble. But
most serious commentators are now demanding more of leisure. A 'fun
ethic' has gained prominence and it has become less controversial than
formerly to propose support for the arts, sport and countryside recreation simply to allow people to enjoy themselves. In recreation provision the emphasis has moved from the control to the quality of life.
Issues are being redefined in terms such as enabling people to be 'at
leisure' in leisure time.[22] The formerly compressed sphere of life has
grown with implications for longer-established institutions, and this
growth has brought new opportunities and dangers. There are dangers
of massification and class domination, but the major problems are
summarised by the concept of anomie. Realising the opportunities
depends upon the potential of leisure being appreciated. Stressing the
need to avoid harmful uses of leisure fails to do justice to the subject.
Pointing to the contribution of recreation facilities to the quality of life
is an improvement. But adequate conceptualisations of leisure need to
encompass and go beyond these statements to grapple with the variety
and improvisation that are now possible in such disparate spheres as
education, the youth culture, the family and the shape of working life.

It is important to recognise them, but it is equally vital not to
overstate the immensity of the changes in process. Society does not
need to be rescued from the verge of collapse by religious or political
zealots, or even by the recreation professions with their state-
sponsored leisure industries. Over-reaction could destroy leisure as we
know it. To exploit the opportunities presented by leisure we do not
need a leisure policy that specifies the end product to be sought and
stipulates means to its attainment. Leisure opens alternative futures.

As a society we could respond to the growth of leisure by charging cadres of recreation professionals with responsibility for filling the public's spare time. We could acquiesce as political, business or religious élites structure the public's life-styles to accord with their own values and interests. These are among the possibilities on the agenda. But before we endorse any of these futures let us realise that there is an alternative. Leisure can be used further to enrich the socio-cultural pluralism that has taken root during the past development of Western societies. This future requires a circumscribed role for public provision and an understanding tolerance rather than alarm at the diversity that leisure permits.

Rather than a comprehensive and stipulative leisure policy, it is more helpful to think in terms of broader values that provide an orientation to action in the society with leisure. The leisure age does not require completely new values, but calls for certain longer-established values to be accorded renewed emphasis; values that together offer a philosophy for the society with leisure. The first value we should emphasise is *hedonism*, the desirability of pleasure. The growth of leisure means that many constraints which have limited pleasure-seeking in the past are no longer necessary. Today pleasure alone can be considered sufficient justification for action without recourse to ulterior motives. Leisure means that individuals can be permitted to pursue their pleasures without the harm resulting that was more likely in times of relative scarcity. If they find them pleasant, individuals can be allowed to use alcohol, other drugs, obtain divorces and enter new marriages. We can afford to rid ourselves of many legal, customary and moral inhibitions that once justifiably limited pleasure-seaking.

The second value is *humanism,* which recognises the variety of experiences that can supply pleasure. The society with leisure can offer its members scope to enjoy all aspects of their natures. Pleasure is not the product solely of sensual and sexual exercises. It is also gained through intellectual, athletic and artistic experiences. The more leisure we have, then the more people can become aware of the full range of their capacities for enjoyment.

The third cardinal value is *liberalism,* acknowledging that each individual is the best judge of what is pleasurable for himself, and that choosing for oneself is an intrinsic quality of leisure. Neither politicians, government bureaucrats nor recreation professionals know how to maximise well-being and sociologists of leisure are no wiser. This is a topic on which the experts should confess their ignorance. Social science can sometimes serve mankind by developing knowledge which is subsequently applied. It can be of equal service, however, when it reminds its audience of what is not known. Like other commentators I cannot prove it, but I also have a hunch that at the moment we are not using our leisure in the most satisfying of all possible ways. I suspect that some of the 19 hours per week with the television could be used to better effect, and that the drives to the countryside that pause only for a stroll around a lay-by could be executed in a more inspiring manner. At the same time, I realise that I cannot recommend alternatives that will satisfy everyone. Nor do I believe that other authorities are any wiser.

The values listed above may appear unbalanced. Why no mention of industry, compassion, altruism and justice? There is no likelihood of leisure becoming synonymous with life in general, and other values will retain relevance in different spheres. But in so far as leisure is growing in importance hedonism, humanism and liberalism deserve renewed emphasis. However individualistic and selfish the list appears when first set out, the society resulting from the application of these values will be a tolerant society. Hedonism, humanism and liberalism require that others be allowed all the freedom that any individual wishes to claim for himself. If we act upon this leisure philosophy, we can develop a social order which not only tolerates but encourages a rich variety of experience.

References

Chapter 1

1. **J. Dumazedier,** *Sociology of Leisure,* Elsevier, Amsterdam, 1974, p. 2.
2. **S. Parker,** *The Sociology of Leisure,* Allen and Unwin, London, 1976, p. 12.
3. **J. Dumazedier,** *op. cit.*
4. **M. Kaplan,** *Leisure: Theory and Policy,* Wiley, New York, 1975, p. 26.
5. See **A. Roadburgh,** 'An enquiry into the meaning of work and leisure', Ph.D. thesis, University of Edinburgh, 1977.
6. **R. W. Malcolmson,** *Popular Recreations in English Society, 1700–1850,* Cambridge U.P., London, 1973, p. 1.
7. **J. Myerscough,** 'The recent history and use of leisure time', in I. Appleton, ed., *Leisure Research and Policy,* Scottish Academic Press, Edinburgh, 1974.
8. **S. de Grazia,** *Of Time, Work and Leisure,* Twentieth Century Fund, New York, 1962.
9. **J. Huizinga,** *Homo Ludens,* Routledge, London, 1949.
10. **R. Callois,** 'The structure and classification of games', *Diogenes,* **12,** 1955, 62–75.
11. **J. W. Keating,** 'Winning in sport and athletics', *Thought,* 1963, 201–10, and 'Sportsmanship as a moral category', *Ethics,* 1964, 25–35.

Chapter 2

1. **H. L. Wilenski,** 'The uneven distribution of leisure: the impact of economic growth on "free time" ', in E. O. Smigel, ed., *Work and Leisure,* College and University Press, New Haven, 1963.
2. **G. Burck,** 'There'll be less leisure than you think', *Fortune,* March 1970.
3. **M. Young** and **P. Willmott,** *The Symmetrical Family,* Routledge, London, 1973.
4. **S. Linder,** *The Harried Leisure Class,* Columbia U.P., New York, 1970.
5. **D. Bell,** *The Coming of Post-Industrial Society,* Basic Books, New York, 1974.
6. **G. Godbey,** 'Anti-leisure and public recreation policy', in S. Parker *et al.,* eds., *Sport and Leisure in Contemporary Society,* Polytechnic of Central London, London, 1975.
7. Organisation for Economic Co-operation and Development, *New Patterns for Working Time,* Paris, 1973.
8. **R. Poor,** *4 Days, 40 Hours,* Pan, London, 1972.
9. **W. D. C. Wright,** 'Some aspects of the economics of leisure', in I. Appleton, ed., *op. cit.* (see ref. 7, Ch. 1.)
10. **M. Young** and **P. Willmott,** *op cit.*
11. BBC TV, *These Young People,* 30 July 1973.
12. **G. Katona** *et al., Aspirations and Affluence,* McGraw-Hill, New York, 1971.
13. See **K. Roberts** *et al.,* 'How many hours in a week?', *Personnel Management,* **6,** 1974, 33–41.
14. **J. M. Kreps,** *Lifetime Allocation of Work and Income,* Duke U.P., North Carolina, 1971.

15. *Ibid.*
16. **M. Kaplan,** *op. cit.* (See ref. 4, Ch. 1.)
17. English Tourist Board and Trades Union Congress, *Holidays: The Social Need,* London, 1976.
18. **Wynford Vaughan Thomas,** addressing the British Mountaineering Conference at Buxton. Reported in *The Guardian,* 29 March 1976.
19. **M. A. Holman,** 'A national time-budget for the year 2000', *Sociology and Social Research,* **46,** 1961.
20. **A. Patmore,** 'The busy world of leisure', *Observer,* 1 December 1974.

Chapter 3

1. **M. Young** and **P. Willmott,** *op. cit.* (See ref. 3, ch. 2.)
2. See **P. Jephcott,** *Time of One's Own,* Oliver and Boyd, Edinburgh, 1967, and **J. Leigh,** *Young People and Leisure,* Routledge, London, 1971.
3. See **R.** and **R. N. Rapoport,** *Leisure and the Family Life-Cycle,* Routledge, London, 1975.
4. British Travel Association/University of Keele, *Pilot National Recreation Survey,* 1967; **K. Sillitoe,** *Planning for Leisure,* HMSO, London, 1969; North-West Sports Council, *Leisure in the North-West,* Salford, 1972.
5. **B. Rodgers,** 'Urbanism, sport and welfare', in M. A. Smith, ed., *Leisure and Urban Society,* Leisure Studies Association, Manchester, 1977.
6. **A. Szalai** *et al., The Use of Time,* Mouton, The Hague, 1972.
7. BBC TV, *Children as Viewers,* London, 1974.
8. **W. Melody,** *Children's TV,* Yale U.P., New Haven, 1973.
9. **M. Bradley** and **D. Fenwick,** *Popular Attitudes to Liquor Licensing Laws in Great Britain,* HMSO, London, 1974.
10. **G. Gorer,** *Sex and Marriage in England Today,* Nelson, London, 1971.
11. **O. Newman,** *Gambling: Hazard and Reward,* Athlone Press, London, 1972.
12. **D. Downes** *et al., Gambling, Work and Leisure,* Routledge, London, 1976.
13. **M. Young** and **P. Willmott,** *op. cit.* (See ref. 3, ch. 2.)
14. **B. Russell,** 'In praise of idleness', in E. Larabee and R. Meyersohn, eds., *Mass Leisure,* Free Press, Glencoe, 1961.
15. **O. Newman,** *op cit.*
16. **M. G. Wilders,** 'Some preliminary observations on the sociology of the public house', in S. Parker *et al.,* eds., *op. cit.* (See ref. 6, ch. 2.)
17. **J. White** and **M. Dunn,** *Recreational Use of the Countryside: A Case Study in the West Midlands,* Research memorandum 33, Centre for Urban and Regional Studies, University of Birmingham, 1974.
18. Reported in *Sunday Times,* 18 April 1976.
19. *Ibid.*
20. **M. Elson,** 'The weekend car', *New Society,* 11 April 1974.
21. **W. R. Burch,** Jr., 'Facilities of leisure and recreation behaviour in an ecological view', Paper presented to the third biennial conference of the International Society for the Study of Behavioural Development, Guildford, 1975.
22. **N. Cheek** *et al., Leisure and Recreation Places,* Ann Arbor Science, Michigan, 1976.
23. For evidence see, for example, South-West Economic Planning Council, *Economic Survey of the Tourist Industry in the South-West,* HMSO, London, 1976.
24. See **J. Walvin,** *The People's Game,* Allen Lane, London, 1975.
25. **L. Turner** and **J. Ash,** *The Golden Hordes,* Constable, London, 1975, p. 42.
26. *Ibid.* p. 43.
27. As observed in **I. G. Simmons,** *Rural Recreation in the Industrial World,* Edward Arnold, London, 1975.
28. See **I. Emmett,** 'The social filter in the leisure field', *Recreation News Supplement,* **4,** 1971, 7–8.

29. **N.** and **J. Parry**, 'Theories of culture and leisure', and **M. A. Smith**, ed., *op. cit.*
30. **E. Bammel**, 'Wilderness and urban society', in **M. A. Smith**, ed., *op. cit.*
31. **K. Roberts** *et al., The Character-Training Industry,* David and Charles, Newton Abbot, 1974.
32. **R.** and **R. N. Rapoport,** *op. cit.*
33. See **M. Abrams**, 'Quality of life studies', in **M. A. Smith**, ed., *op. cit.*
34. *Ibid.*
35. **D. R. Dunn**, 'Recreation in the urbanising world: no models to mimic', *Society and Leisure,* 1976.
36. **J. Hall** and **N. Perry,** *Aspects of Leisure in Two Industrial Cities,* Occasional papers in survey research, **5,** SSRC, London, 1974.

Chapter 4

1. **B. Groombridge,** *Television and the People,* Penguin, Harmondsworth, 1972.
2. **P. Golding,** *The Mass Media,* Longman, London, 1974.
3. **A. J. Lee,** *The Origins of the Popular Press 1855–1914,* Croom Helm, London, 1976.
4. **J. Tunstall,** *The Media are American,* Constable, London, 1977.
5. **S. Giner,** *Mass Society,* Martin Robertson, London, 1976.
6. **P. Golding,** *op. cit.,* p. 2.
7. **B. Rosenberg**, 'Mass culture revisited', in B. Rosenberg and D. M. White, eds., *Mass Culture Revisited,* Van Nostrand Reinhold, New York, 1971.
8. **S. Hood**, 'The politics of television', in D. McQuail, ed., *Sociology of Mass Communication,* Penguin, Harmondsworth, 1972.
9. **H. L. Wilenski**, 'Mass society and mass culture: interdependence or independence', *American Sociological Review,* **29,** 1964, 173–97.
10. **E. van den Haag**, 'A dissent from the consensual society', in B. Rosenberg and D. M. White, eds., *op. cit.*
11. **M. McCluhan** and **Q. Fiore,** *The Medium is the Message,* Penguin, Harmondsworth, 1967.
12. **J. Galtung** and **M. H. Ruge**, 'The structure of foreign news', in J. Tunstall, ed., *Media Sociology,* Constable, London, 1970.
13. **J. Bensman** and **R. Lilienfield**, 'The journalistic attitude', in B. Rosenberg and D. M. White, eds., *op. cit.*
14. **D. Halloran** *et al., Demonstrations and Communication,* Penguin, Harmondsworth, 1970.
15. **J. Whale,** *The Half-Shut Eye,* Macmillan, London, 1969. See also **J. Whale,** *The Politics of the Media,* Fontana, London, 1977.
16. **P. Elliott**, 'Selection and communication in a television production – a case study', in J. Tunstall, ed., *op. cit.*
17. See **J. Tunstall,** *The Westminster Lobby Correspondents,* Routledge, London, 1970.
18. *Ibid.*
19. **T. Burns,** *The BBC,* Macmillan, London, 1977.
20. **J. Tunstall,** *Journalists at Work,* Constable, London, 1971.
21. See **P. Golding,** *op. cit.*
22. **L. Taylor** and **K. Williams**, 'The actor and his world', *New Society,* 29 July 1971.
23. **H. Smith,** *The Russians,* Times Books, London, 1976, p. 175.
24. *Ibid.* p. 173.
25. **B. Groombridge,** *op. cit.*
26. **A. Clayre**, 'The media and cultural change', in M. A. Smith, ed., *op. cit.* (See ref. 5, ch. 3.)
27. These arguments are developed in **A. Clayre,** *op. cit.* (See ref. 5, ch. 3.)
28. *Ibid.*

29. U. **Bronfenbrenner**, *Two Worlds of Childhood, USA and USSR*, Allen and Unwin, London, 1971.
30. **R. Williams**, *Culture and Society*, Chatto and Windus, 1958, and **R. Williams**, *The Long Revolution*, Chatto and Windus, London, 1961.
31. **R. Hoggart**, *The Uses of Literacy*, Chatto and Windus, London, 1957.
32. **J. Baggaley** and **S. Duck**, *Dynamics of Television*, Saxon House, Farnborough, 1976.
33. See **D. McQuail**, 'The television audience: a revised perspective', in D. McQuail, ed., *op. cit*; and **J. Curran** and **J. Tunstall**, 'Mass media and leisure', in M. A. Smith *et al.*, eds., *Leisure and Society in Britain*, Allen Lane, London, 1973.
34. **J. B. Carey**, 'Changing courtship patterns in the popular song', in R. S. Denisoff and R. A. Petersen, eds., *The Sounds of Social Change*, Rand McNally, Chicago, 1972.
35. **P. Robinson** and **P. M. Hirsch**, 'Teenage response to rock and roll protest songs'; and **R. S. Denisoff** and **M. Levine**, 'Brainwashing or background noise; the popular protest song', both in R. S. Denisoff and R. A. Petersen, eds., *op. cit.*
36. **R. A. Petersen** and **D. G. Berger,** 'Three eras in the manufacture of popular music lyrics', in **R. S. Denisoff** and **R. A. Petersen,** eds., *op. cit.*
37. **H. J. Gans**, 'Popular culture in America', in **H. S. Becker**, ed., *Social Problems: a Modern Approach*, Wiley, New York, 1961.
38. **E. Shils**, 'Mass society and its culture', in B. Rosenberg and D. M. White, eds., *op. cit.*
39. **R. Hoggart**, *op. cit.*
40. **R. Williams**, *Culture and Society, op. cit;* and *The Long Revolution, op. cit.*
41. **S. Hall** and **P. Whennel**, *The Popular Arts*, Hutchinson, London, 1964.
42. **H. J. Gans**, *op. cit.*
43. See **R. W. Malcolmson**, *op. cit.* (See ref. 6, ch. 1.)
44. **D. F. Wright**, 'Musical meaning and its social determinants', *Sociology*, **9**, 1975, 419–35. See also **H. S. Becker**, 'Art as collective action', *American Sociological Review*, **39**. 1974, 767–76.
45. **J. Clarke**, 'Framing the arts', Paper presented at the *Symposium on Sport and Leisure*, Polytechnic of Central London, 1975.
46. *Ibid.*
47. **D. L. Phillips**, 'Social participation and happiness', *American Journal of Sociology*, **72**, 1967, 479–88.
48. See **J. Myerscough**, *op. cit.* (See ref. 7, ch. 1.)
49. These and the following figures are taken from **B. Silcock**, 'Anatomy of the British Boozer', *Sunday Times*, 18 December 1977.
50. *New Survey of London Life and Labour*, Vol 9, *Life and Leisure*, King, London, 1935.
51. **W. A. Belson**, *The Impact of Television*, Crosby Lockwood, London, 1967.
52. **R. Meyersohn**, 'Television viewing and other uses of leisure', *Public Opinion Quarterly*, **32**, 1968, 102–11.
53. **K. E. Rosengren** and **S. Windahl**, 'Mass media consumption as a functional alternative', in D. McQuail, ed., *op. cit.*
54. **C. J. Goodhardt** *et al.*, *The Television Audience, Saxon House, Farnborough, 1975.*
55. **D. McQuail**, 'The television audience: a revised perspective', *op. cit.*
56. See **R. A.** and **A. H. Bauer**, 'America, mass society and mass media', *Journal of Social Issues*, **16**, 1960, 3.
57. **S. Giner**, *op. cit.*

Chapter 5

1. Classic statements of this type of argument are to be found in **D. Bell**, *The End of Ideology*, Free Press, New York, 1960; **C. A. R. Crosland**, *The Future of Socialism*, Cape, London, 1956; **R. Dahrendorf**, *Class and Class Conflict in Industrial*

Society, Routledge, London, 1959; **S. M. Lipset,** *Political Man,* Doubleday, New York, 1960.

2. For proper expositions of this case see **J. Foster,** *Class Struggle in the Industrial Revolution,* Weidenfeld and Nicholson, London, 1974; **R. Miliband,** *The State in Capitalist Society,* Weidenfeld and Nicolson, London, 1969; **H. F. Moorhouse,** 'The political incorporation of the British working class', *Sociology,* **7,** 1973, 341–59.
3. **S. Chibnall,** 'The crime reporter', *Sociology,* **9,** 1975, 49–66.
4. **D. Murphy,** *The Silent Watchdog,* Constable, London, 1976.
5. **J. Whale,** *The Half-Shut Eye, op. cit.* (See ref. 15, ch. 4.)
6. **S. Hood,** *op. cit.* (See ref. 8, ch. 4.)
7. **P. Morley,** 'Industrial conflict and the mass media', *Sociological Review,* **24,** 1976, 245–68.
8. Glasgow University Media Research Group, *Bad News,* Routledge, London, 1976.
9. **W. Braden,** 'LSD and the press', in S. Cohen and J. Young, eds., *The Manufacture of News,* Constable, London, 1973.
10. See **J. Young,** *The Drugtakers,* MacGibbon and Kee, London, 1971.
11. Aims of Industry, *Television and Industry,* London, 1972.
12. **A. Jay,** 'What's to become of the BBC?' *Sunday Times,* 19 November 1972.
13. **T. Lane** and **K. Roberts,** *Strike at Pilkingtons,* Fontana, London, 1971.
14. **M. Warner,** 'Organisational context and control of policy in the television newsroom', *British Journal of Sociology,* **22,** 1971, 283–94.
15. **J. Tunstall,** *The Westminster Lobby Correspondents, op. cit.* (See ref. 17, ch. 4.)
16. **K. Kumar,** 'Holding the middle ground', *Sociology,* **9,** 1975, 67–88.
17. **P. Morley,** *op. cit.*
18. **S. Cohen** and **J. Young,** eds., *op. cit.*
19. **J. Young,** *op. cit.*
20. **S. Cohen,** *Folk Devils and Moral Panics,* MacGibbon and Kee, London, 1972.
21. **J. D. Halloran** *et al., op. cit.* (See ref. 14, ch. 4.)
22. See **J. Hargreaves,** 'The political economy of mass sport', in S. Parker *et al.,* eds., *op. cit.* (See ref. 6, ch. 2.)
23. **J. Young,** *op. cit.*
24. **W. Bacon,** 'Social caretaking and leisure provision', in S. Parker *et al.,* eds., *op. cit.* (See ref. 6, ch. 2.)
25. **H. W. Morton,** 'Soviet sport in the 1960s', in J. W. Loy and G. S. Kenyon, eds., *Sport, Culture and Society,* Macmillan, New York, 1969.
26. **B. M. Petrie,** 'Sport and politics', in D. W. Ball and J. W. Loy, eds., *Sport and Social Order,* Addison-Wesley, Mass., 1975.
27. **R. Williams,** *Television: Technology and Cultural Form,* Fontana, London, 1974.
28. **R. S. Gruneau,** 'Sport, social differentiation and social inequality', in D. W. Ball and J. W. Loy, eds., *op. cit.*
29. See **B. M. Petrie,** *op. cit;* and **G. H. Sage,** 'An occupational analysis of the college coach', in D. W. Ball and J. W. Loy, eds., *op. cit.*
30. **P. Bourdieu** and **J. C. Passerson,** *Reproduction in Education, Society and Culture,* Sage, London, 1977. See also **G. Murdock,** 'Class stratification and cultural consumption', in M. A. Smith, ed., *op. cit.* (See ref. 5, ch. 3.)
31. **P. Bourdieu** and **J. C. Passerson,** *op. cit.,* p. 5.
32. *Ibid.,* p. 4.
33. *Ibid.,* pp. 152–3.
34. See **S. Hall** and **T. Jefferson,** eds., *Resistance Through Rituals,* Hutchinson, London, 1975, and G. Mungham and G. Pearson, eds., *Working Class Youth Culture,* Routledge, London, 1976.
35. **G. Murdock,** 'Culture and classlessness: the making and unmaking of a contemporary myth', in J. Haworth and M. A. Smith, eds., *Work and Leisure,* Lepus Books, London, 1975.
36. **P. Willis,** *Learning to Labour,* Saxon House, Farnborough, 1977.
37. **S. Cohen,** *op. cit.*

38. **G. Murdock,** 'Culture and classlessness', *op. cit.*
39. **P. Cohen,** 'Subcultural conflicts and working class community', in M. Hammersley and P. Woods, ed., *The Process of Schooling,* Routledge, London, 1976.
40. **C. Wright-Mills,** *White Collar,* Galaxy, New York, 1956, p. xvii.
41. **L. Pearson,** 'You've got to be happy', Unpublished manuscript, University of Birmingham, 1976.
42. **A. C. Ingham,** 'Occupational subcultures in the work-world of sport', in D. W. Ball and J. W. Loy, eds., *op. cit.* See also **R. K. Haerle,** 'Career patterns and career contingencies of professional baseball players: an occupational analysis', in D. W. Ball and J. W. Loy, eds., *op. cit.*
43. See the contributions in **S. Cohen,** ed., *Images of Deviance, Penguin, Harmondsworth, 1971. For an application of these arguments to the youth culture see* **P. Willis,** *op. cit.*

Chapter 6

1. Albermarle Report, *The Youth Service in England and Wales,* HMSO, London, 1960.
2. **H. L. Dunlop,** 'Games, sports, dancing and other vigorous recreational activities and their function in Samoan culture', in J. W. Loy and G. S. Kenyon, eds., *op. cit.* (See ref. 25, ch. 5.)
3. **J. M. Roberts** and **B. Sutton-Smith,** 'Child-training and game involvement'; **B. Sutton-Smith, J. M. Roberts** and **R. M. Kozelka,** 'Game involvement in adults', both in J. W. Loy and G. S. Kenyon, *op. cit.* (See ref. 25, ch. 5.)
4. **E. Gross,** 'A functional approach to leisure analysis', in E. O. Smigel, ed., *op. cit.* (See ref. 1, ch. 2.)
5. **P. Gardner,** *Nice Guys Finish Last,* Allen Lane, London, 1974.
6. **J. A. Patmore,** *Land and Leisure,* Penguin, Harmondsworth, 1972.
7. **C. S. Van Doren** and **L. Hodges,** *America's Park and Recreation Heritage,* US Department of the Interior, Washington, 1975.
8. English Tourist Board and Trades Union Congress, *Holidays: The Social Need,* London, 1976.
9. **C. Smith,** 'The emergence of leisure as a policy issue for central government and the administrative response', in S. Parker and J. Haworth, eds., *Leisure and Public Policy,* Leisure Studies Association, University of Birmingham, 1975.
10. **G. Godbey** and **S. Parker,** *Leisure Studies and Services, an Overview,* Saunders, Philadelphia, 1976.
11. **M. Blaug** and **K. King,** 'Is the Arts Council cost-effective?' *New Society,* 3 January 1974.
12. **S. Mennell,** *Cultural Policy in Towns,* Council of Europe, Strasbourg, 1976.
13. **E. Derrick** *et al., Schoolchildren and Leisure: Interim Report,* Working paper 19, Centre for Urban and Regional Studies, University of Birmingham, 1973.
14. **I. R. Taylor,** 'Soccer consciousness and soccer hooliganism', in S. Cohen, ed., *Images of Deviance,* Penguin, Harmondsworth, 1971.
15. **N. Petryszak,** 'The appeal of violence in spectator sport – a bio-social perspective,' in M. A. Smith, ed., *op. cit.* (See ref. 5, ch. 3.)
16. See **K. Roberts** *et al., The Fragmentary Class Structure,* Heinemann, London, 1977.
17. **P. Bandyopadhyay,** 'The holiday camp', in M. A. Smith *et al.,* eds., *Leisure and Society in Britain,* Allen Lane, London, 1973.
18. **D. Dallas,** *The Travelling People,* Macmillan, London, 1971.
19. **I. Cullen,** 'A day in the life of . . .' *New Society,* 11 April 1974.
20. **L. Srole,** 'Social integration and certain corollaries: an exploratory study', *American Sociological Review,* **21,** 1956, 709–16.
21. **E. Durkheim,** *The Division of Labour in Society,* Free Press, New York, 1964.
22. **H. Cohen,** 'The anomia of success and the anomia of failure', *British Journal of Sociology,* **23,** 1972, 229–43.

23. **N. Anderson,** *Work and Leisure,* Routledge, London, 1967.
24. **C. Davies,** *Permissive Britain,* Pitman, London, 1975.
25. **R. Glasser,** *Leisure: Penalty or Prize,* Macmillan, London, 1970; and 'A case of robot's cramp', *Guardian,* 1 February 1974.
26. **J. Raban,** *Soft City,* Hamish Hamilton, London, 1974, p. 245.
27. *Ibid.,* p. 9.
28. *Ibid.,* p. 245.
29. **R. Sennett,** *The Uses of Disorder,* Penguin, Harmondsworth, 1973.
30. **J. Jacobs,** *The Death and Life of Great American Cities,* Random House, New York, 1961.
31. **J. Haworth,** 'Leisure and the individual', in S. Parker *et al.,* eds., *op. cit.* (See ref. 6, ch. 2.)

Chapter 7

1. **R.** and **R. N. Rapoport,** *op. cit.* (See ref. 3, ch. 3.)
2. This investigation was conducted with financial support from the Social Science Research Council.
3. **C. Bell** and **P. Healey,** 'The family and leisure', in M. A. Smith *et al.,* eds., *Leisure and Society in Britain, op. cit.* (See ref. 17, ch. 6.)
4. **I. Cullen,** *op. cit.* (See ref. 19, ch. 6.)
5. **H. Gavron,** *The Captive Wife,* Routledge, London, 1966.
6. **N. C. A. Parry** and **D. Johnson,** *Leisure and Social Structure,* Hatfield Polytechnic, 1974.
7. **A. Booth,** 'Sex and social participation', *American Sociological Review,* **37,** 1972, 183–92.
8. **R.** and **R. N. Rapoport,** *op cit.* (See ref. 3, ch. 3.)
9. **K. Sillitoe,** *Planning for Leisure,* HMSO, London, 1969.
10. **N. C. A. Parry** and **D. Johnson,** *op cit.*
11. Including **C. Bell** and **P. Healey,** *op. cit.* (See ref. 17, ch. 6.)
12. **J. Platt,** 'Some problems in measuring the jointness of conjugal relationships', *Sociology,* **3,** 1969, 287–97.

Chapter 8

1. **A. Giddens,** 'Notes on the concepts of play and leisure', *Sociological Review,* **12,** 1964, 73.
2. **P. Golding,** *op. cit.,* p. 15. (See ref. 2, ch. 4.)
3. **E. Hughes,** 'Work and the self', in J. H. Rohrer and M. Sherif, eds., *Social Psychology at the Crossroads,* Harper and Row, New York, 1951.
4. See **R. Sennett** and **J. Cobb,** *The Hidden Injuries of Class,* Random House, New York, 1972.
5. **P. Berger** *et al., The Homeless Mind,* Penguin, Harmondsworth, 1973.
6. **P. Berger,** *The Human Shape of Work,* Macmillan, New York, 1964.
7. **H. L. Wilenski,** 'Work as a social problem', in H. S. Becker, ed., *op. cit.* (See ref. 37, ch. 4.)
8. **G. Friedmann,** *The Anatomy of Work,* Heinemann, London, 1961.
9. **S. Parker,** *The Future of Work and Leisure,* MacGibbon and Kee, London, 1971.
10. **G. Salaman,** 'Two occupational communities: examples of a remarkable convergence of work and non-work', *Sociological Review,* **19,** 1971, 389–407. See also G. Salaman, *Community and Occupation,* Cambridge U.P., London, 1974.
11. **J. Dumazedier,** *op. cit.,* p. 26. (See ref. 1, ch. 1.)
12. *Ibid.,* p. 122.
13. *Ibid.,* p. 121.

14. **H. Gavron,** *op. cit.* (See ref. 5, ch. 7.)
15. **F. Musgrove,** *The Migratory Elite,* Heinemann, London, 1963.
16. **P. Mann,** 'Survey of a theatre audience: findings', *British Journal of Sociology,* **18,** 1967, 75.
17. **A. Clayre,** *Work and Play,* Weidenfeld and Nicolson, London, 1975.
18. **P. D. Anthony,** *The Ideology of Work,* Tavistock, London, 1977.
19. **D. Bell,** *The Cultural Contradictions of Capitalism,* Heinemann, London, 1976.
20. *Ibid.,* p. 53.
21. *Ibid.,* pp. 71–2.

Chapter 9

1. **J. Myerscough,** *op. cit.* (See ref. 7, ch. 1.)
2. **M. Elson,** *op. cit.,* and **E. H. Scheuch,** 'Family cohesion in leisure time', *Sociological Review,* **8,** 1960, 37–61.
3. **N. Foote,** 'Sex as play', *Social Problems,* **1,** 1954, 159–63. See also **G. Godbey and S. Parker,** *op. cit.* (See ref. 10, ch. 6.)
4. **G. Gorer,** *Sex and Marriage in England Today,* Nelson, London, 1971.
5. **M. Schofield,** *The Sexual Behaviour of Young Adults,* Allen Lane, London, 1973.
6. See **R. O. Blood** and **D. M. Wolfe,** *Husbands and Wives,* Free Press, New York, 1965.
7. **M. Young** and **P. Willmott,** *op. cit.* (See ref. 3, ch. 2.)
8. **R.** and **R. N. Rapoport,** *Dual Career Families,* Penguin, Harmondsworth, 1971.
9. **M. Mead,** *Male and Female,* Penguin, Harmondsworth, 1962.
10. **R. Collins,** 'A Conflict theory of sexual stratification', *Social Problems,* **19,** 1971, 3–21.
11. **H. Z. Lopata,** *Occupation Housewife,* Oxford U.P., New York, 1971.
12. **A. Oakley,** *The Sociology of Housework,* Martin Robertson, London, 1974.
13. **M. Young** and **P. Willmott,** *Family and Kinship in East London,* Routledge, London, 1957; **C. Bell,** *Middle Class Families,* Routledge, London, 1968.
14. **R. Firth** *et al., Families and their Relatives,* Routledge, London, 1969.
15. **M. Abrams,** *The Teenage Consumer,* London Press Exchange, London, 1961; **N. Millward,** 'Family status and behaviour at work', *Sociological Review,* **16,** 1968, 149–64.
16. **D. Barker,** 'Young people and their homes', *Sociological Review,* **20,** 1972, 569–90.
17. **G. Murdock,** 'Culture and classlessness: the making and unmaking of a contemporary myth', *op. cit.* (See ref. 35, ch. 5.)
18. **K. Fogelman,** ed., *Britain's Sixteen Year Olds,* National Children's Bureau, London, 1976.
19. **D. Barker,** *op. cit.*
20. **R. Mills,** *Young Outsiders,* Routledge, London, 1973; **A. Rigby,** *Alternative Realities,* Routledge, London, 1974.
21. **C. Reich,** *The Greening of America,* Penguin, Harmondsworth, 1972.
22. **F. Musgrove,** *Ecstasy and Holiness,* Methuen, London, 1974.
23. *Ibid.,* p. 19.
24. *Ibid.,* p. 115.
25. **E. Derrick** *et al., op. cit.* (See ref. 13, ch. 6.)
26. **D. Jary,** 'Evenings at the ivory tower', in M. A. Smith *et al.,* eds., *Leisure and Society in Britain, op. cit.* (See ref. 33, ch. 4.)
27. **G. Swift,** 'An approach to leisure: satisfying wants not needs', in J. Haworth and A. J. Veal, eds., *Leisure and the Community,* Leisure Studies Association, University of Birmingham, 1976.
28. **C. Jencks** *et al., Inequality,* Allen Lane, London, 1973.
29. **F. Musgrove,** *op. cit.*

30 This trend towards flexibility is evident in all the advanced industrial societies. The OECD report, *New Patterns of Working Time,* Paris, 1973, notes the international reduction in working hours, and also notes and generally approves the growth of choice in the number of hours that individuals work each day, week, year and throughout their life-times.
31. **E. Clarke,** 'Life at the middle', *New Society,* 11 January 1973.
32. **C. Davies,** *op. cit.* (See ref. 24, ch. 6.)

Chapter 10

1. **T. Burns,** 'Leisure in industrial society', in M. A. Smith *et al.,* eds., *Leisure and Society in Britain, op. cit.* (See ref. 33, ch. 4.)
2. **A. W. Bacon,** 'The embarrassed self', *Society and Leisure,* **4,** 1972, 23–39.
3. **M. Kaplan,** *op. cit.,* p. 216. (See ref. 4, ch. 1.)
4. **J. Dumazedier,** *op. cit.,* p. 240. (See ref. 1, ch. 1.)
5. *Ibid.,* p. 42.
6. **O. Newman,** 'Leisure and life-style', *Ontario Psychologist,* **8,** 1976, 28–34.
7. **L. Turner** and **J. Ash,** *The Golden Hordes,* Constable, London, 1975.
8. *Ibid.,* p. 14.
9. **J. Young,** *op. cit.* (See ref. 10, ch. 5.)
10. **W. K. Richmond,** Foreword to **T. Husen,** *The Learning Society,* Methuen, London, 1974.
11. See **R. K. Brown** *et al.,* 'Leisure in work', in M. A. Smith *et al.,* eds., *Leisure and Society in Britain, op. cit.* (See ref. 33, ch. 4.)
12. See **P. Warr** and **T. Wall,** *Work and Well-being,* Penguin, Harmondsworth, 1975; **N. A. B. Wilson,** *On the Quality of Working Life,* Manpower paper No 7, Department of Employment, London, 1973; **A. B. Cherns** and **L. E. Davis,** eds., *The Quality of Working Life,* 2 Vols, Free Press, New York, 1976.
13. **H. L. Wilenski,** 'Work as a social problem', *op. cit.* (See ref. 7, ch. 8.)
14. **A. Fox,** 'The meaning of work', in *Occupational Categories and Cultures,* DE 351, Open University, Milton Keynes, 1976.
15. See **H. Beynon,** *Working for Ford,* E. P. Publishing, Wakefield, 1975.
16. **J. H. Goldthorpe** *et al.,* *The Affluent Worker, Vol 1. Industrial Attitudes and Behaviour,* Cambridge U.P., London, 1968.
17. **J. K. Galbraith,** *The Age of Uncertainty,* BBC/Andre Deutsch, London, 1977, pp. 329–30.
18. **D. Ravitch,** *The Great School Wars,* Basic Books, New York, 1974.
19. **A. W. Bacon,** 'Parent power and professional control', *Sociological Review,* **24,** 1976, 577–97.
20. **R. Wippler,** 'Private and public modes of spending leisure and their relevance for ecological problems', Paper presented to the *Third Biennial Conference of the ISSBD,* Guildford, 1975.
21. **D. Lane,** *The Socialist Industrial State,* Allen and Unwin, London, 1976; **M. Matthews,** *Class and Society in Soviet Russia,* Allen Lane, London, 1972.
22. **R. E. Miles,** *Awakening from the American Dream,* Marion Boyars/Open Forum, London, 1977.
23. **F. Hirsch,** *The Social Limits to Growth,* Routledge, London, 1977.
24. **D. Bell,** *The Cultural Contradictions of Capitalism, op. cit.* (See ref. 19, ch. 8.)
25. **D. Bell,** *The Coming of Post-Industrial Society, op. cit.* (See ref. 5, ch. 2.)

Chapter 11

1. **S. Mennell,** *op. cit.* (See ref. 12, ch. 6.)

2. **F. M. M. Lewes** and **S. J. Mennell,** *Leisure, Culture and Local Government,* University of Exeter, 1976.

3. For example, see **M. Blaug** and **K. King,** *op. cit.* (See ref. 11, ch. 6.)

4. **S. Mennell,** *op. cit.* (See ref. 12, ch. 6.)

5. **D. R. Dunn,** *op. cit.* (See ref. 35, ch. 3.)

6. **J. Hall** and **N. Perry,** *op. cit.* (See ref. 36, ch. 3.)

7. **L. F. Pearson,** 'Working class non-work time and social policy', in J. Haworth and A. J. Veal, eds., *op. cit.* (See ref. 27, ch. 9.)

8. See **S. Mennell,** *op. cit.* (See ref. 12, ch. 6.)

9. See **I. M. Seeley,** *Outdoor Recreation and the Urban Environment,* Macmillan, London 1973; **G. A. C. Searle,** ed., *Recreational Economics and Analysis,* Longman, London, 1975.

10. **G. Swift,** *op. cit.* (See ref. 27, ch. 9.)

11. **R.** and **R. N. Rapoport,** *Leisure and the Family Life-Cycle, op. cit.* (See ref. 3, ch. 3.)

12. **B. Gillinson,** 'The problems of designing for leisure', in J. Haworth and M. A. Smith, eds., *op. cit.* (See ref. 27, ch. 9.)

13. **J. L. Crompton,** 'Problems of provision and planning in leisure', in J. Haworth and M. A. Smith, eds., *op. cit.* (See ref. 35, ch. 5.)

14. See **G. Swift,** *op. cit.* (See ref. 27, ch. 9.)

15. As noted by **F. M. M. Lewes** and **S. J. Mennell,** *op. cit.*

16. **J. Murphy** *et al., Leisure Delivery Systems: a Modern Perspective,* Lea and Febiger, Philadelphia, 1973, p. 206.

17. *Ibid.,* p. 78.

18. **A. Kingsbury,** 'Animation', in J. Haworth and A. J. Veal, eds., *op. cit.* (See ref. 27, ch. 9.)

19. **F. M. M. Lewes** and **S. J. Mennell,** *op. cit.,* p. 9.

20. **H. C. Baldry,** 'Community arts', in J. Haworth and A. J. Veal, eds., *op cit.* (See ref. 27, ch. 9.)

21. See **I. Emmett,** *Youth and Leisure in an Urban Sprawl,* Manchester U.P., 1971.

22. **J. Murphy,** *Concepts of Leisure,* Prentice-Hall, New Jersey, 1974.

Bibliography

Note: *op. cit.* refers to references listed in this bibliography.

M. **Abrams,** *The Teenage Consumer,* London Press Exchange, London, 1961.

M. **Abrams,** 'Quality of life studies', in M. A. Smith, ed., *Leisure and the Urban Society, op. cit.*

Aims of Industry, *Television and Industry,* London, 1972.

Albermarle Report, *The Youth Service in England and Wales,* HMSO, London, 1960.

N. **Anderson,** *Work and Leisure,* Routledge, London, 1967.

P. D. **Anthony,** *The Ideology of Work,* Tavistock, London, 1977.

I. **Appleton,** ed., *Leisure Research and Policy,* Scottish Academic Press, Edinburgh, 1974.

BBC TV, *These Young People,* 30 July 1973.

BBC TV, *Children as Viewers,* London, 1974.

A. W. **Bacon,** 'Parent power and professional control', *Sociological Review,* **24,** 1976, 577–97.

A. W. **Bacon,** 'The embarrassed self', *Society and Leisure,* **4,** 1972, 23–39.

A. W. **Bacon,** 'Social caretaking and leisure provision', in S. Parker *et al.,* eds, *op. cit.*

J. **Baggaley** and S. **Duck,** *Dynamics of Television,* Saxon House, Farnborough, 1976.

H. C. **Baldry,** 'Community arts', in J. Haworth and A. J. Veal, eds., *op. cit.*

D. W. **Ball** and J. W. **Loy,** eds., *Sport and Social Order,* Addison-Wesley, Mass., 1975.

E. C. **Bammel,** 'Wilderness and urban society', in M. A. Smith, ed., *Leisure and Urban Society, op. cit.*

P. **Bandyopadhyay,** 'The holiday camp', in M. A. Smith *et al.,* eds., *Leisure and Society in Britain, op. cit.*

D. **Barker,** 'Young people and their homes', *Sociological Review,* **20,** 1972, 569–90.

R. A. **Bauer** and A. H. **Bauer,** 'America, mass society and mass media', *Journal of Social Issues,* 1960, **16,** 3.

H. S. **Becker,** 'Art as collective action', *American Sociological Review,* **39,** 1974, 767–76.

C. **Bell,** *Middle Class Families,* Routledge, London, 1968.

C. **Bell** and P. **Healey.** 'The family and leisure', in M. A. Smith *et al.,* eds., *Leisure and Society in Britain, op. cit.*

D. **Bell,** *The End of Ideology,* Free Press, New York, 1960.

D. **Bell,** *The Coming of Post-Industrial Society,* Basic Books, New York, 1974.

D. **Bell,** *The Cultural Contradictions of Capitalism,* Heinemann, London, 1976.

W. A. **Belson,** *The Impact of Television,* Crosby Lockwood, London, 1967.

J. **Bensman** and R. **Lilienfield,** 'The journalistic attitude', in B. Rosenberg and D. M. White, eds., *op. cit.*

P. **Berger,** *The Human Shape of Work,* Macmillan, New York, 1964.

P. **Berger** *et al. The Homeless Mind,* Penguin, Harmondsworth, 1973.

H. **Beynon,** *Working for Ford,* E. P. Publishing, Wakefield, 1975.

M. **Blaug** and K. **King,** 'Is the Arts Council cost-effective?' *New Society,* 3 January 1974.

R. O. **Blood** and D. M. **Wolfe,** *Husbands and Wives,* Free Press, New York, 1965.

A. **Booth,** 'Sex and social participation', *American Sociological Review,* **37,** 1972, 183–92.

P. **Bourdieu** and **J. C. Passeron,** *Reproduction in Education, Culture and Society,* Sage, London, 1977.

W. **Braden,** 'LSD and the press', in S. Cohen and J. Young, eds., *op. cit.*

M. **Bradley** and **D. Fenwick,** *Popular Attitudes to Liquor Licensing Laws in Great Britain,* HMSO, London, 1974.

British Travel Association/University of Keele, *Pilot National Recreation Survey,* 1967.

U. **Bronfenbrenner,** *Two Worlds of Childhood, USA and USSR,* Allen and Unwin, London, 1971.

R. K. **Brown** *et al.,* 'Leisure in work', in M. A. Smith *et al.,* eds., *Leisure and Society in Britain, op. cit.*

W. R. **Burch** Jr., 'Facilities of leisure and leisure behaviour in an ecological view', paper presented to 3rd biennial conference of the *International Society for the Study of Behavioural Development,* Guildford, 1975.

G. **Burck,** 'There'll be less leisure than you think', *Fortune,* March 1970.

T. **Burns,** 'Leisure in industrial society', in M. A. Smith *et al.,* eds., *Leisure and Society in Britain, op. cit.*

T. **Burns,** *The BBC,* Macmillan, London, 1977.

T. L. **Burton,** *Recreation Research and Planning,* Allen and Unwin, London, 1970.

R. **Callois,** 'The structure and classification of games', *Diogenes,* **12,** 1955, 62–75.

J. B. **Carey,** 'Changing courtship patterns in the popular song', in R. S. Denisoff and R. A. Peterson, eds., *op. cit.*

N. **Cheek** *et al., Leisure and Recreation Places,* Ann Arbor Science, Michigan, 1976.

A. B. **Cherns** and **L. E. Davis,** eds., *The Quality of Working Life,* 2 Vols., Free Press, New York, 1976.

S. **Chibnall,** 'The crime reporter,' *Sociology,* **9,** 1975, 49–66.

E. **Clark,** 'Life at the middle', *New Society,* 11 January 1973.

J. **Clarke,** 'Framing the arts', Paper presented at the *Symposium on Sport and Leisure,* Polytechnic of Central London, 1975.

A. **Clayre,** *Work and Play,* Weidenfeld and Nicholson, London, 1975.

A. **Clayre,** 'The media and cultural change', in M. A. Smith, ed., *Leisure and Urban Society, op. cit.*

H. **Cohen,** 'The anomia of success and the anomia of failure', *British Journal of Sociology,* **23,** 1972, 229–43.

P. **Cohen,** 'Subcultural conflicts and working class community', in M. Hammersley and P. Woods, eds., *The Process of Schooling,* Routledge, London, 1976.

S. **Cohen,** ed., *Images of Deviance,* Penguin, Harmondsworth, 1971.

S. **Cohen,** *Folk Devils and Moral Panics,* MacGibbon and Kee, London, 1972.

S. **Cohen** and **J. Young,** eds., *The Manufacture of News,* Constable, London, 1973.

R. **Collins,** 'A conflict theory of sexual stratification', *Social Problems,* **19,** 1971, 3–21.

J. L. **Crompton,** 'Problems of provision and planning in leisure', in J. Haworth and M. A. Smith, eds., *Work and Leisure, op. cit.*

C. A. R. **Crosland,** *The Future of Socialism,* Cape, London, 1956.

I. **Cullen,** 'A day in the life of . . .', *New Society,* 11 April 1974.

J. **Curran** and **J. Tunstall,** 'Mass media and leisure', in M. A. Smith *et al.,* eds., *Leisure and Society in Britain, op. cit.*

R. **Dahrendorf,** *Class and Class Conflict in Industrial Society,* Routledge, London, 1959.

D. **Dallas,** *The Travelling People,* Macmillan, London, 1971.

C. **Davies,** *Permissive Britain,* Pitman, London, 1975.

R. S. **Denisoff** and **M. Levine,** 'Brainwashing or background noise; the popular protest song', in R. S. Denisoff and R. A. Petersen, eds., *op. cit.*

R. S. **Denisoff** and **R. A. Petersen,** eds., *The Sounds of Social Change,* Rand McNally, Chicago, 1972.

E. **Derrick** *et al., Schoolchildren and Leisure: Interim Report,* Working Paper 19, Centre for Urban and Regional Studies, University of Birmingham, 1973.

D. **Downes** *et al., Gambling, Work and Leisure,* Routledge, London, 1976.

J. **Dumazedier,** *Sociology of Leisure,* Elsevier, Amsterdam, 1974.

H. L. **Dunlop,** 'Games, sports, dancing and other vigorous recreational activities and their function in Samoan culture', in J. W. Loy and G. S. Kenyon, eds., *Sport, Culture and Society*, Macmillan, New York, 1969.

D. R. Dunn, 'Recreation in the urbanising world: no models to mimic', *Society and Leisure*, 1976.

E. Durkheim, *The Division of Labour in Society*, Free Press, New York, 1964.

P. Elliott, 'Selection and communication in a television production – a case study', in J. Tunstall, ed., *Media Sociology, op. cit.*

M. Elson, 'The weekend car', *New society*, 11 April 1974.

I. Emmett, *Youth and Leisure in an Urban Sprawl*, Manchester University Press, 1971.

I. Emmett, 'The Social filler in the leisure field', *Recreation News Supplement*, **4**, 1971, 7–8.

English Tourist Board and Trade Union Congress, *Holidays: The Social Need*, London, 1976.

R. Firth, J. Hubert and **A. Forge,** *Families and Their Relatives*, Routledge, London, 1969.

K. Fogelman, ed., *Britain's Sixteen Year Olds*, National Children's Bureau, London, 1976.

N. Foote, 'Sex as play', *Social Problems*, **1**, 1954, 159–63.

J. Foster, *Class Struggle in the Industrial Revolution*, Weidenfeld and Nicolson, London, 1974.

A. Fox, 'The meaning of work', in *Occupational Categories and Cultures*, DE351, Open University, Milton Keynes, 1976.

G. Friedmann, *The Anatomy of Work*, Heinemann, London, 1961.

J. K. Galbraith, *The Age of Uncertainty*, BBC/Andre Deutsch, London, 1977.

J. Galtung and **M. H. Ruge,** 'The structure of foreign news', in J. Tunstall, ed., *Media Sociology, op. cit.*

H. J. Gans, 'Popular culture in America', in H. S. Becker, ed., *Social Problems: A Modern Approach*, Wiley, New York, 1961.

P. Gardner, *Nice Guys Finish Last*, Allen Lane, London, 1974.

H. Gavron, *The Captive Wife*, Routledge, London, 1966.

A. Giddens, 'Notes on the concepts of play and leisure', *Sociological Review*, **12**, 1964, 73.

B. Gillinson, 'The problems of designing for leisure', in J. Haworth and M. A. Smith, eds., *Work and Leisure, op. cit.*

S. Giner, *Mass Society*, Martin Robertson, London, 1976.

Glasgow University Media Research Group, *Bad News*, Routledge, London, 1976.

R. Glasser, *Leisure: Penalty or Prize*, Macmillan, London, 1970.

R. Glasser, 'A case of robot's cramp', *Guardian*, 1 February 1974.

G. Godbey, 'Anti-leisure and public recreation policy', in S. Parker *et al.*, eds., *op. cit.*

G. Godbey and **S. Parker,** *Leisure Studies and Services: An Overview*, Saunders, Philadelphia, 1976.

P. Golding, *The Mass Media*, Longman, London, 1974.

J. H. Goldthorpe *et al.*, *The Affluent Worker, Vol. 1, Industrial Attitudes and Behaviour*, Cambridge U.P., London, 1968.

C. J. Goodhardt *et al.*, *The Television Audience*, Saxon House, Farnborough, 1975.

G. Gorer, *Sex and Marriage in England today*, Nelson, London, 1971.

S. de Grazia, *Of Time, Work and Leisure*, Twentieth Century Fund, New York, 1962.

B. Groombridge, *Television and the People*, Penguin, Harmondsworth, 1972.

E. Gross, 'A functional approach to leisure analysis', in E. O. Smigel, ed., *Work and Leisure*, College and University Press, New Haven, 1963.

R. S. Gruneau, 'Sport, social differentiation and social inequality', in D. W. Ball and J. W. Loy, eds., *op. cit.*

R. K. Haerle, 'Career patterns and career contingencies of professional baseball players: an occupational analysis', in D. W. Ball and J. W. Loy, eds., *op. cit.*

J. Hall and **N. Perry,** *Aspects of Leisure in Two Industrial Cities*, Occasional papers in survey research, **5**, SSRC, London, 1974.

S. Hall and **T. Jefferson,** eds., *Resistance Through Rituals*, Hutchinson, London, 1975.

S. Hall and P. Whennel, *The Popular Arts*, Hutchinson, London, 1964.

J. D. Halloran *et al.*, *Demonstrations and Communication*, Penguin, Harmondsworth, 1970.

J. Hargreaves, 'The political economy of mass sport', in S. Parker *et al.*, eds., *op. cit.*

R. J. Havighurst, 'The leisure activities of the middle aged', *American Journal of Sociology*, **63**, 1957, 152–62.

R. J. Havighurst and K. Feigenbaum, 'Leisure and life-style', *American Journal of Sociology*, **64**, 1959, 396–405.

J. T. Haworth, 'Leisure and the individual', in S. Parker *et al.*, eds., *op. cit.*

J. Haworth and M. A. Smith, eds., *Work and Leisure*, Lepus Books, London, 1975.

J. Haworth and A. J. Veal, eds., *Leisure and the Community*, Leisure Studies Association, University of Birmingham, 1976.

F. Hirsch, *The Social Limits to Growth*, Routledge, London, 1977.

R. Hoggart, *The Uses of Literacy*, Chatto and Windus, London, 1957.

M. A. Holman, 'A national time-budget for the year 2000', *Sociology and Social Research*, **46**, 1961.

S. Hood, 'The politics of television', in D. McQuail, ed., *op. cit.*

E. Hughes, 'Work and the Self', in J. H. Rohrer and M. Sherif, eds., *Social Psychology at the Crossroads*, Harper and Row, New York, 1951.

J. Huizinga, *Homo Ludens*, Routledge, London, 1949.

R. Hutchinson, 'Provision for the arts', in S. Parker and J. Haworth, eds., *op. cit.*

A. G. Ingham, 'Occupational subcultures in the work-world of sport', in D. W. Ball and J. W. Loy, eds., *op. cit.*

J. Jacobs, *The Death and Life of Great American Cities*, Random House, New York, 1961.

D. Jary, 'Evenings at the ivory tower', in M. A. Smith *et al.*, eds., *Leisure and Society in Britain*, *op. cit.*

A. Jay, 'What's to become of the BBC?', *Sunday Times*, 19th November 1972.

C. Jencks *et al.*, *Inequality*, Allen Lane, London, 1973.

P. Jephcott, *Time of One's Own*, Oliver and Boyd, Edinburgh, 1967.

M. Kaplan, *Leisure: Theory and Policy*, Wiley, New York, 1975.

G. Katona *et al.*, *Aspirations and Affluence*, McGraw-Hill, New York, 1971.

J. W. Keating, 'Winning in sport and athletics', *Thought*, 1963, 201-10.

J. W. Keating, 'Sportsmanship as a moral category', *Ethics*, 1964, 25–35.

A. Kingsbury, 'Animation', in J. Haworth and A. J. Veal, eds., *op. cit.*

J. M. Kreps, *Lifetime Allocation of Work and Income*, Duke U.P., North Carolina, 1971.

K. Kumar, 'Holding the middle ground', *Sociology*, **9**, 1975, 67–88.

D. Lane, *The Socialist Industrial State*, Allen and Unwin, London, 1976.

T. Lane and K. Roberts, *Strike at Pilkingtons*, Fontana, London, 1971.

A. J. Lee, *The Origins of the Popular Press 1855—1914*, Croom Helm, London, 1976.

J. Leigh, *Young People and Leisure*, Routledge, London, 1971.

F. M. M. Lewes and S. J. Mennell, *Leisure, Culture and Local Government*, University of Exeter, 1976.

S. Linder, *The Harried Leisure Class*, Columbia U.P., New York, 1970.

S. M. Lipset, *Political Man*, Doubleday, New York, 1960.

H. Z. Lopata, *Occupation Housewife*, Oxford U.P., New York, 1971.

J. W. Loy Jr. and G. S. Kenyon, eds., *Sport, Culture and Society*, Macmillan, New York, 1969.

M. McLuhan and Q. Fiore, *The Medium is the Message*, Penguin, Harmondsworth, 1967.

D. McQuail, 'The audience for television plays', in J. Tunstall, ed., *op. cit.*

D. McQuail, ed., *Sociology of Mass Communications*, Penguin, Harmondsworth, 1972.

D. McQuail, 'The television audience: a revised perspective', in D. McQuail, ed., *op. cit.*

R. W. Malcolmson, *Popular Recreations in English Society, 1700—1850*, Cambridge U.P., London, 1973.

P. H. Mann, 'Survey of a theatre audience: findings', *British Journal of Sociology*, **18**, 1967, 75.

M. Matthews, *Class and Society in Soviet Russia*, Allen Lane, London, 1972.

M. **Mead,** *Male and Female,* Penguin, Harmondsworth, 1962.

W. **Melody,** *Children's TV,* Yale U.P., New Haven, 1973.

S. **Mennell,** *Cultural Policy in Towns,* Council of Europe, Strasbourg, 1976.

R. **Meyersohn,** 'Television viewing and other uses of leisure', *Public Opinion Quarterly,* **32,** 1968, 102–11.

R. E. **Miles,** *Awakening From the American Dream,* Marion Boyars/Open Forum, London, 1977.

R. **Miliband,** *The State in Capitalist Society,* Weidenfeld and Nicolson, London, 1969.

R. **Mills,** *Young Outsiders,* Routledge, London, 1973.

N. **Millward,** 'Family status and behaviour at work', *Sociological Review,* **16,** 1968, 149–64.

H. F. **Moorhouse,** 'The political incorporation of the British working class', *Sociology,* **7,** 1973, 341–59.

P. **Morley,** 'Industrial conflict and the mass media', *Sociological Review,* **24,** 1976, 245–68.

H. W. **Morton,** 'Soviet sport in the 1960s', in J. W. Loy and G. S. Kenyon, eds., *op. cit.*

G. **Mungham** and G. **Pearson,** eds., *Working Class Youth Culture,* Routledge, London, 1976.

G. **Murdock,** 'Culture and classlessness: the making and unmaking of a contemporary myth', in J. Haworth and M. A. Smith, eds., *Work and Leisure, op. cit.*

G. **Murdock,** 'Class stratification and cultural consumption', in M. A. Smith, ed., *Leisure and Urban Society, op. cit.*

D. **Murphy,** *The Silent Watchdog,* Constable, London, 1976.

J. F. **Murphy** *et al., Leisure Delivery Systems: A Modern Perspective,* Lea and Febiger, Philadelphia, 1973.

J. F. **Murphy,** *Concepts of Leisure,* Prentice-Hall, New Jersey, 1974.

P. W. **Musgrave,** 'How children use television', *New Society,* 20 February 1969.

F. **Musgrove,** *The Migratory Élite,* Heinemann, London, 1963.

F. **Musgrove,** *Ecstasy and Holiness,* Methuen, London, 1974.

J. **Myerscough,** 'The recent history and use of leisure time', in I. Appleton, ed., *op. cit.*

New Survey of London Life and Labour, Vol. 9 *Life and Leisure,* King, London, 1935.

O. **Newman,** *Gambling: Hazard and Reward,* Athlone Press, London, 1972.

O. **Newman,** 'Leisure and life-style', *Ontario Psychologist,* **8,** 1976, 28–34.

North West Sports Council, *Leisure in the North West,* Salford, 1972.

A. **Oakley,** *The Sociology of Housework,* Martin Robertson, London, 1974.

Organisation for Economic Co-operation and Development, *New Patterns for Working Time,* Paris, 1973.

S. **Parker,** *The Future of Work and Leisure,* MacGibbon and Kee, London, 1971.

S. **Parker,** *The Sociology of Leisure,* Allen and Unwin, London, 1976.

S. **Parker,** *et al.,* eds., *Sport and Leisure in Contemporary Society,* Polytechnic of Central London, 1975.

S. **Parker** and J. **Haworth,** eds., *Leisure and Public Policy,* Leisure Studies Association, Birmingham, 1975.

N. **Parry** and J. **Parry,** 'Theories of culture and leisure', in M. A. Smith, ed., *Leisure and Urban Society, op. cit.,*

N. C. A. **Parry** and D. **Johnson,** *Leisure and Social Structure,* Hatfield Polytechnic, 1974.

J. A. **Patmore,** *Land and Leisure,* Penguin, Harmondsworth, 1972.

A. **Patmore,** 'The busy world of leisure', *Observer,* 1 December 1974.

L. F. **Pearson,** 'Working class non-work time and social policy', in J. Haworth and A. J. Veal, eds., *op. cit.*

L. F. **Pearson,** 'You've got to be happy', *Unpublished manuscript, University of Birmingham,* 1976.

R. A. **Petersen** and D. G. **Berger,** 'Three eras in the manufacture of popular music lyrics', in R. S. Denisoff and R. A. Petersen, eds., *op., cit.*

B. M. **Petrie,** 'Sport and politics', in D. W. Ball and J. W. Loy, eds., *op. cit.*

N. **Petryszak,** 'The appeal of violence in spectator sport – a bio-sociological perspective', in M. A. Smith, ed., *Leisure and Urban Society, op. cit.*

D. L. Phillips, 'Social participation and happiness', *American Journal of Sociology,* **72,** 1967, 479–88.

J. Platt, 'Some problems in measuring the jointness of conjugal role relationships', *Sociology,* **3,** 1969, 287–97.

R. Poor, *4 Days, 40 hours,* Pan, London, 1972.

J. Raban, *Soft City,* Hamish Hamilton, London, 1974.

R. and R. N. Rapoport, *Dual Career Families,* Penguin, Harmondsworth, 1971.

R. and R. N. Rapoport, *Leisure and the Family Life-cycle,* Routledge, London, 1975.

D. Ravitch, *The Great School Wars,* Basic Books, New York, 1974.

C. Reich, *The Greening of America,* Penguin, Harmondsworth, 1972.

D. Rich, 'Spare time in the Black Country', in L. Kuper, ed., *Living in Towns,* Cresset, London, 1953.

K. W. Richmond, Foreword to T. Husen, *The Learning Society,* Methuen, London, 1974.

D. Riesman, 'Leisure and work in post-industrial society', in E. Larrabee and R. Meyersohn, eds., *Mass Leisure,* Free Press, Glencoe, 1958.

A. Rigby, *Alternative Realities,* Routledge, London, 1974.

A. Roadburg, *An Enquiry into the Meanings of Work and Leisure,* Ph.D. thesis, University of Edinburgh, 1977.

J. M. Roberts and **B. Sutton-Smith,** 'Child-training and game involvement', in J. W. Loy and G. S. Kenyon, eds., *op. cit.*

K. Roberts, *Leisure,* Longman, London, 1970.

K. Roberts, 'Society of leisure: myth and reality', in S. Parker *et al.,* eds., *op. cit.*

K. Roberts *et al., The Character—Training Industry,* David and Charles, Newton Abbot, 1974.

K. Roberts *et al.,* 'How many hours in a week?', *Personnel Management,* **6,** 1974, 33–41.

K. Roberts *et al., The Fragmentary Class Structure,* Heinemann, London, 1977.

J. P. Robinson and **P. M. Hirsch,** 'Teenage response to rock and roll protest songs', in R. S. Denisoff and R. A. Petersen, eds., *op. cit.*

B. Rodgers, 'Urbanism, sport and welfare', in M. A. Smith, ed., *Leisure and Urban Society, op. cit.*

B. Rosenberg, 'Mass culture revisited', in B. Rosenberg and D. M. White, eds., *op. cit.*

B. Rosenberg and **D. M. White,** eds., *Mass Culture Revisited,* Van Nostrand Reinhold, New York, 1971.

K. E. Rosengren and **S. Windahl,** 'Mass media consumption as a functional alternative', in D. McQuail, ed., *op. cit.*

B. Russell, 'In praise of idleness', in E. Larabee and R. Meyersohn, eds., *Mass Leisure,* Free Press, Glencoe, 1961.

F. Rust, *Dance and Society,* Routledge, London, 1969.

G. H. Sage 'An occupational analysis of the college coach', in D. W. Ball and J. W. Loy, eds., *op. cit.*

G. Salaman, 'Two occupational communities: examples of a remarkable convergence of work and non-work', *Sociological Review,* **19,** 1971, 389–407.

G. Salaman, *Community and Occupation,* Cambridge U.P., London, 1974.

E. H. Scheuch, 'Family cohesion in leisure time', *Sociological Review,* **8,** 1960, 37–61.

M. Schofield, *The Sexual Behaviour of Young Adults,* Allen Lane, London, 1973.

G. A. C. Searle, ed., *Recreational Economics and Analysis,* Longman, London, 1975.

I. M. Seeley, *Outdoor Recreation and the Urban Environment,* Macmillan, London, 1973.

R. Sennett, *The Uses of Disorder,* Penguin, Harmondsworth, 1973.

R. Sennett and **J. Cobb,** *The Hidden Injuries of Class,* Random House, New York, 1972.

E. Shils, 'Mass society and its culture', in B. Rosenberg and D. M. White, eds., *op. cit.*

B. Silcock, 'Anatomy of the British boozer', *Sunday Times,* 18 December 1977.

K. Sillitoe, *Planning for Leisure,* HMSO, London, 1969.

I. G. Simmons, *Rural Recreation in the Industrial World,* Edward Arnold, London, 1975.

C. Smith, 'The emergence of leisure as a policy issue for central government and the administrative response', in S. Parker and J. Haworth, eds., *op. cit.*

H. **Smith**, *The Russians,* Times Books, London, 1976.

M. A. **Smith** *et al.,* eds., *Leisure and Society in Britain,* Allen Lane, London, 1973.

M. A. **Smith**, ed., *Leisure and Urban Society,* Leisure Studies Association, Manchester, 1977.

South-West Economic Planning Council, *Economic Survey of the Tourist Industry in the South-West,* HMSO, London, 1976.

L. **Srole**, 'Social integration and certain corollaries: an exploratory study', *American Sociological Review,* **21,** 1956, 709–16.

B. **Sutton-Smith,** J. M. **Roberts** and R. M. **Kozelka,** 'Game involvement in adults', in J. W. Loy and G. S. Kenyon, eds., *op. cit.*

G. **Swift,** 'An approach to leisure: satisfying wants not needs', in J. Haworth and A. J. Veal, eds., *op. cit.*

A. **Szalai** *et al.,* *The Use of Time,* Mouton, The Hague, 1972.

I. R. **Taylor,** 'Soccer consciousness and soccer hooliganism', in S. Cohen, ed., *op. cit.*

L. **Taylor** and K. **Williams,** 'The actor and his world', *New Society,* 29 July 1971.

J. **Tunstall,** ed., *Media Sociology,* Constable, London, 1970.

J. **Tunstall,** *The Westminster Lobby Correspondents,* Routledge, London, 1970.

J. **Tunstall,** *Journalists at work,* Constable, London, 1971.

J. **Tunstall,** *The Media are American,* Constable, London, 1977.

L. **Turner** and J. **Ash,** *The Golden Hordes,* Constable, London, 1975.

E. **Van den Haag,** 'A dissent from the consenual society', in B. Rosenberg and D. M. White, eds., *op. cit.*

C. S. **Van Doren** and L. **Hodges,** *America's Park and Recreation Heritage,* US Department of the Interior, Washington, 1975.

J. **Walvin,** *The People's Game,* Allen Lane, London, 1975.

M. **Warner,** 'Organisational context and control of policy in the television newsroom', *British Journal of Sociology,* **22,** 1971, 283–94.

P. **Warr** and T. **Wall,** *Work and Well-being,* Penguin, Harmondsworth, 1975.

J. **Whale,** *The Half-Shut Eye,* Macmillan, London, 1969.

J. **Whale,** *The Politics of the Media,* Fontana, London, 1977.

J. **White** and M. **Dunn,** *Recreational Use of the Countryside: A Case Study in the West Midlands,* Research memorandum 33, Centre for Urban and Regional Studies, University of Birmingham, 1974.

M. G. **Wilders,** 'Some preliminary observations on the sociology of the public house', in S. Parker *et al.,* eds., *op. cit.*

H. L. **Wilenski,** 'The uneven distribution of leisure: the impact of economic growth on "free time" ', in E. O. Smigel, ed., *Work and Leisure,* College and University Press, New Haven, 1963.

H. L. **Wilenski,** 'Mass society and mass culture: interdependence or independence', *American Sociological Review,* **29,** 1964, 173–97.

H. L. **Wilenski,** 'Work as a social problem', in H. S. Becker, ed., *Social Problems: A Modern Approach,* Wiley, New York, 1966.

R. **Williams,** *Culture and Society,* Chatto and Windus, London, 1958.

R. **Williams,** *The Long Revolution,* Chatto and Windus, London, 1961.

R. **Williams,** *Television: Technology and Cultural Form,* Fontana, London, 1974.

P. **Willis,** *Learning to Labour,* Saxon House, Farnborough, 1977.

N. A. B. **Wilson,** *On the Quality of Working Life,* Department of Employment, Manpower paper No. 7, 1973.

R. **Wippler,** 'Private and public modes of spending leisure and their relevance for ecological problems', Paper presented to the *3rd Biennial Conference of the ISSBD,* Guildford, 1975.

D. F. **Wright,** 'Musical meaning and its social determinants', *Sociology,* **9,** 1975, 419–35.

W. D. C. **Wright,** 'Some aspects of the economics of leisure', in I. Appleton, ed., *op. cit.*

C. **Wright-Mills,** *White-Collar,* Galaxy, New York, 1956.

J. **Young,** *The Drugtakers,* MacGibbon and Kee, London, 1971.

M. **Young** and P. **Willmott,** *Family and Kinship in East London,* Routledge, London, 1957.

M. **Young** and P. **Willmott,** *The Symmetrical Family,* Routledge, London, 1973.

Index